Seven Cherokee Myths

Seven Cherokee Myths

Creation, Fire, the Primordial Parents,
the Nature of Evil, the Family,
Universal Suffering, and
Communal Obligation

G. KEITH PARKER

Forewords by Joyce Dugan and Paul Brutsche

McFarland & Company, Inc., Publishers
Jefferson, North Carolina, and London

LIBRARY OF CONGRESS CATALOGUING-IN-PUBLICATION DATA

Parker, G. Keith
    Seven Cherokee myths : creation, fire, the primordial parents,
the nature of evil, the family, universal suffering, and communal
obligation / G. Keith Parker ; forewords by Joyce Dugan and Paul
Brutsche.
        p.   cm.
    Includes bibliographical references and index.

    ISBN 0-7864-2364-1 (softcover : 50# alkaline paper) ∞

    1. Cherokee mythology.   2. Cherokee Indians—Rites and
ceremonies.   3. Cherokee Indians—Psychology.   I. Title.
E99.C5.P29   2006
                                                    2005032985

British Library cataloguing data are available

On the cover: Figure found at Etowah Mounds, northwest Georgia,
historic Cherokee homeland (photograph by Marilyn Angel Wynn
©2005 Nativestock Images)

Manufactured in the United States of America

McFarland & Company, Inc., Publishers
    Box 611, Jefferson, North Carolina 28640
    www.mcfarlandpub.com

For Jonlyn,
whose Selu nourishment is eternal

Acknowledgments

This work has benefited from the help of many people, including family, friends, colleagues, and associates in many walks of life. Not all can be named but several should be noted for their extra support, without which this book would never have been completed. My deep thanks go to all, named and unnamed. First of all, my warmest thanks go to my own family for their patience, editing, feedback, technical help with computers and photos, as well as encouragement: Paul and Gai Parker have given extensive computer and other technical help. Leslie Borhaug and Kym Sebranek have done crucial reading and made helpful suggestions. Carroll Parker and Pat Brunner of the Brunnner Studio in Berea, with Scharme, Gwen and Jerry as well as Warren, have given technical assistance. Nadine Ashe has typed much. Above all, for her patience through many years of research and writing, for the solid feedback and serious editing, as well as for grasping the deeper meanings of these stories, I am forever grateful to my loving wife, Jonlyn.

Many in Cherokee, North Carolina, have given invaluable help over the years with their encouragement, crucial guidance and wise advice. I am indebted especially to the late Tom Underwood, the late Robert Bushyhead, the late Mary and G.B. Chiltosky, Geneva "Mama Gene" Jackson, Amy Walker, Walker Calhoun, Lloyd Arneach, Freeman Owle, Lynn Lossiah, Joyce Dugan, B. Lynne Harlan, and Ben and Jean Bushyhead. Special thanks go to Ed Sharpe of Cherokee Publications, and Kay Sharpe of Medicine Man Crafts, who have given priceless guidance, help and support. The assistance of the staff of the Museum of the Cherokee Indian has been noteworthy, especially that of Bo Taylor, archivist, and Barbara Duncan, education director. One enrolled Cherokee and longtime friend, Glenn Rogers, has been a solid support. My thanks also go to the Eastern Band of Cherokee Indians

Cultural Resources Office and Cherokee Language Program as well as their research committee, who approved my program.

My warm thanks go also to significant persons in Zurich, Switzerland, who encouraged the project: Paul Brutsche, Ursula Dohrn, Dirk Evers and the late John Mattern. My thanks go also to the C.G. Jung Institut in Kuesnacht, Zurich, Switzerland, to the former director of studies, John Granrose, and to the many international students who attended my lectures there on some of this material in 2002. Their feedback from experiencing Cherokee myths on a multicultural level was enlightening and most helpful. Likewise, I am indebted to Brevard College for the invitation to present some of the material at the Purgason Distinguished Scholar Lectures in 1994. The helpful feedback and active participation of students at the Blue Ridge Community College deserves my warm thanks. There have been multiple other presentations, especially with "Jung" groups in Chapel Hill, N.C. (Triad Area), Charlotte, N.C. and several churches; to each of those groups I give my sincere thanks for your engaging with, and learning from, these myths, and thus for learning with me about the breadth and depth of their meanings.

Contents

Foreword

by Paul Brutsche

Myths contain, in symbolic language, predications about a people in the particular historical and geographical scope of their own experiences and world outlook. But myths also contain a treasure of generally valid wisdom that extends far beyond the limited context of a people and a culture. They touch upon universal human experiences that people everywhere have always been exposed to, as well as existential, fundamental questions for which they have always sought answers. In this, their archetypal dimensions, they have found their eternal, living reality. In myths we encounter parts of ourselves here and now.

G. Keith Parker's book leads in both of these directions: it brings the reader in an empathic way close to the spiritual world and the history of the Cherokee Indians as they see themselves in their magnificent myths, and it allows them to be revealed through the subtle interpretations of the universally valid meanings of these myths.

The myths may also impart to today's people something of a knowledge and insight that affects them as individuals, even when in many respects they may stand totally elsewhere. In the depths of one's existence, one is exposed to similar experiences and challenges, as they plainly apply to every individual for life and for spiritual development. And myths refer, as do legends, fairy tales and other vessels and expressions of the collective unconscious, to the fundamental experiences of humanity.

That makes the engagement with them exciting and interesting; one will be absorbed by a fascinating story, but at the same time, whether consciously or unconsciously, will be touched by the therein crafted spiritual profundities.

Parker deliberately works through the psychological significance of seven Cherokee myths, and deduces from them insights and directives of a general nature. The proposed meanings are never conclusive, but rather full of respect for the fabric of the myths themselves. They are to be thought of as pointers, encirclements, as offers for understanding and not as final interpretations that become immobile or claim validity for everyone. They inflict no violence to the myths; rather, they allow them to release their rich meanings and come into their own worth.

Even though the author approaches the myths as a counselor, and declaredly armed with the analytical psychology of C.G. Jung, he succeeds without difficult technical language in convincingly shedding light on the myths. The book is therefore not reserved for only the narrower circle of specialists, but instead turns towards a wider public, without having resorted to lowering the quality of the work.

In the book one perceives the great value the author places on the culture and the history of the Cherokee, with whose world he has had contact since childhood. This respect for the deep wisdom of the myths is shared with the reader, and it goes almost unnoticed that that influence is substantial.

I wish for this beautiful work to have many readers who are willing to allow themselves to be touched by the wisdom of these old Cherokee myths, and to let themselves be challenged.

> Paul Brutsche, Ph.D.
> Past President, Curatorium
> C.G. Jung Institute
> Zurich, Switzerland

Foreword

by Joyce Conseen Dugan

G. Keith Parker has analyzed the stories of the Cherokee people through his life experience not only as a Jungian analyst and counselor but also as a mountain resident who has walked the paths of the stories and experienced the landscape of the ancient mountains.

I read with great interest these stories of old and began to contemplate a deeper message in each of them. Often we view these stories as simple myths or fairy tales, understanding the human message but relenting to our twenty-first century minds. Keith has renewed an interest in these stories both for their overt message and for the sublime.

What is most important about Keith's analysis is the context of continuing mountain traditions that reflect old stories, not only among the Cherokee but among other highlanders as well. This analysis demonstrates the importance of the environment in explaining our social mores and patterns of behavior.

This work is important in a world context because it gives those outside the realm of the Cherokee an opportunity to experience our culture through our stories. I hope you will take away from this analysis a better understanding of the humanity of the Cherokee, that continues among us today.

> Joyce Conseen Dugan
> Principal Chief
> Eastern Band of the Cherokee Indian
> 1995–1999

Preface

This book is about some very old stories, called myths, of the Cherokee Indians, from their homeland in the Appalachian mountain region of the United States. It deals briefly with Cherokee history and interaction with European settlers and the U.S. government as well as the perception that some Cherokee myths and traditions loosely resemble some Judeo-Christian practices. The major focus is on seven myths and how they express not only world views and cultural perspectives of these early Appalachian natives, but also deeper human issues that are found as common themes in the myths and fairy tales of all cultures. Insights are given from analytical psychology as developed by C.G. Jung, while avoiding much of the technical language of that school of depth psychology. These ancient stories are held with respect and are honored for their uniqueness by the Cherokee people collectively and individually. They are also noteworthy for their contribution to all peoples in that they carry universal, or archetypal, wisdom.

These stories are important in that they provide little-known insight into Native American traditions and especially into the depth of that culture. In recent years, interest in Native Americans has risen tremendously as seen in the opening of the new National Museum of the American Indian in September 2004 in Washington, D.C., and in the shift in movies, books and other programs from the old negative stereotypes to more humane portrayals of most Indians as persons. Historians, ethnologists, anthropologists and others have debated the impact of Native Americans on U.S. history, government and culture. During one visit to the U.S., Dr. Carl Jung noted the powerful influence the "Red Indians" had on the American psyche as well. In recent years the written and televised work of Joseph Campbell in comparative ethnology has stimulated awareness of common cultural themes found worldwide. For Americans (North and South) to grasp something of the Native Americans is not only to understand the Indians better, but also themselves.

Many factors attracted me to this work, not the least of which was growing up with Cherokee, as well as living on the geographical site of one of these myths, and very close to the locations of several others, as my family had for generations. This is to say that I grew up with Cherokee traditions, concepts and local mountain folkways. In college I found myself confronting the stereotypes found in history books about the Cherokee. While living and teaching overseas for over two decades, the Cherokee story came more alive for me, especially during my personal analysis and study at the C.G. Jung Institute in Zurich, Switzerland. Working with dreams and the unconscious were vital parts of that training, but the deeper human insights found in myths and fairy tales inspired me to look further into their meaning. As the great European, African and Asian myths, fairy tales and legends yielded wisdom from the depths, I rediscovered and revisited the Cherokee stories from my own Appalachian heritage.

In order to research the topic, I used both academic study and contextual fieldwork. In Switzerland some research was begun at the C.G. Jung Institute library, and in North Carolina most research was at the archives of the Museum of the Cherokee Indian in Cherokee, as well as the Hunter Library at Western Carolina University in nearby Cullowhee. I worked also in the Native American section of the library of the University of Arizona, Tuscon, as well as in the smaller libraries in Transylvania, Haywood, Henderson, Jackson and Buncombe counties. In the context of the Eastern Band of Cherokee Indians, I interviewed over a period of several years local experts in Cherokee culture (though all would deny such "expert" status), including some elders, ministers, historians, linguists, and "regular folks" living on the Indian reservation in Cherokee, properly called the Qualla Boundary.

Many scholars and their writings influenced me. In my doctoral work I note especially the guidance of Glenn Hinson and Penrose St. Amant in history, and Wayne Oates in the psychology of religion. The classic study by William James, *Varieties of Religious Experience*, and writings by Mircea Eliade, Otto Rank, Alfred Adler, Sigmund Freud and others, stimulated my interest in fairy tales and myths as being something more than "just stories." My later studies at the Jung Institute in

Zurich, however, gave the opportunity not only to attend lectures and to engage with many Jungian scholars, but also to learn from their research and books. Most notable was the late Marie-Louise von Franz whose multiple books, lectures, seminars and other presentations have placed her as possibly the primary interpreter of practical Jungian understandings of myths and fairy tales.

Many books have been written in Europe amplifying and interpreting human behavior in the light of Grimm's Fairy Tales, ancient Greek myths, Scandinavian tales, and stories from around the world. In North America, some popular works have emphasized the clinical issues focusing on such concepts as the "Peter Pan Syndrome," regarding persons who do not grow up. Likewise, popular books by Jungian analysts such as Thomas Moore have used myths to capture the imagination of their readers in dealing with certain life issues. There are numerous books on Native American spirituality, history, and myths. One notable work, by William Stolzman, is titled *The Pipe and Christ: A Christian-Sioux Dialogue*, it compares the compatibilities and incompatibilities of the Sioux and Christian religions. The classical research of Scandinavian ethnologist Ake Hultkrantz titled *Soul and Native Americans* differentiates how many Native Americans, including the Cherokee, experience "soul" or "spirit." Of course, the many publications of C.G. Jung as found in *The Collective Works of C.G. Jung* as well as in other works have been major resources for this work.

Some authors make reference occasionally to a Cherokee myth, usually woven into a story line or movie theme. Barbara R. Duncan and Brett H. Riggs, folklore specialist and archeologist, respectively, have put together the book *Cherokee Heritage Trail Guidebook*, a guide to Cherokee historical sites that includes pictures and many myths as told by modern Cherokee story tellers. One book, *Dreamquest: Native American Myth and the Recovery of Soul*, by Morton Kelsey, has a similar approach to that of this book, in that he considers Seneca myths using Jungian psychology and comparative religion, as well as world mythology. Any reference to my work or any study about the Cherokee would be inadequate without appropriate tribute to the massive contribution of James Mooney who worked for the American Bureau of Ethnology and lived with Cherokee, east and west, recording their lives, history and stories in the 1880s and 1890s. Considered the major primary source for Cherokee studies, these formerly separate reports to the Bureau of American Ethnology have been made available to the public in *James Mooney's History, Myths and Sacred Formulas of the Cherokees*. The seven myths used for this work are taken unchanged from Mooney.

These seven myths were chosen because they give a balanced perspective of essential Cherokee and archetypal, or universal, thought. (1) The creation story is foundational to Cherokee thinking for it underlines their deep tie to the natural world, especially to the Appalachian mountains as created by the wings of the Great Buzzard. (2) The story of the first fire is sought and obtained by the lowly spider. (3) The first parents, the Cherokee equivalent to Adam and Eve in Paradise, are portrayed in the lengthy and intensive story of Kana'ti and Selu: the origin of game and corn, the main food of the Cherokee, and the loss of the paradise setting due to the immaturity of their two sons. This lengthy and intensive myth presents not only the martyrdom of the mother and a circuitous pilgrimage but also an eventual maturing process and final family reunion. (4) Because Cherokee story tellers cross-referenced them in their telling, I have combined into one chapter the stories of Spear-finger and Stone Man to illustrate the reality of evil, betrayal and deception. The two stories are combined not only due to their many similarities but also to show that evil can come in masculine and feminine forms. (5) Perhaps the most misunderstood story, especially by early sensational writers, is that of Judaculla or Tsul'Kalu, the Slant-Eyed Giant. A kind of Beauty and the Beast story, this hero tale portrays many everyday family tensions and developmental issues for all. (6) Kana'sta, or Connestee, is about an entire village that disappeared, choosing to follow spiritual guides into nearby Pilot Knob to find peace in troubled times. It underlines the reality of a community facing universal suffering and sharing with others. (7) Tsuwe'nahi is the "poor rich man" story of the lazy hunter who also found refuge in Pilot Knob through a personal pilgrimage in spite of his humiliation by his community, a contrast to the Kana'sta story. The last three stories share close geographic sites in the mountains of western North Carolina in what is now Transylvania, Haywood and Jackson counties, on or near the Blue Ridge Parkway.

There are well over 100 myths recorded by Mooney; stories of animals, plants, people and encounter with others, far beyond the scope of this work. Notable are the trickster stories, also told as "Uncle

Remus" stories elsewhere. Many animal stories are very humorous, containing comical encounters between animals and reasons for some of their physical or behavioral features. For a comprehensive consideration of all the myths, the reader is advised to visit the classic work by Mooney as noted in this preface. I have chosen these particular seven myths in order to focus on their archetypal or universal application and to demonstrate that the Cherokee people have ancient wisdom stories like other great peoples.

A final note should be made about religion and spirituality. One of Dr. Jung's notable contributions to both psychology and psychiatry was his observation that religion is a phenomenon in human nature and thus worthy of scientific study. In his cross-cultural research and clinical studies it became an important dimension in dealing more holistically with persons. The Cherokee, like most Native Americans, see themselves as connected to the religious or spiritual world and to separate that dimension from them is to deny their essence. In the decades of my association with the Cherokee, the most consistent complaint about published works concerning them was that their spiritual side was ignored or demeaned. This work does not attempt to put into a system any spiritual or theological position. It simply accepts the stories' deeper meanings, which are both psychological and spiritual. Because early visitors among the Cherokee saw many parallels to Jewish and Christian beliefs and because most Cherokee today are Christian in belief, my theological reflections and comments are simply meant to observe similarities between their ancient stories and biblical traditions. There are also some clinical observations that I hope will stir interest for psychotherapists, pastoral counselors, social workers and other mental health professionals.

The old stories give meaning for life with its suffering and hope, its pain and refuge. There is wisdom there.

G. Keith Parker
Connestee
Brevard, North Carolina

Introduction

THE APPALACHIAN CHEROKEE

Long, long ago, before the Old World knew about the New World, before the United States existed, before there were states called the Carolinas, Georgia, Tennessee, the Virginias, Kentucky or Alabama, before there was a Blue Ridge Parkway traversing the southern Appalachian Mountains, before the white settlers settled those mountains, and before the Christian missionaries arrived, the native Cherokee people raised families, hunted and cultivated food, traded goods and practiced their own native spirituality, something never separated from all other life activities. Like peoples of all the earth, they shared their traditions, their life understanding, and their deeper truths through stories. Those deeper truths were also passed down from generation to generation by means of legend, myth, song, dance, and religious and healing ritual. With the creation of Cherokee writing by the genius Sequoyah, some of these were recorded on the "talking leaves" of books.

Most of those stories are also tied to local geographic settings, giving credence to unexplainable phenomena, giving respect and awe to the beauty and mystery of their surroundings and to life itself. Powerful psychological and spiritual dynamics are part of the homeland settings of these stories. Modern tourists see the natural beauty of the mountains mostly from the convenience of modern roads and trails but have no idea they are traversing the settings of great Cherokee myths from long ago, the holy ground of ancient peoples. In the 1733 Mosely map, the southern Appalachians are identified as the "Cherokee Mountains," underlining what early white explorers perceived about the occupants and their territory. The modern convenience of the Blue Ridge Parkway south of Asheville, North Carolina, cuts through the

heart of that land, ending in the Qualla Boundary of the Eastern Band
of Cherokee. This small reservation occupied by a remnant band of
Eastern Cherokee belies their once large territory, which covered over
40,000 square miles and parts of the eight states noted earlier. The
Parkway section through the Pisgah Ranger District of the Pisgah
National Forest and further west gives various views (close or distant)
of some Cherokee mythological settings: Looking Glass Rock, Shining
Rock, Kana'sta (Connestee), Pilot Knob, the so-called Devil's Court-
house and nearby Judaculla Old Fields, Caney Fork (with the Judaculla
Rock), and many others.

There is an undeniable revival of interest in Native Americans in
Europe, North America and other parts of the world. Museums of
American Indians have been popular in Europe for years and now
Native Americans have one on their own continent in Washington,

Judaculla Rock, on Caney Fork, Jackson County, North Carolina, with petroglyphs (rock carvings) chalked in for contrast. Dated about 3000–1000 B.C., the
rock is tied to the Judaculla myth. The man in the picture is Milas Parker
(1873–1946) who farmed the area and whose family cared for the rock until
donating it to Jackson County in 1959. Courtesy of the North Carolina Office of
Archives and History, Raleigh, North Carolina, and the descendants of Milas
Parker.

D.C., the nation's capital. Increasing numbers of people have stepped beyond curious tourist interest into participating in ceremonies, making drums and seeking to learn from the wisdom of these native peoples. The Cherokee are very much part of that revival of interest and the name "Cherokee" is one of many marketing devices, used on merchandise from automobiles to clothing, attempting to play on a certain mystique. With this interest increasing in modern Western society, and to a degree in Asian and other societies, one sees studies, research and the use of Native American ideas in such diverse areas as business, history, religion, philosophy, anthropology, archeology, and story telling, not to speak of movies and literature.

Both in Europe and in North America, the portrayal of the early natives and settlers is a mixed one, often distorted by Hollywood or pop psychology, if not by historical revisionists who have an ideological axe to grind. One can speak of two extremes: the Native Americans portrayed as "noble savages," or "Red Hebrew" cousins being confronted by decadent European settlers; at the other extreme, they may be shown as heathens or animals worthy only of destruction or conquest by a superior people with that God-given right. The truth is not found in stereotypes on either side, for both the native peoples and the early settlers had their unique strengths and weakness, and their cultural nuances little understood by the other; they were simply different, and each had much to learn from the other.

HISTORICAL PERSPECTIVES

There were, however, some very clear examples of the extremes in leadership positions in the young American nation. President George Washington started a national policy of assimilation in 1789, and expected that all 85 tribes east of the Mississippi would be acculturated within 50 years. The plan was that, once they became self-supporting as farmers and spoke English, they would be admitted into the republic as full and equal citizens.[1] Even President Thomas Jefferson declared in 1785, "I believe the Indian then in body and mind equal to the white man."[2] But the hopes for such integration were dashed by 1833 when the rough frontiersman Andrew Jackson became president and declared to the U.S. Congress that the Cherokee were "established in the midst of a superior race and without appreciating the causes of their inferiority

or seeking to control them, they must yield to the force of circumstances and ere long disappear."[3]

The Cherokee did not necessarily prosper after the Washington policy, and during the Jackson era the discovery of gold in Cherokee territory had tragic consequences, especially in Georgia where they lost all
rights and their lands. Businesses and properties were confiscated and
given to whites. A treaty of sorts was worked out at New Echota to give
a so-called legal base for removal to the west. Chief John Ross, with a del-
egation from the Cherokee Nation, presented lengthy evidence about the
injustices in Georgia when he spoke to the U.S. House of Representatives
in Washington City on the twenty-first of June, 1836. His comments
underlined the sense of betrayal by Jackson after they not only had been
taught to think and feel as American citizens, but had been scrupulous
in observing treaties and had made great advances in civilization. Now
they were about to be "despoiled by their guardian" and would become
strangers and wanderers in the land of their fathers. Underlining the fraud-
ulent nature of the supposed treaty made by a handful of unauthorized
Cherokee, he noted that over 15,000 had protested against such.[4]

Most cogent and moving is the conclusion of Chief Ross in antic-
ipation of the tragedy to come and the deep grief felt in the loss of the
original policy of George Washington. He said: "The Cherokees cannot resist the power of the United States, and should they be driven
from their native land, then will they look in melancholy sadness upon
the golden chains presented by President Washington to the Cherokee
people as emblematic of the brightness and purity of the friendship
between the United States and the Cherokee people."[5]

The words of John Ross were prophetic. By 1838 the forced
removal was carried out by Jackson in spite of great opposition, even
that of the United States Supreme Court, where the removal was
declared unconstitutional; it was the only time in U.S. history that a
president opposed that high court. As a result of the removal today's
Cherokee are split into the major Eastern and Western bands with
smaller groups scattered in such places as Alabama, Texas and
Arkansas. The Western Band is in Oklahoma, formerly Indian Territory. That tragic removal is called the "Trail of Tears" due to the pain,
suffering, and loss of life, estimated to be upwards of 4,000 out of the
12,000 who began the trip. The remnants in the mountains of western
North Carolina eventually were able to stay and live on the Qualla

Boundary around or not too far from Cherokee, North Carolina. There are of course some self-declared Cherokee Indians to be found in many other places with various names.

The Cherokee are part of the revival of interest in North American Indians or Native Americans, although it has not been there long. Until the current generation, mainly anthropologists, missionaries and a few historians took the Cherokee seriously. Until very recently, many of Cherokee heritage in the east were reluctant to confess their ties, due in part to the racism and in part to fears left from the forced removal in the nineteenth century. What this revival of interest represents today is a modern confrontation of cultures, of modern Euro-Asian-African-Americans with Cherokee Americans, few of whom know much about their own heritage. This is rapidly changing with cultural and language programs now in the schools and tribal programs. There is a human tendency to project back into history personal needs, ideals and prejudices. People in the southeast United States are profoundly affected not only by remnant Cherokee names and European names, but also by a common flow of thoughts over two centuries of cultural blending.

The Cherokee call themselves the *Ani'Yun'wiya'*, or Principal People, or Real People. Many tribes use some form of "principal" or "the" to refer to themselves in their own language.[6] Most peoples, not only in Native American cultures but also in other lands, ended up with names given them by other peoples. The more commonly known name, Cherokee, is not from their own language but from others. When used among the Cherokee it is *Tsa'la gi* or *Tsa'ra gi*. It was recorded by many travelers including in a 1557 Portuguese document from De Soto's expedition as *Chalaque*. It may come from a trade language from a Choctaw word, *Choluk* or *Chiluk*, having to do with a cave or pit.[7] Both the Iroquois and Catawba names for the Cherokee had to do with caves, or coming out of the ground.[8] This tie to the sense of refuge inside the mountains plays a key role in Cherokee mythology.

The Cherokee also look back to one central town called Kituhwa that was destroyed, and the land taken away, many years ago. The land was reacquired in 1996 and is a very special place for Cherokee everywhere, named by most as their foremost "mother town." In fact many Cherokee groups prefer to call themselves the *Ani-Kitu'hwagi*, the people of Kituhwa. The largest and most important of the towns along the Tuckaseegee River valley, "Kittowah" is listed on the 1721 census as having 143 men, 93 women and 47 children. British troops burned the town and surrounding crops of corn in 1761.[9] The U.S. government forced them to cede the Tuckaseegee River land in 1819 and eventually it was in the hands of whites who evicted the remaining Cherokee. This is the cradle of Cherokee society and the name Kituhwa is used to preserve Cherokee heritage. Various groups and events utilize the name as well. Listed since 1973 on the National Register of Historic Places, the site covers about 65 acres including several archeological sites. A recent magnetic image of the main mound shows clearly buried council houses. Archeologists have located burned houses, ditches, grave sites (not excavated, out of respect for the dead), and other items.[10]

THE FOCUS

Who were those people, those original Appalachian mountaineers? How did they face suffering, life and death? How did they face family tensions and become individuals in light of, and in spite of, family and community conflict? How was spirituality pictured for them? How did they see their place in the world? How was this world created? These ancient myths show the same issues seen in myths from all over the world, for they deal with archetypal, i.e. universal, issues faced by all peoples and dealt with in the wisdom stories from all cultures, couched in the clothing of each unique culture. The ancient themes have existed for millennia and affect all cultures profoundly as they are portrayed in stories, movies, art, music or technology. Scholars have studied myths from Egypt and Greece, and tales gathered by the Brothers Grimm in Europe and others around the world, to learn more about basic human nature, both good and bad. This work focuses on the Cherokee in the context of their mountain homeland and some of the ancient wisdom kept within their homes and villages for centuries, before the influence of Europeans and the Christian missionaries who worked so effectively among them. They are ancient and yet amazingly modern in their understanding of human personality development, of family dynamics, of community solidarity, and the reality of religion or a spirituality. The truths are universal and yet grounded in the very soil that one tills, the mountains that one climbs, the rivers that one rides, the air one breathes.

AN ANALYTICAL PSYCHOLOGICAL PERSPECTIVE

The pioneer psychiatrist C.G. Jung noted that these archetypes, these basic human impulses, are inbred in all humans and are seen in ordinary everyday life. Their "ceaseless activity is everywhere apparent even in a rationalistic age like ours."[11] Some of the basic archetypal identities that work in all persons are mother, father, child, wife, husband and so on. Thus the archetype of family lies deep within everyone and carries deep emotional energy, both positive and negative. Most religious symbols express similar archetypal power and thus have much unconscious influence through music, worship forms, art and narrative. Significant dreams, as well as the ancient stories carried for generations, often carry these primitive or archetypal themes and with them universal lessons, or, as the ancients in every society and in biblical days said, "messages from God."

The myths, legends and old stories are also documents of the Indian folk. Some of those are from the historical times, some much older and carried down through the generations in the minds and oral tradition of the people. These are artifacts of the soul. In reference to these ancient myths Bill Moyers said, "The remnants of all that stuff line the walls of our interior system of belief, like shards of broken pottery in an archeological site."[12] Dr. Jung also noted that myths and symbols arise automatically "in every corner of the earth and yet are identical, because they are fashioned out of the same world-wide human consciousness, whose contents are infinitely less variable than are races and individuals."[13]

These Cherokee myths are from a culture different from European culture and myths, and yet they contain many of the same deep, relevant human issues. And when seen for their symbolism, they contain some themes similar to Judeo-Christian traditions. In reference to myths, Jung underlined that "whatever explanation or interpretation does to it, we do to our own souls as well, with corresponding results for our own well-being. The archetype — let us never forget this — is a psychic organ present in all of us."[14]

The historical fact is that the Cherokee were open and generally hospitable to early European settlers. Some of that attitude of hospitality is reflected in these stories. Also, many Cherokee intermarried with early settlers in these mountains, losing their traditional identities. Several white churches still had Cherokee members on their active membership rolls after the deadly forced removal of 1838. Although traditional ways may have been lost in blending with local early settlers, the "shards" of thinking remain in the minds and psyches of many mountain folk. There is a linguistic parallel in listening to local mountain English dialect where one can pick up (though few really recognize) remnants from the days of Chaucer and Shakespeare, such words as "agin, fer, ary, britches, chawed, herrn, yourn, ourn, holp" and so on.[15] Many of the Cherokee words that remain in the public mind are place names: Toxaway, Cullowhee, Nantahala, Tuckaseegee, Kanuga, Connestee, Tanasee Bald, Tennessee, Tomassee, Keowee, and Judaculla Rock. But deep within the collective mountain psyche there remain thought patterns, deep feelings shared by both modern Cherokee and other traditional Appalachian mountain folk. The closeness to, and respect for, the earth, the relatedness to animals, both in hunting and protecting them, the need for balance and individuality in harmony with community with great respect for others, are only some of many shared principles. In the broader U.S. context, 23 of the states bear Native American names and so do thousands of rivers, counties, towns, mountains and lakes, including four of the five Great Lakes.[16] Although the names are remnants, the question is raised as to the broader psychological impact. Jung was convinced that Americans were, in fact, affected far more than they realized.

Jung's observations of American psychology in the 1920s and 1930s during his visits, and in later years of patients and pupils working with him, were very pointed in drawing contrasts to their European counterparts. He was convinced that the "Red Indians" and "Negroids" had a major impact on the American mind, and that most Americans were unaware of it. He commented in 1934:

> Is this American white man nothing but a simple white man, or is he in some way different from the European representative of the species? I believe there is a marked difference between them within as well as without. European magazines have recently published pictures of well-known Americans in Indian headdress, and some Red Indians in European costume in the opposite column, with the question: Who are the Indians?[17]
>
> This is not just a joke. There is something in it that can hardly be denied. It may seem mysterious and unbelievable, yet it is a fact that can be observed in other countries just as well. Man can be assimilated by a country.[18]
>
> That would mean that the spirit of the Indian gets at the American from within and without.[19]

Dr. Jung was not the only psychologist or observer to note that Europeans (and others) settling in North America were greatly affected by the New World. Perhaps the term most widely used of Americans is "frontier mentality," capturing a multitude of strengths and weaknesses from the history of conquering several frontiers across the continent. After the European settlers crossed the ocean, the next major barriers were the formidable Appalachian Mountains, and the Cherokee were the inhabitants of the southern portion of those mountains.

This work is written with the author's interpretation of analytical psychology as developed by C.G. Jung and with some theological comparisons as well. The intention is to speak more to the average person who is untrained in Jungian depth psychology and thus there is an attempt to avoid technical language. Those more trained or well-read in Jung will easily recognize principal concepts without such terms. For those unfamiliar with the work of the pioneer psychiatrist C.G. Jung, appendix A gives a brief summary. Some Jungian concepts are woven into the text for clarity. There are also several clinical references made from counseling settings or family settings. Some theological comments and biblical cross-references will be made at the end of each section both to underline the current reality that many modern Cherokee are unapologetically Christian and to show why the spiritual and psychological nature of the Cherokee folk would be open to and trusting of the early missionary message. The work focuses on the Cherokee in the original Appalachian homeland before the removal of 1838. The geographical setting of the myths is not far from the home of the Eastern Band of Cherokee Indians today but before European settlers pushed them away from these locations. The terms "Native Americans" and "Indians" will be used interchangeably. Most of the modern Cherokee refer to themselves and other Native Americans as Indians, as seen in their official name, the Eastern Band of Cherokee Indians.

One of Jung's practical contributions was his typology that has been expanded by many others, most notably seen in the popular Myers-Briggs Type Inventory, used by many universities, colleges and business organizations. His understanding of the four functions focused on how persons take in information and how they process what they have taken in. These are seen in two sets of opposites, with each bearing some preference. Gathering information is seen in the sensing function (all five senses) and in the intuitive function, the "sixth sense."

Decisions are made about what is obtained is primarily by the thinking function (rational thought) or the feeling function (emotions).
Since these are in opposites and preference is given by different individuals, he encouraged patients to also get in touch with all four functions and not just the superior ones. The inferior functions end in the
unconscious and can create many problems. For example, those who
prefer sensing and thinking (rational) may be overwhelmed by their
feelings if they are not connected to them.

A balanced approached to these myths would thus call for using all
four functions, as far as is possible. In lay terms, and in Cherokee terms,
this means listening with both head and heart. In real life the stories
were, and are, simply told and experienced, not analyzed. Their deeper
meanings apply to each individual in unique ways, as do all myths.

CHEROKEE STORY TELLERS

The Cherokee are like most Native American groups and folk
groups around the world whose story telling, narrations of the past,
and sacred legends show a wealth of history and meaning. Cherokee
migration stories are practically nonexistent but other stories of a cosmological nature are common. Hero figures, personified evil figures,
tricksters and animal stories are rich and exciting. The sacred myths
were told with proper ritual and place. It is said that the myth keepers
and medicine men told them at night in the *asi* (pronounced "o'shi"),
a log winter sleeping house or sweat lodge built very low, often half
underground. They met all night in the *asi* with a low fire burning in
the middle. At daybreak the hearers ran to the cold running streams,
stripped themselves, were scratched with a hard comb and then dipped
seven times in the water, facing the rising sun. This ritual has some remnants today in other practices and in relation to sacred myths. The low,
almost womblike *asi* lodge plays a role in the Judaculla myth.

The sacred myths were kept in oral tradition, passed from generation to generation as were the oldest scriptures in most religious traditions. In the nineteenth century many stories were recorded by
ethnologists who for years worked hard to get them from the myth
keepers themselves and in the original languages. James Mooney worked
many years among the Cherokee and was the main ethnologist for the
Bureau of American Ethnology. The key Cherokee he used as references

were (a.) A'yuni'ni' (Swimmer), born ca. 1835, who spoke no English and was a priest, doctor and keeper of tradition; (b.) John Ax, born ca. 1800, keeper of tradition and tales, especially wonder stories, also not an English speaker; (c.) Suyette (the Chosen One), a Baptist preacher who spoke no English and specialized in animal stories; and (d.) others including James and David Blythe and James Wafford, scholar, believer in the Nunnehi and distant relative of Sequoyah, who made Cherokee a written language.[20]

The old stories are still told today with some variations, as is true of all such tales. Many are given historical, Christian or other interpretative twists and some are combined in modern reflections: all that is perfectly normal in the evolving of the deeper truths found in them. Those myths chosen keep the forms recorded by Mooney because of their age and because of the apparent minimal influence by Europeans. Because these old stories, are so dynamic and deep, so powerful and universal, they speak for themselves to each individual person. Like fairy tales or good modern stories, they speak different messages to each hearer.

MYTHS, DREAMS AND SYMBOLS

Lest the average reader be hindered by the use of the term "myth," a word of clarification is in order. One is faced with the old tradition in the use of the word only in a negative sense, in essence that myths are trivial and blatantly untrue. In fact, there was a biblical warning by the Apostle Paul to avoid "godless and silly myths,"[21] often misinterpreted to mean that all myths are godless and silly. However, the important role of myths for the studies of anthropology, comparative religion, archeology, history of religions, language and literature, in addition to depth psychology, has been amplified tremendously in recent years. Myths are special stories, but not histories or just prescientific ways of looking at the world. They give certain insights into reality in all societies, ancient and recent. Some of these special stories may be sacred to the people and some may be explanations for things not understood, giving meaning and purpose if not hope, to life. They may give important life values, morals, lessons or warnings. They are not verifiable and in that sense are "not true," but the truths they carry is of a deeper kind than simply rational provability. A parallel might be seen in any attempt to establish the "truth" of poetry, music, art, love or beauty.

These old stories, which exist and continually evolve in all cultures, carry some fundamental truths about the universe and our place in it. All societies, however advanced or primitive, have myths in some form. Not all people are consciously aware of them. American mentality was and is very much affected by the frontier mentality and the many myths associated with it, mixed with bits and pieces of literal history. Modern American myths include those of inevitable progress, economic success (with enough work), and freedom from suffering. People build not only great monuments to their leaders of the past but also great myths to polish their heroic status. Names like George Washington, Abraham Lincoln, John Henry, Davy Crockett, the Alamo, Paul Bunyan, Star Wars, John Wayne, and many others bring about images of fantasy and myth as much as actual history. Art, music, literature and the film industry play on those American myths with powerful results, both positive and negative.

The language of myths is symbolic, filled with images that can have many meanings to the story teller and listener. Many of those symbols are archetypal, that is, they are very deep, ancient, universal motifs that all peoples everywhere share. All peoples have heroes, mothers and fathers (both good and bad) as well as families with problems and with success. There is trouble and suffering, with hopes of avoiding such. Another way to look at the symbolic images is to see them as metaphors or parables, using images in poetic and picture language. This is in contrast to literal language. For example, the Cherokee myths that take people into Pilot Knob describe more of a life pilgrimage than a literal climbing into that mountain. Jung emphasized that to understand the world of the unconscious and to understand dreams and myths, one must see this difference between the symbolic meaning and literal meaning. In one of his essays he said that even Jesus tried to help Nicodemus see that difference. Nicodemus could see only the literal meaning of the words, "Ye must be born again," and asked how a man could enter his mother's womb a second time and be born. Jesus translated it from the literal into symbolic meaning by noting the symbolic meaning to be born of water and the Spirit.[22]

Some specialists have divided approaches to myths into three categories: functional (justifying social facts, i.e., why a tribe fishes), symbolic (a way of communication in poetic language to give deeper meaning, i.e., loving help from angelic figures) and structural (the interplay of opposites and a way to resolve them, i.e., war vs. peace, health vs. sickness).[23] This work will blend these three elements with a heavier focus on the symbolic possibilities.

Many have underlined the differences between myths, fairy tales and legends, putting a more cosmological, universal emphasis on myths, and a more personal, localized twist on fairy tales and local legends. Von Franz noted that the differences are not always so clear, since all these stories deal with archetypal material at some level.[24] As noted, the language of myths, fairy tales, and legends is symbolic rather than literal, much like the language of dreams. Jung noted that myths are experienced, not invented.[25] Many myths sound like dreams that people have had throughout the ages. Dreams, like myths, are not limited to normal references of time, space and morals. They shock, wake up, correct, give hope and warning. Most of the time they compensate for situations one experiences in the "outer" world. Not only in the Bible but also in history and all cultures, dreams played a very important role and were seem as a divine voice. Anxiety, however, causes some people to fear that the message is less than divine, and they proclaim that the messages are from the devil. In analytical psychology one works with dreams to listen to the inner world of persons coming for help or guidance along life's pilgrimage. Once when Dr. Jung was asked if myths were to be equated with a collective dream, he responded:

Strictly speaking, a myth is a historical document. It is told, it is recorded, but it is not in itself a dream. It is the product of an unconscious process in a particular social group, at a particular time, at a particular place. This unconscious process can naturally be equated with a dream. Hence anyone who "mythologizes," that is tells myths, is speaking out of this dream, and then what is retold or actually recorded is the myth.[26]

He goes on to underline that the group is caught up in such a process that the myth development can take even thousands of years. In another place he notes:

Myths are original revelations of the preconscious psyche, involuntary statements about unconscious psychic happenings, and anything but allegories of physical processes. Such allegories would be an idle amusement for an unscientific intellect. Myths, on the contrary, have a vital meaning. Not merely do they represent, they *are* the psychic life of the primitive tribe, which immediately falls to pieces and decays when it loses mythological heritage, like a man who has lost his soul.[27]

Some myths and dreams may have deeply religious or spiritual messages or points. Some may have powerful feeling tones for the person, a numinous feeling that somehow this was divine or a "word from the Lord." The language is symbolic and may not be the exact same language that one hears in the outer, Western-educated, rational world. In other words, it may not be the "language of Zion" that some grew up with, or the dogmatic teachings of a particular church or religious group. One is reminded of many times in Eastern Europe during the Communist era while attending worship services, be it in the USSR or Romania or another land, when someone would offer a poem or dream that was "given" to them during the recent week. The collective silence and reverence was amazing as the others hung on the importance of these inner spiritual messages. Rarely did such happen in the West where more logical, rational and intellectual functioning seemed to deny the movement of inner spirits.

THE NUNNEHI: CHEROKEE ANGELS

The Nunnehi, the spirit folk, appear directly or indirectly in these stories and are part of Cherokee thought. They are the "people who live anywhere," but mostly in the high mountain country. They are experienced as normal folk when they want to be, or they can be invisible. Their town houses can be invisible and one can hear their drumming, dancing and merrymaking. In the old days, they were often experienced as friendly heroes who helped the lost to find their way home or helped the warrior in battle against his enemy. They took hurt folk home to nurse them to health and returned them to their families in good health. There are many stories about the Nunnehi, sometimes in the form of beautiful maidens, coming to a dance to lighten the hearts of sad warriors or a struggling hunter, as in the story about Pilot Knob. Even though they live anywhere, usually high in the mountains, they have special places like Pilot Knob, Tsuwa'tel'da, and the old Nikwasi mound in what is now Franklin, N.C. For native Appalachian mountaineers, they are often equated with the angels of Christianity. If one felt one had experienced them in some crisis the good church people would say they were just angels by another other name. Today, as in Mooney's day, Cherokee when asked about the Nunnehi will tell about experiences *others* have had with the Nunnehi, rarely sharing their own.

THE LITTLE PEOPLE: CHEROKEE ELVES

The "Little People," or the "Yun'wi, Tsundi'," are not to be confused with the Nunnehi. The Little People are the fairylike people who are less than knee high and live inside the mountains. They can be friendly and helpful but also can cast spells and cause havoc. Closely associated with animals, they also dress and look like the Cherokee. They can be tricksters or healers and are as sensitive as the animals with whom they live. For some years Appalachian children who thought they saw the Little People learned not to say much about it, because they were seen as being like elves in some "Catholic superstition from Ireland." Not unlike the European elves, trolls or gnomes, the Little People are deeply imbedded in Cherokee culture and widespread among other tribes. One scholar notes that this phenomenon is so extensive that it "cannot easily be explained as a product of European diffusion."[28] There is no archeological evidence of dwarfism among the Cherokee, but if the literal-minded need some prototype there has been some evidence of dwarfism among the prehistoric peoples in Alabama. Even today, when one asks some Cherokee if they believe in the Little People, they will not give a direct yes or no but tell you a story of someone they know or heard of who experienced one, with some detail of the events.[29]

CHEROKEE RELIGION: EUROPEAN AND AMERICAN VIEWS

There are two major historical viewpoints about the Cherokee religion that have been expressed in a variety of ways and are always intertwined with political decisions by the conquering powers. One is a positive, if not idealized, perspective; the other is a negative, "heathen" concept. As noted above, early leaders saw them differently: Washington and Jefferson sought to make them full citizens while Jackson saw the Indians as not belonging anywhere near the whites who settled their lands; he reversed the policy and sent most of them west.

The more idealized, positive view is best captured in the widely used work of James Adair, who lived among and around the Cherokee for over 30 years, starting in 1735. He also spent time with the Catawba, Chickasaw and Choctaw, and is one of the first historians to record firsthand accounts, as well as learning the language while living with the Cherokee. With an education in theology and Hebrew, he studied their myths, stories and especially their language, concluding that the Indians were of Jewish origin, specifically one of the ten lost tribes of Israel. His work, entitled *Cherokee Beliefs and Practices of the Ancients*, published in London in 1775, was used extensively by many others both as an early primary document as to beliefs and to see the aboriginal people of America as lost spiritual kinfolk.[30]

Adair was not the first to theorize that Indians of both North and South America came from the lost tribes of Israel. Garcia in 1607 was followed by several other writers in French, Spanish and English in the 1600s until the 1800s. Significant early American preachers and leaders such as Cotton Mather, Roger Williams, Jonathan Edwards, and William Penn shared the view.[31] The most extensive work done was that of Lord Viscount Kingsborough, who published in London from 1830 to 1848 nine volumes, including much material from French, Spanish and Mexican manuscripts. He wrecked his fortune and died a debtor for his work that "confirmed" the veracity of Adair's work.[32] Modern historians and ethnologists praise the early reports but not always the "Ten Tribism" theory. Significant historical Cherokee leaders such as Elias Boudinot and the charismatic Chief John Ross used the theory to help acculturate their people to the overwhelming tide of European settlers.

The more negative view that the Indians were at best heathen, if not animals, was also hard to separate from the white man's greed for land, farms, game and gold. Early missionary activity was supported, if not sponsored, by the federal government to "civilize" the Cherokee and to thus integrate them into the growing American society. To be "Christian" was to be "civilized" and vice versa. Schools were started that focused not only on white values—reading, writing and domestic life of settlers—but also on a Christian faith. Some Cherokee ignored, some adopted and some adapted that faith to their own system of belief and lifestyle. The most progressive changes occurred in the 50 years 1789–1839, during which massive cultural transformation took place, according to historian William G. McLoughlin.[33] His summary focuses on six major areas as follows.

First, he notes the economic transformation from fur trading to farming, which included the "rise of an elite who profited from owning slaves and developing commercial activities such as trading stores, taverns, ferries, gristmills, cotton gins, turnpikes, etc."[34] In some areas of the frontier the Cherokee were more successful at these commercial ventures than their European settler counterparts, feeding into many tensions and increased racism. In some areas, such as northern Georgia, this factor played a major role in removal. White settlers were quick to take over farms and businesses as soon as the Cherokee were removed.

Second, McLoughlin lists the massive changes in familial roles and kinship transformations, which meant the "shift from a matrilineal, exogamous clan system to a patriarchal nuclear family system with a concomitant shift from communal cooperation to individualism."[35] In practical terms this meant that the schools, both governmental and mission, worked to take the women from the fields and put them into the home and kitchen and to take the men from the hunt and put them into the fields. Records show the attempt to make them look and act like their white mentors, who could not grasp that the kinship ties and ownership of most goods were through the mother, not the father.[36]

Third, he underlines the social and ethical transformations that resulted in the "decline of hospitality and harmony ethics, the accumulation of private family wealth through patrilineal inheritances, the development of class and educational distinctions."[37] With the rise of individualism as a higher value and with the education of some, but not all, came inevitable classes created among the Cherokee. The older idea of sharing and seeking harmony above all was lost. Yet the older ideas remained as traditional Cherokee tried to hold on, often in conflict with the newer wealthy, educated families.

Political transformation is the fourth massive cultural transformation McLoughlin lists. This included the "centralization of authority and the adoption of an elective, bicameral legislative system with courts and police able to coerce all individuals to conform to tribal laws."[38] Within their old system, there were hundreds of small villages, each able to deal with their own agreed-upon rules. Since harmony within the community was so highly valued, matters were dealt with at a local level, usually within the family or local group.

Fifth, he notes the massive religious transformation, which meant the "shift to religious pluralism and the adaptation of Christian views and practices while retaining certain traditional beliefs, customs and ceremonies, especially in the medical and conjuring arts."[39] Perhaps in no other area is tension as high in Eastern Cherokee faith communities as in this one, often posed in the question: "Can one be Christian and still go to the old dances?" One of the persistent traditions, little known and oft denied by modern Cherokee, is that of the Ani-kuta'ni, an ancient people or priestly class among them whom they massacred. Mooney documents various sources and variations of who these people were, citing the authority they apparently had over the people.[40]

Last, McLoughlin notes the transformation from an oral to a written tradition that came about "after Sequoyah found a way of writing Cherokee, though it began earlier among those familiar with English."[41]

Each of these changes in Cherokee life was massive in itself, but the old, traditional ways lingered on. The old stories, dances and treatments were still strong when Mooney did his research in the late 1800s. With the mixed marriages with settlers, many tensions arose between the more traditional full-bloods and those with mixed parents. Some of those tensions remain today. Also, not only the missionaries but also many teachers and federal agents never knew where the Cherokee individuals were in their belief systems. They had no problem making all the behavioral changes of good Christians and still were able to play Indian ball and dance to the drums, both of which upset the conservative missionaries. Historian McLoughlin concludes that they could adapt to the Christian ways and still practice many traditions such as conjuring arts without seeing any conflict.[42]

The assertive, more rational, left-brain theology of many American churches still appears today not to have a final answer. Many of the underlying Cherokee world views, their cosmology and old traditional stories are still there. Many are "good Christians" and faithful in their church participation, yet have still a deep spiritual connection to the old ways, or at least some respect for them. There are some who struggle with divided loyalty, but also some who feel no conflict. Outsiders, and some well-intentioned preachers, may have problems with the drums, the dances and old stories. One ancient elder, Walker Calhoun, who keeps up the old dances, explained how much a part of his life they were; he never knew there might be any question about them until he went to Oklahoma and heard a preacher saying the old dances were "heathen."[43]

What exists today is a syncretism of old and new religions, a long process of blending ancient Cherokee beliefs with Christian beliefs, and others. This harmonizing was clearly at work in 1826 when Elias Boudinot was raising money for his printing press and spoke of blending the best of both the old and the new:

They ... cannot be called idolators, for they never worshiped Images. They believed in a Supreme Being, the Creator of all, the God of the white, the red, and the black man. They also believed in the existence of an evil spirit who resided, as they thought, in the setting sun, the future place of all who in their lifetime had done iniquitously. Their prayers were addressed alone to the Supreme Being, and if written would fill a large volume and display much sincerity, beauty, and sublimity. When the ancient customs of the Cherokee were in their full force, no warrior [was] thought secure unless he had addressed his guardian angel; no hunter could hope for success unless, before the rising sun, he had asked for the assistance of his God and on his return at eve had offered sacrifice to him.[44]

For some theologians, the word "syncretism" or the idea of blending anything with Christian doctrine is close to heresy. Yet from the history of missions, even from biblical times, the missionary is always faced with the question of how the Divine, by whatever name, might have been revealed to the people. The modern Cherokee, like their ancestors, are open to the Great Spirit, the Creator, because they are open to creation and to spiritual things. They generally do not try to harmonize the old ways but feel so many parallels that they feel comfortable. As one Cherokee elder, also a minister, said to me, "We find the seeds of the Gospel in the old stories, even the seeds to understanding the Trinity. The Great Spirit is the Holy Spirit but really God one Creator."[45]

Western rational theology has a long history of dogma, of teachings formed with clear lines and conclusions. The Cherokee way is much more Eastern, much more like the days of Jesus, when parables and stories carried the truth in them, with meaning for each person who heard. They did not have to be reduced to the "truth" by a singular person. While working in Communist Eastern Europe, this author noted the difference between Western European (and American) thinking, especially the further east one went. Westerners would often ask a direct question to a Russian or Siberian and get a story as an answer. The Westerner would ask, in frustration, "Why doesn't he give me a straight answer?" The usual answer was, "He did. It is in the story. Listen to it and you have your answer." Likewise, one can hear in these old stories some ancient truth, some message that may not fit the strictly rational or linear categories. For each person it may be slightly different or very different, just as in biblical stories. Many images not only of a personal, family nature but also of a religious or spiritual nature may come up. One does not have to subscribe to the "Ten Tribism" theory to see that many parallels to early Christian beliefs do exist. The vast cultural changes in their world did lead the Cherokee to move strongly into Christian traditions, but not without great losses. Missionary activities, especially with their own Cherokee ministers, were effective, especially during the times of great tragedies, such as the Trail of Tears, famine and smallpox epidemics. There were spiritual heroes like Reverend Jesse Busheyhead, a Cherokee Baptist pastor who ministered to Cherokee folk during the removal and traveled to several white congregations to try to stop the removal, in addition to helping some of those congregations deal with their loss of the Cherokee members.[46] Such leaders, like the ancient Cherokee wisdom stories, can help one face overwhelming circumstances with faith and dignity.

The Cherokee Country — Adapted from the map by James Mooney (1900), Bureau of American Ethnology, Nineteenth Annual Report, plate III. After page 22 in *James Mooney's History, Myths, and Sacred Formulas of the Cherokees.*

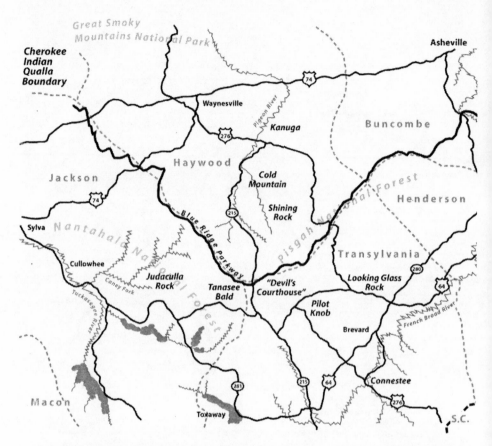

Cherokee Myth Locations — The geographical sites of several myths as identified by Mooney, located in one part of western North Carolina, especially in the counties of Transylvania, Jackson and Haywood.

1

The Cherokee Creation Story

HOW THE WORLD WAS MADE: THE MYTH

The earth is a great island floating in a sea of water, and suspended at each of the four cardinal points by a cord hanging down from the sky vault, which is of solid rock. When the world grows old and worn out, the people will die and the cords will break and let the earth sink down into the ocean, and all will be water again. The Indians are afraid of this.

When all was water, the animals were above in Galun'lati, beyond the arch; but it was very much crowded, and they were wanting more room. They wondered what was below the water, and at last Dayunisi, "Beaver's Grandchild," the little water beetle, offered to go and see if it could learn. It darted in every direction over the surface of the water, but could find no firm place to rest. Then it dived to the bottom and came up with some soft mud, which began to grow and spread on every side until it became the island which we call the earth. It was afterward fastened to the sky with four cords, but no one remembers who did this.

At first the earth was flat and very soft and wet. The animals were anxious to get down, and sent out different birds to see if it was yet dry, but they found no place to alight and came back again to Galun'lati. At last it seemed to be time, and they sent out the Buzzard and told him to go and make ready for them. This was the Great Buzzard, the father of all the buzzards we see now. He flew over all the earth, low down near the ground, and it was still soft. When he reached the Cherokee country, he was very tired, and his wings began to flap and strike the ground, and wherever they struck the earth there was a valley, and where they turned up again there was a mountain. When the animals above saw this, they were afraid that the whole world would be mountains, so they called him back, but the Cherokee country remains full of mountains to this day.

When the earth was dry and the animals came down, it was still dark, so they got the sun and set it in a track to go every day across the island from east to west, just overhead. It was too hot this way and Tsiskagili, the Red Crawfish, had his shell scorched a bright red, so that his meat was spoiled; and the Cherokee do not eat it. The conjurors put the sun another hand-breadth higher in the air, but it was still too hot. They raised it another time, and another, until it was seven hand-breadths high and just under the sky arch. Then it was right and they left it so. This is why the conjurors call the highest place Gulkwa'gine Di'galun'latiyun', "the seventh height," because it is seven hand-breadths above the earth. Every day the sun goes along under this arch, and returns at night on the upper side to the starting place.

There is another world under this, and it is like ours in every-thing — animals, plants, and people — save that the seasons are different. The streams that come down from the mountains are the trails by which we reach this underworld, and the springs at their heads are the doorways by which we enter it, but to do this one must fast and go to water and have one of the underground people for a guide. We know that the seasons in the underworld are different from ours, because the water in the springs is always warmer in winter and cooler in summer than the outer air.

When the animals and plants were first made — we do not know by whom — they were told to watch and keep awake for seven nights, just as young men now fast and keep awake when they pray to their medicine. They tried to do this, and nearly all were awake through the first night, but the next night several dropped off to sleep, and the third night others were asleep, and then others, until, on the seventh night, of all the animals only the owl, the panther, and one or two more were still awake. To these were given the power to see and to go about in the dark, and to make prey of the birds and animals which must sleep at night. Of the trees only the cedar, the pine, the spruce, and holly, and the laurel were awake to the end, and to them it was given to be always green and to be greatest for medicine, but to the others it was said: "Because you have not endured to the end you shall lose your hair every winter."

How the World Was Made — The Great Buzzard whose wings formed the Cherokee mountains and valleys is depicted by Cherokee artist Lynn Lossiah.

Men came after the animals and plants. At first there were only a brother and sister until he struck her with a fish and told her to multiply and so it was. In seven days a child was born to her, and thereafter every seven days another, and they increased very fast until there was danger that the world could not keep them. Then it was made that a woman should have only one child in a year, and it has been so ever since.

THE CHEROKEE CREATION STORY

When people enter the modern Museum of the Cherokee Indian in Cherokee, North Carolina, they are presented with a brief film about the creation myth, setting the stage for visiting the history and culture of the Cherokee. In most public presentations of other myths it is important to use the creation myth to lay a basic foundation for understanding the rest. Jung's close associate and specialist in fairy tales and myths, Marie-Louise von Franz, says that creation myths are in a different class from other myths. She says that "when they are told there is always a certain *solemnity* that gives them a central importance; they convey a mood which implies that what is said will concern the basic things of existence."[1] She goes on to say that, concerning the emotional and mood accompanying them, "creation myths are the deepest and most important of all."[2] The telling of creation stories is frequently portrayed as vital since they have to do with "the ultimate meaning, not only of our existence, but of the existence of the whole cosmos."[3]

The creation story is for every group and for every person some form of coming to an awareness of their own existence, their world and their place in the world. Because there are so many unknowns, so many things on the periphery of our understanding, humans tend to create images and explain those in some fashion, both for themselves and for their children. People project those images on their world, even as their ancestors drew maps of the New World that had greater distortions the farther from their known world they went. At the edge of old maps were serpents and other fearful, demonic creatures. Von Franz comments that such maps show that "wherever known reality stops, where we touch the unknown, there we project an archetypal image."[4] She says further that creation myths "represent unconscious and pre-conscious processes which describe not the origin of our cosmos, but *the origin of man's conscious awareness of the world*"[5] (italics von Franz's).

That conscious awareness of the world as seen in its origins speaks to the many expressions in the artwork of the Cherokee. B. Lynne Harlan, former cultural resources director for the Eastern Band of Cherokee Indians, says that the creation story lives among the Cherokee "not as a single story but as a complex of ideas and knowledge woven into our history and life-ways." Contemporary beliefs challenge the stories, and the interpretations vary as much as the individuals. Many of those stories, Harlan says, "have come down to us through shell gorgets taken from graves, pottery shards from past home sites, and from earthworks that still touch our imagination today." Today's artists "continue to be driven by the same pride, understanding, knowledge and camaraderie of those who came before us and left behind reminders of our collective Cherokee family."[6]

Harlan's reference to gorgets, ancient shell neck ornaments, is related to one popularly portrayed image that comes from another Cherokee myth about the origin of fire. That tiny water beetle that brought the first fire has become the emblem for the Museum of the Cherokee Indian (see following chapter).

As one experiences the Cherokee creation story, one can get a sense of their inner world, the deeper awareness of their place not only in the mountains of Appalachia and in the world itself, but also of their rightful individual existence. As Lynne Harlan noted, interpretations are as varied as individuals, and each person hears what is important to them at each hearing of the myth.

GLOBAL STATUS: IN SUSPENSION AND SUSPENSE

> *The earth is a great island floating in a sea of water, and suspended at each of the four cardinal points by a cord hanging down from the sky vault, which is of solid rock. When the world grows old and worn out, the people will die and the cords will break and let the earth sink down into the ocean, and all will be water again. The Indians are afraid of this.*

The opening paragraph of this creation story gives the current status of the world: the earth place is an island floating in water, yet tied to the heavens above. There is a tension between above and below and humans are in between. The heavens above are solid rock, a sky vault that gives more security and the most stability from above, the spirit world. The fragile nature of the earth is noted, with the real possibility of becoming "worn out." The geographic reality is emphasized, namely that most of the world is water. And as one elder explained to this author, "You are mostly water, your body is not only made up of it but it is crucial to your survival; honor it, respect it [the water]."[7] The Cherokee tie to water is a theme that arises in the myths repeatedly.

From a psychological perspective it captures the deepest anxiety of every human: the possibility of nonexistence when all is lost, when the world sinks beneath and when all life ceases to exist. This is deeper than a fear of death; this is *Ur-Angst*, that most primitive and fearful of all fears that humans are born with: the possibility of not existing. It is the core fear of life: nonlife. It is being and nonbeing caught in the tension of opposites. It has to do with life and death but is much deeper than living or dying. The Cherokee admit such a basic human fear at the start of their powerful understanding of creation itself. It is something one never really loses and becomes part of one's survival reaction when danger is present. But for some suffering people, that core fear spills over into sensing danger when they feel they are not loved or are not accepted. It is as if they are fearful that the very cords of life are about to break, even if the actual danger is small.

This sky vault tension has a different twist in several other more northern tribes in whose stories the earth rests on the back of a turtle, as in many other world cultures. Many tribes use the term "turtle island" for this world. That sense of world-support also carries some sense of security and longevity for both heaven and earth. The turtle shows up in the Lazy Hunter myth considered later.

EARTH FORMATION: FROM THE WATERY DEPTHS

> When all was water, the animals were above in Galun'lati, beyond the arch; but it was very much crowded, and they were wanting more room. They wondered what was below the water, and at last Dayunisi, "Beaver's Grandchild," the little water beetle, offered to go and see if it could learn. It darted in every direction over the surface of the water, but could find no firm place to rest. Then it dived

to the bottom and came up with some soft mud, which began to grow and spread on every side until it became the island which we call the earth. It was afterward fastened to the sky with four cords, but no one remembers who did this.

The second step in this seven-step story presents the problem of crowding, and of the animals who exist before humans. They are creatures residing above the sky arch, but they need room. Their curiosity leads them to wonder about the depths of the water, what might be down there. Then the lowly, humble water beetle, that insect gifted like the beaver in that it can not only skim the surface but also dive to the depths, volunteers to check it out. It not only learns but acts and brings forth substance from the bottom, real earth that not only forms an island but grows and grows. The reality of the earth as a living, changing being is shown. Then the four cardinal ties are made to the strong sky arch, the heavens above. No credit is given to who does it, but it is done; the tie to the sky above is crucial. Without that heavenly support, all is lost.

From a depth psychological perspective, this calls for a plunge into the deep, into the unconscious for both source and substance for "grounding." The search for more room in life, for psychological space, is not only a community need but also a personal need, when life is too crowded. Superficial searches lead one to many fads or quick fixes as one skims about the surface. But only when, like the lowly water beetle, persons look deeper can they be rewarded with substantive material, real stuff that has potential for growth and stability. Even with the earth being formed, the connection to the solid heavenly arch above is crucial for balance.

CHEROKEE COUNTRY: A FLYING FORMATION

At first the earth was flat and very soft and wet. The animals were anxious to get down, and sent out different birds to see if it was yet dry, but they found no place to alight and came back again to Galun'lati. At last it seemed to be time, and they sent out the Buzzard and told him to go and make ready for them. This was the Great Buzzard, the father of all the buzzards we see now. He flew over all the earth, low down near the ground, and it was still soft. When he reached the Cherokee country, he was very tired, and his

wings began to flap and strike the ground, and wherever they struck
the earth there was a valley, and where they turned up again there
was a mountain. When the animals above saw this, they were afraid
that the whole world would be mountains, so they called him back,
but the Cherokee country remains full of mountains to this day.

The third paragraph is perhaps the most emotional and powerful
for it demonstrates the tie of the Cherokee to their beloved homeland,
the Appalachian Mountains. The theme of the mountains as a source
of strength, as refuge and even in some sense as paradise is picked up
in several myths. The name "Cherokee" itself seems to tie them closely
to mountains and caves. This creation strongly captures the heavenly
nature of that creation as the Great Buzzard is chosen finally to make
ready, after other birds had checked it out, not unlike in the biblical
flood story. The massiveness of this spirit creature, this father of all the
giant buzzards today, emphasizes for Cherokee that the Great Spirit
created the mountains and valleys so well known today. But the call-
back of the Great Buzzard is unique in that even the community of
animals did not want all land to be mountains; there had to be space
for other creatures, those not adapted to mountains, but other types
of landscape. A sense of toleration, or respect for different spaces is
implied.[8]

This can also be a metaphor for human development in terms of
emotional space, as creation of the psychological landscape in formation during one's lifetime. Early on, persons are malleable, able to be
formed into a unique shape, as individuals, as families and as communities. In the history of all peoples, such as the Cherokee, this dynamic
of ongoing formation exists. The psychological formation, collectively
and individually, is always in formation, adapting to the many new
"spirits" that enter. The adaptability of the Cherokee to changes in time
has played a major role in their survival.

LIGHT, WARMTH AND TIME: THE SUN AND DAYS

When the earth was dry and the animals came down, it was
still dark, so they got the sun and set it in a track to go every day
across the island from east to west, just overhead. It was too hot this
way and Tsiskagili, the Red Crawfish, had his shell scorched a bright
red, so that his meat was spoiled; and the Cherokee do not eat it.

*The conjurors put the sun another hand-breadth higher in the air,
but it was still too hot. They raised it another time, and another,
until it was seven hand-breadths high and just under the sky arch.
Then it was right and they left it so. This is why the conjurors call
the highest place Gulkwa'gine Di'galun'latiyun', "the seventh
height," because is it seven hand-breadths above the earth. Every day
the sun goes along under this arch, and returns at night on the upper
side to the starting place.*

This next phase has to do with the sun and the setting of the days.
The handbreadth is a figurative expression used in many sacred formulas. The theme of successive removals of the sun in order to mod-
ify the excessive heat is found in other tribes, according to Mooney.[9]
The seven heights or seven heavens is found in widespread cosmology
around the world, most noted in India and Polynesia. (For the Aztecs
and ancient Scandinavians the sacred number was nine.)[10] Likewise,
every culture or tribe has sacred numbers. For Christianity they are
usually three and seven. For the Cherokee they are four and seven, used
in many formulas, in the seven tribal clans, and in prayers. Reference
to the four cardinal directions is made in prayers and dances. In terms
of direction, the Cherokee have not only the four sacred cardinal ones
that all Indians have (north, south, east and west), but also their sacred
seven adds three more: above, below and "here" in the center.[11]

The Red Crawfish becomes a symbol and reminder of the imbalance of heat and light. The correct height is seven hands, that special,
sacred number.

The adjustment of the sun's height and its effect on the creation is
powerful in its modern and ancient sense. With debates over global
warming, with crops and weather and other natural issues of major
concern, here the ancient wisdom of the Cherokee noted their dependence on the right amount of sunlight, the length of days as set by the
sun, the most basic source of light and warmth. From a psychological
perspective, the meaning of light in life and the sense of an adequate
amount of light as insight may be the key points. Not only having too
little insight, but sometimes too much, is harmful. For example, too
much analysis, too much intensity may well scorch and burn. Some topics, like the Red Crawfish, cannot be digested because they have been
subjected to too much intensity and heat. Better to back off and find
the "seventh handbreadth" or correct height. It may well be a different

level for different people. So it is in psychotherapy: not every person is at the same place. Like a conjurer, the therapist searches constantly for the right "height" that will bring light and life without damage.

THE UNDERWORLD: ENTRANCE INTO OPPOSITES

There is another world under this, and it is like ours in every-thing — animals, plants, and people — save that the seasons are different. The streams that come down from the mountains are the trails by which we reach this underworld, and the springs at their heads are the doorways by which we enter it, but to this one must fast and go to water and have one of the underground people for a guide. We know that the seasons in the underworld are different from ours, because the water in the springs is always warmer in winter and cooler in summer than the outer air.

The fifth segment of this story comes back to the current world, to explain some of its mysteries. The world under this world captures the belief that within the mountains, under the ground as it were, there exists another world like the outer in all ways except the seasons are different. The pathways are the streams themselves, tying again the role of water to their deeper world in the context of the mountains. The guides from that domain are probably either the Little People or the Nunnehi. Fasting is a major issue in several myths, including others considered here.

Going to water is that important ritual performed usually in the early morning as a part of giving thanks and preparation for every sort of special activity, from the powerful stick ball games to war parties. In earlier years it was an annual rite of purification to celebrate the new year. The ceremony included prayers, chants with the entire community entering the flowing water, and dipping under four times, once in each of the four cardinal directions. In the oldest traditions they also took off their old clothes, letting them float away, and donned fresh clothes when leaving the water. They went to the fire kept by the priest and got a new flame to carry to their homes to rekindle their home fires. The purpose of all this was "to restore harmony and good feelings among all members of the community by washing away bad relations."[12] It can also carry a meaning of one being naive if one had not been to water.

From a Jungian perspective, this underground image of the spring captures the role of the unconscious as being very real, as well as noting the need for access to that reality, usually by dreams or visions. In Jungian therapy dreams, art, word association, active imagination and other methods often present symbolic images from the unconscious as if from "under the earth" or under water. What is striking is that those images are often in opposite forms from the conscious world or "above the ground." The best known is Jung's concept of the "shadow," which is made up of all those things one has suppressed or repressed into the unconscious. He defined the shadow as "everything that the subject refuses to acknowledge about himself and yet is always thrusting itself upon him directly or indirectly, for instance, inferior traits of character and other incompatible tendencies."[13] When they are not recognized or brought into the conscious world, these negative or darker parts of the personality are then projected onto others as "evil." In the Cherokee story, what appears to be warm on the outside may well be quite cold in the underworld, especially with regard to feelings. To enter that world one is often guided by other messengers, parts of one's own being that guide one into deeper sources of learning. Those guides to the inner world of the unconscious may be in the form of angels, or other "spirit forms." Some form of the anima, the feminine part of the person, may take on that task. (Or the animus, the masculine form, may apply.) Anima is the Greek word for spirit and is an important archetypal force for Jung.

People are often drawn to water literally, for mysterious, unknown reasons, and sit on a bank and meditate, or wade into the water and fish; many find healing near the water. Personalized rituals with water are common even when not attached to some known religious tradition. Some can experience it as is a kind of returning to the womb, a place of peace and tranquility. Also the question could be asked: What kind of individual, family or community rituals provide cleansing for a new start? Perhaps to some degree, the community dinners and family reunions capture a little of that. For some, the act of swimming or fishing takes on a ritual, cleansing power.

PLANTS AND ANIMALS: REWARDS FOR FAITHFUL FASTING

When the animals and plants were first made — we do not know
by whom — they were told to watch and keep awake for seven nights,

just as young men now fast and keep awake when they pray to their medicine. They tried to do this, and nearly all were awake through the first night, but the next night several dropped off to sleep, and the third night others were asleep, and then others, until, on the seventh night, of all the animals only the owl, the panther, and one or two more were still awake. To these were given the power to see and to go about in the dark, and to make prey of the birds and animals which must sleep at night. Of the trees only the cedar, the pine, the spruce, and holly, and the laurel were awake to the end, and to them it was given to be always green and to be greatest for medicine, but to the others it was said: "Because you have not endured to the end you shall lose your hair every winter."

The sixth segment reverts back to the formative stages in creation of plants and animals, letting the Cherokee know that they have different features for a very specific reason. They are told to fast and pray for the special seven days and seven nights, as some people still do. As is shown in one of the later myths, not all are able to hold out but some do: the owl, the panther and other nocturnal animals do, as well as the cedar, pine, spruce, holly and laurel. As a reward, the night animals could feed on the others and the plants not only kept their "hair" each winter, but also provided medicine for healing for all.

The sense of endurance is also an issue here, for the call to pilgrimage demands sacrifice and has its rewards for those few who can hold out to the end. The kind of healing that can come from the medicine within is only one reward. Being able to see in the darkness when others cannot is another reward, for darkness is all around. Survival in the dark world, i.e., having eyes that can see, is a crucial psychological metaphor. The gift (and skill) of differentiation is one of the goals of therapy and psychological growth. For example, it is a gift to be able to "see" or differentiate those shadow or complex items that are one's own and to withdraw one's projection of them onto others. Another reward metaphor is captured in the endurance of the evergreens: In dream interpretation, as well as in myths and fairy tales, the symbol of hair often represents one's thoughts. This would also imply that the ability to keep one's thoughts focused "year-round" or most of the time is also a great gift.

HUMAN BEINGS: BIRTH AND LIMITS

Men came after the animals and plants. At first there were only a brother and sister until he struck her with a fish and told her to multiply and so it was. In seven days a child was born to her, and thereafter every seven days another, and they increased very fast until there was danger that the world could not keep them. Then it was made that a woman should have only one child in a year, and it has been so every since.

In the seventh and final stage, humans are created after plants and animals, in the same order as the biblical accounts. One has no way of knowing that the terms "brother and sister" are literal or symbolic uses of the terms but it seems more likely to be the latter due to the strong incest taboo set by the Cherokee clan system, which carefully governed such matters. This first male and female story has him striking her with a fish, which is a symbol of the depths. In any case he tells her to multiply and she does so every seven days. The fear of overpopulation comes soon and the timing is set so that a child only came once yearly.

As in most Native American myths, humans have no priority over other creatures, for they came last. A sense of superiority of humans is not declared, only mutual existence with other creatures. The bringing of other human life is given but only responsibly, only the number that can be sustained. Here is a powerful early fear of overpopulation. Even as balance and harmony were core issues for the individual and community, so it was in creation. Psychologically, one may choose to have children or not, for at the start there were only the two. If one so chooses one is responsible not to have more than the number for whom one can provide. A key symbol here is the fish, a sign so often in antiquity for fertility and sexuality. But it is also used as a sign of resurrection and immortality. Life goes on in children.

In depth psychology the fish appears as a symbol with key meaning from the unconscious. It often appears in dreams as a symbol for the Self, that unique central guiding core in each person, as well as the totality of the personality. Many meanings appear for this creature, such as vigilance and humility.

THEOLOGICAL COMMENTS

The biblical creation story and its variations have some parallels that may be clear to many. Some obvious parallels include the creation of land as separate from the water, and especially light from the darkness.[14] Some biblical similarities are seen in the setting out of allotted times. The plants and animals are also preexistent; all is good, in harmony and in balance. When the role of water is noted in relationship to "going to water," the crucial role of baptism in the history of Christianity can be seen. Also, in some Christian traditions, the ritual of sprinkling holy water is a part of worship ritual. The brother and sister story, of course, is similar to the story of Adam and Eve in paradise, especially in the account of Eve coming from Adam's rib; one as close as a sister. However, there is certainly no first-creation priority for the man in the Cherokee story, rather a sense of equality in keeping with the equal role of women in Cherokee thinking.[15]

The role of the fish, of course, is significant in Christian history and art. In Christian history the use of the fish symbol was a statement of faith, as the sign of the fish was a kind of acronym from the Greek word for fish: *ichthus*, i.e., Jesus Christ, Son of God, savior (*Iesous Christos, Theou Uios, Soter*). Christ is pictured as a fisherman and his followers are called to be "fishers of men."[16] He eats fish in his post resurrection appearance.[17] Numerous biblical uses for the fish gave it a key role in most religious traditions. Christ multiplied the loaves and fishes to feed the multitudes.[18] The ancient story of Jonah being swallowed by a big fish carries powerful psychological and religious symbolism of a being taken down into depths and "resurrected" into new life.[19] In therapy, many people suffering from depression or difficult life crises identify with the Jonah story, feeling they too were "swallowed up" by the great fish of depression.

The fish symbol captures not only fruitfulness and birth but also life after death, even meaning for baptism. So, the symbol for birth and rebirth is captured in the Cherokee myth, coming close to some of the Christian images for fish. In many religions, the fish had a sacred nature, one implying wisdom and knowledge. In antiquity, the fish itself was often a symbol of life and fertility because of all the eggs it could produce. All of these aspects give special meaning to giving life to other beings, to having children as a sacred act, and certainly puts this "fish" action into a religious perspective.

In a similar vein, the powerful implications for the seven directions of the Cherokee (east, west, north, south, up, down, and here in the center of the person) bring much greater depth to one's self-understanding, both psychologically and spiritually. The four standard directions are horizontal and the others are vertical with the last being the center of all. This is captured in the image of the cross, which is not only the major Christian symbol but also used in many forms of other religions. As noted, the ancient Cherokee gorget with the art form for the water beetle has a cross in the middle. Also, the ancient symbol for the sun, a cross with angled arms on each leg, called a swastika, is one of the most universal cross symbols not only among Native Americans but across Asia and most of the globe. It carries religious meaning for different cultures.[20] From this Cherokee sense of direction one can note that when one is torn in many directions, not knowing which way to turn, one is also reminded to look "up" to the holy, to the spiritual possibilities, to listen for that "still small voice." Persons are also reminded to look down into the depths of the soul, to seek the wisdom from the unconscious, to listen to the messages from dreams and the creative inner world. Most of all one is reminded to look for that "here" in the center, to get in touch with that core of one's being, that Self that can allow connection with the Divine. This question, "Who am I?" is the one asked by many in their search for meaning and hope. Jung noted that for the first half of life most are looking outwardly toward education, work, family and life orientation (the first four Cherokee directions) and the last half looking inward for meaning to it all (the last three Cherokee directions).

Perhaps the most notable difference between the biblical account and the Cherokee one is the consistent declaration in Genesis that "God created" or acted in other ways, and that God saw that creation was good. In the Cherokee story it is said that "no one remembers who did this." However there is an implied "good"[21] in the very positive sense of the creation itself. They saw it as good and much of their remnant belief system is to see that beauty of creation and to give thanks daily for it. In response to a question about his faith, one elder said, "It is to wake each day, and to really see what the Great Spirit has created and to truly give thanks for that. Each day is a gift from above and to be appreciated."[22]

2

The First Fire

In the beginning, there was no fire, and the world was cold, until the Thunders (Ani'-Hyuntikwala'ski), who lived up in Galun'lati, sent their lightning and put fire into the bottom of a hollow sycamore tree that grew on an island. The animals knew it was there, because they could see the smoke coming out at the top, but they could not get to it on account of the water, so they held a council to decide what to do. This was a long time ago.

Every animal that could fly or swim was anxious to go after the fire. The Raven offered, and because he was so large and strong they thought that he could surely do the work, so he was sent first. He flew high and across the water and alighted on the sycamore tree, but while he was wondering what to do next, the heat had scorched all his feathers black, and he was frightened and came back without the fire. The little Screech Owl (Wa'huhu') volunteered to go, and reached the place safely, but while he was looking down into the hollow tree a blast of hot air came up and nearly burned out his eyes. He managed to fly home as best he could, but it was a long time before he could see well, and his eyes are red to this day. Then the Hooting Owl (U'guku') and the Horned Owl (Tskili') went, but by the time they got to the hollow tree the fire was burning so fiercely that the smoke nearly blinded them, and the ashes carried up by the wind made white rings about their eyes. They had to come again without the fire, but with all their rubbing they were never able to get rid of the white rings.

Now no more of the birds would venture, and so the little Uksu'hi snake, the black racer, said he would go through the water *and bring back some fire. He swam across to the island and crawled through the grass to the tree, and went in by a small hole at the bottom. The heat and smoke were too much for him, too, and after dodging about blindly over the hot ashes until he was almost on fire himself he managed by good luck, to get out again at the same hole, but his body had been scorched black, and he has ever since had the habit of darting and doubling on his track as if trying to escape from close quarters. He came back, and the great blacksnake, Gule'gi, "the Climber," offered to go for the fire. He swam over to the island and climbed up the tree on the outside, as the blacksnake always does, but when he put his head down into the hole the smoke choked him so that he fell into the burning stump, and before he could climb out again he was as black as the Uksu'hi.*

Now they held another council, for still there was no fire, and the world was cold, but birds, snakes and four-footed animals all had some excuse for not going, because they were all afraid to venture near the burning sycamore, until at last Kanane'ski Amai'yehi (the Water Spider) said she would go. This is not the water spider that looks like a mosquito, but the other one, with black downy hair and red stripes on her body. She can run on top of the water or dive to the bottom, so there would be no trouble to get over to the island, but the question was, how could she bring back the fire? "I'll manage that," said the Water Spider; so she spun a thread from her body and wove it into a tusti bowl, which she fastened on her back. Then she crossed over to the island and through the grass to where the fire was still burning. She put one little coal of fire into the bowl, and came back with it, and ever since we have had fire, and the Water Spider still keeps her tusti bowl.

THE GIFT OF FIRE: OUT OF REACH

In the beginning there was no fire, and the world was cold, until the Thunders (Ani'-Hyuntikwala'ski), who lived up in Galun'lati, sent their lightning and put fire into the bottom of a hollow sycamore tree that grew on an island. The animals knew it was there, because they could see the smoke coming out at the top, but they could not get to it on account of the water, so they held a council to decide what to do. This was a long time ago.

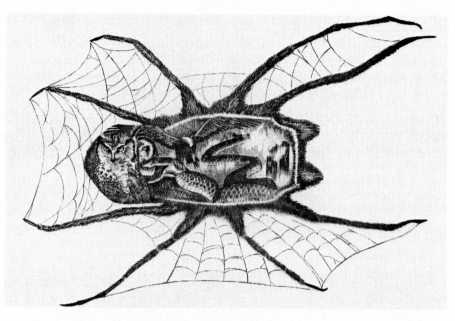

The First Fire Myth: The Water Spider — The water spider, successful in obtaining the first fire, as depicted by Cherokee artist Lynn Lossiah, who includes also those birds and reptiles who tried, but failed.

This short story is like a continuation of the Cherokee creation story in that it is part of the creation process and the obtaining of that essential tool of humanity, the gift of fire. As is true in most Native American stories, little difference is made between the animals and humans; there is a connectedness and here all the players are animals.

The statement of the first problem is that the world is cold, implying that all the inhabitants also are cold. Galun'lati, that place above the great arch in the sky, is where the fire source is located and sent by none other than the Thunders, who will be introduced in the myth of Kana'ti and Selu later. The connection of thunder and lightning is important as a phenomenon not only in mythology but also in the practical experience of humans and animals alike. The creation of natural fires and the subsequent burning of woodlands and great prairies were universal experiences. Early ancestors of most cultures attached gods to such acts. Even the names of most days in the English calendar carry references to those gods, such as Thursday for the Norse god Thor, who sends thunder. More explicit is the German name for the same day, *Donnerstag*, literally "thunder-day."

Mooney gives variations of the story including failed tries by the buzzard and possum with subsequent physiological results. He also compares Creek and Jicarilla stories in obtaining the first fire.[1] The main point is the vital nature of fire for Native Americans and early cultures everywhere. Ancient peoples kept fires not just for warmth and cooking, but also for spiritual or religious reasons. Many groups even today have an "eternal flame" to carry on a tradition or memory of persons and events. Carrying fire from the homeland on the Trail of Tears, and then back, was special in its deeper connection. In ancient Cherokee culture, many ceremonies were made with or around fire as a purifier and special act. Connected to ancestors and traditions, the council fires were, and are, special events. As in the myth, the connection to the heavens above put it in a special holy dimension, as in many cultures.[2]

The second problem presented in the story is that, even though the solution is seen, it is beyond their reach, the fire having landed at the bottom of a hollow sycamore tree on an island. The smoke coming out of the tree is the evidence for such, but the water prevents access. The symbolism of the tree itself is powerful and universal, i.e., archetypal. There are many symbolic possibilities, and all cultures have stories connected to a tree or many trees, such as the tree of knowledge, mother as a tree, the family tree, tree of history, and so on. This use seems to capture the transcendent nature of the tree as connecting three areas: the earth, under the earth, and the heavens, also a psychological parallel to the outer, everyday world, the unconscious and the spiritual world. Inside this tree, like a mother, is the source of warmth, but it must be obtained with much effort. The council will decide just how that is possible.

From a depth psychological level, this seeking of fire concerns more than escape from the cold, for most ancients considered fire to be a basic element, one essential for life, along with wind, water and earth. All those elements are carried in this short Cherokee story. The ancient Greeks saw fire as a "theft from the gods" and Zeus, god of thunder and lightning, punished Prometheus for that theft.[3] Fire is both life-giving and destructive. It warms and purifies. It calms and excites. To be "fired up" is to have enthusiasm. Fire and blood are often associated. Many levels of ambivalence are also carried in this story: they need the fire but it can be harmful. Fire is also associated with the hearth, the center of the home, with hospitality and family warmth. In some ways it is as if this part of the creation story for the Cherokee is the reminder that the gift of warm, family hospitality is also a gift from above, one grasped only with some suffering.

FLYING ANIMAL ATTEMPTS: MARKED FOR LIFE

Every animal that could fly or swim was anxious to go after the fire. The Raven offered, and because he was so large and strong they thought that he could surely do the work, so he was sent first. He flew high and across the water and alighted on the sycamore tree, but while he was wondering what to do next, the heat had scorched all his feathers black, and he was frightened and came back without the fire. The little Screech Owl (Wa'huhu') volunteered to go, and reached the place safely, but while he was looking down into the hollow tree a blast of hot air came up and nearly burned out his eyes. He managed to fly home as best he could, but it was a long time before he could see well, and his eyes are red to this day. Then the Hooting Owl (U'guku') and the Horned Owl (Tskili') went, but by the time they got to the hollow tree the fire was burning so fiercely that the smoke nearly blinded them, and the ashes carried up by the wind made white rings about their eyes. They had to come again without the fire, but with all their rubbing they were never able to get rid of the white rings.

Those who can fly or swim have more energy and enthusiasm to get the fire, so the birds make the first try. The raven, with his size and strength, is invested with their expectations. He only partially accomplishes the task for he crosses the water and lands on the tree, but does nothing more. He is trying to develop a plan, to decide what to do when the heat gets to him and scorches him. Fear overcomes him and he returns without the prized fire. In the human arena, this has many parallels and could speak to those who have the appearance of size and strength and who go to attack major tasks, but cannot think beyond the expectations of others. They cannot step "out of the box" of what they thought they could do. Fear can so easily paralyze them and leave them blackened or marked on their very bodies by this experience.

Next, three owls make their try, the little screech owl, the hooting owl and the horned owl. The first goes one step further than the raven, for he looks into the tree to figure out a way, but in the process, burns his eyes, marking him uniquely with red eyes. The next two owls try but the fire has become fierce, with much more smoke coming up and nearly blinding them. The ashes from the fire give them white rings around their eyes which cannot be rubbed away. Their trip is also a failure. As night creatures, owls are associated with death, wisdom and even witchcraft, among other things. But here their gifts, whatever they may be, are to no avail.

Symbolically, these mysterious night creatures can represent the highly specialized and gifted people who can accomplish great things not "seen" by others. They seem to have sharp night vision that allows them to go into places and accomplish tasks no other humans could; for example, the specialized doctor, lawyer or computer engineer who can accomplish major deeds in their field that others cannot "see" in the normal light of day. But it is often assumed that because they are good in that area that they are also able to "obtain the fire" or to do great things in other areas. Wise as they are, they cannot do all things as they or others may assume.

REPTILIAN RECOVERY: BLACKENED DEFEAT

Now no more of the birds would venture, and so the little Uksu'hi snake, the black racer, said he would go through the water and bring back some fire. He swam across to the island and crawled through the grass to the tree, and went in by a small hole at the bottom. The heat and smoke were too much for him, too, and after dodging about blindly over the hot ashes until he was almost on fire himself he managed by good luck, to get out again at the same hole, but his body had been scorched black, and he has ever since had the habit of darting and doubling on his track as if trying to escape from close quarters. He came back, and the great blacksnake, Gule'gi, "the Climber," offered to go for the fire. He swam over to the island and climbed up the tree on the outside, as the blacksnake always does, but when he put his head down into the hole the smoke choked him so that he fell into the burning stump, and before he could climb out again he was as black as the Uksu'hi.

With the failure of the flying creatures the swimmers take their turn, using their skills in the water and on the land. The black racer, a common, swift snake in the Cherokee world, promises to do the task. He is confident and does cross the water, negotiate the grass and even finds a hole to enter the tree at the bottom. But, alas, it is more than he reckons for, and he even finds himself on hot ashes, luckily finding the hole to escape, but being burned black forever. In addition to that, he moves in such a way today as if trying to escape from close quarters. From a psychological perspective this has human parallels in that some people, such as stereotypical politicians, who promise big results but spend their time dodging about, trying to escape the "close quarters" of questions, or answerability. Often they can get to the "bottom" of an issue, but do not have the ability to bring home what the community needs. In couples' counseling this can also be the case where one or the other skirts about by word or deed, avoiding real issues and their own failures in bringing home the warmth needed for fruitful relationship.

Finally, the blacksnake, apparently learning from his colleague's experience, makes the goal but climbs up the tree, not directly into the hole. The smoke chokes him when his head goes into the hole so he falls into the burning stump. He can climb out, but is also blackened for life, and leaves without the precious fire. One psychological parallel could be the persons who launch out with very good intentions and massive efforts, but are blinded in their (good) pursuit and fall into an inferno of loss and difficulty. Countless debts, bankruptcy, and darkened relationships with friends and family "blacken" them for life. And they had so much potential. The feeling of helplessness now is high in the story as it is in real life. Some element of hope is needed.

THE WEBBED WARRIOR: A CHARIOT OF FIRE FOR ALL

Now they held another council, for still there was no fire, and the world was cold, but birds, snakes and four-footed animals all had some excuse for not going, because they were all afraid to venture near the burning sycamore, until at last Kanane'ski Amai'yehi (the Water Spider) said she would go. This is not the water spider that looks like a mosquito, but the other one, with black downy hair and red stripes on her body. She can run on top of the water or dive to the bottom, so there would be no trouble to get over to the island, but the question was, How could she bring back the fire? "I'll manage that," said the Water Spider; so she spun a thread from her body and wove it into a tusti bowl, which she fastened on her back. Then she crossed over to the island and through the grass to where the fire was still burning. She put one little coal of fire in the bowl, and came back with it, and ever since we have had fire, and the Water Spider still keeps her tusti bowl.

The community meets once again, but this time the animals have no enthusiasm for rescue, only excuses for not going. Fear rules. The burning sycamore has become something other than the blessing it had originally appeared to be; it now appears to be a curse to be avoided. Finally the most unlikely, most lowly creature steps forward. It is not the mighty flying raven or the swimming and climbing snake, but the tiny water spider. She has the skill and has a plan. She can both go on the top of the water and under the water, if needed. And she can spin a *tusti* bowl for her back in which she can carry a coal of fire. She brings warmth into the cold world.

That symbol of this water spider is popular among Cherokee artists who use different media to express the beauty of this otherwise unappreciated creature. A 1,000-year-old gorget, or decorative necklace, was uncovered years ago, and an artistic rendition of it is used as the official symbol of the Museum of the Cherokee Indians in Cherokee, North Carolina. The spider carries many cross-cultural meanings, especially about weaving and spinning. Not always a positive figure in the sense of entrapment or ensnaring other figures, this creature did and does have a very positive image among rural Appalachian and Indian peoples. Not only do they help capture unwanted insects (flies, mosquitoes and the like), but also the web is used in healing wounds. Spiders often appear in dreams of clients, sometimes with a healing purpose.

What is striking about this story is that the saving person is not only the lowly spider, but a

Museum of the Cherokee Indian logo (used by permission)

"she," a feminine creature. More than a linguistic note, this demonstrates the strong role that women played in Cherokee society. This topic is considered in a later myth but this fact, combined with the womblike symbolism of the hollow tree and the warmth of the fire itself, suggests a high psychological role for the feminine in Cherokee thinking. It also alludes to the role of the feminine in men. Jung taught that men have a feminine part to their personalities, the anima, and women have a masculine part, the animus. This story implies that in order to accomplish such a touchy, difficult, symbolic task as this, a man needs to call on his feminine side, his "water spider" as it were. A clinical example would be when a father is faced with a runaway teenager and needs to rescue her or him from a "burning" situation like drug addiction. His approach may well be a lowly, gentle one rather than a flying, high-profile attack.

Often in family therapy, the real hero (heroine) that holds the family together emotionally, if not economically, is the tiny, unnoticed, feminine creature (either the wife, the daughter or the gentler, feminine side of the husband or son). When all the attempts to accomplish the needed tasks with male testosterone fail, she humbly "crosses the water" to obtain the prize, which she shares with all those needing its warmth. The symbolic "basket" (*tusti*) she carries is her badge of courage, her mark of distinction for life. She does it when no one else can.

From a Jungian perspective, this figure of the water spider expresses a powerful, living mandala. She is clearly a living creature, and the circle and cross capture both masculine and feminine features. Mandala is a word from Sanskrit meaning "magic circle." A mandala usually has a circle and square with divisions. In Jungian and other depth analysis, mandalas often appear in the dreams and paintings of patients as objects of healing. Jung noted that many psychiatric patients, especially schizophrenics, when they were moving toward wholeness, spontaneously drew mandalas. Some people use mandalas from their own traditions to help move toward wholeness when they are fragmented or in crisis. Christians may meditate on the cross, especially the Celtic cross, which has a configuration similar to the mandala. Jung saw the mandala as an expression of the Self, the center of the psyche.[4] He also saw the Self as the psychological image carrier of the God-image. It is where man could connect to God.

Theological Comments

Although there are no direct parallels in biblical materials to *obtaining* fire, the use of fire and symbolism concerning fire is most extensive. Popular expressions of religious fervor would lead one to think that scriptures only speak of fire and brimstone and the destructive nature of fire.[5] There are many stories of how destructive fire is, even concepts of hell as a place of fire. As in the Cherokee myth, that fear of fire is expressed, but the positive side is also noted. A pillar of fire leads the children of Israel, and the light of Israel will become a fire.[6] Many expressions of God speak of manifestations in fire, like Moses and the burning bush,[7] the pillar of fire in the Tabernacle[8] and even God's word: "Is not my word like fire? saith the Lord."[9] Even Jesus' transfiguration on the mountain is associated with fire.[10] But the need for fire as warmth is seen in two notable stories. One is when Peter denies Christ while warming by a fire and the other is when Paul is shipwrecked on Malta and the very hospitable natives build a fire to warm him.[11]

Perhaps the main point of the lowly spider sharing the fire is captured in the Judeo-Christian tradition of a loving community, usually expressed in terms of warmth. Hers was a motherly deed, and a "mother" church, congregation or community that feeds and cares for its people shares that fire from above, in a symbolic sense. In most faith groups a test of welcome is often couched in terms of temperature metaphors, or whether the folks are "warm" or "cold." Also, one of the strongest biblical condemnations of the church in Laodicea was that it was lukewarm, neither hot nor cold.[12]

The image of the lowly water spider so captured in art also carries religious symbolism. As noted, the mandala appears in all cultures and plays a role in calming and in healing troubled souls. This ancient Cherokee water spider figure contains the mandala elements with the circle and cross. The cross itself is a crucial part of Christian theology and history. In the spider artwork the cross is where the saving warmth of the coal of fire is carried, a parallel to the theology of the warmth, love and sacrifice of the crucifixion. Even the arms of the spider that enabled her to walk across the water seem open to acceptance, underlining the warmth of the hospitality offered by the (Cherokee) fire.

3

Kana'ti and Selu: The Origin of Game and Corn

THE MYTH

When I was a boy this is what the old men told me they had heard when they were boys.

Long years ago, soon after the world was made, a hunter and his wife lived at Pilot Knob with their only child, a little boy. The father's name was Kana'ti (the Lucky Hunter), and his wife was called Selu (Corn). No matter when Kana'ti went into the woods, he never failed to bring back a load of game, which his wife would cut up and prepare, washing off the blood from the meat in the river near the house. The little boy used to play down by the river every day, and one morning the old people thought they heard laughing and talking in the bushes as though there were two children there. When the boy came home at night his parents asked him who he had been playing with all day. "He comes out of the water," said the boy, "and he calls himself my elder brother. He says his mother was cruel to him and threw him into the river." Then they knew that the strange boy had sprung from the blood of the game that Selu had washed off at the river's edge.

Every day when the little boy went out to play the other would join him, but as he always went back into the water the old people never had a chance to see him. At last one evening Kana'ti said to his son, "Tomorrow, when the other boy comes to play, get him to wrestle with you, and when you have your arms around him hold on to him and call for us." The boy promised to do as he was told, so the next day as soon as his playmate appeared he challenged him to a wrestling match. The other agreed at once, but as soon as they had their arms around each other, Kana'ti's boy began to scream for his father. The old folks at once came running down, and as soon as the Wild Boy saw them he struggled to free himself and cried out, "Let me go; you threw me away!" but his brother held on until his parents reached the spot, when they seized the Wild Boy and took him home with them. They kept him in the house until they tamed him, but he was always wild and artful in his disposition, and was the leader of his brother in every mischief. It was not long until the old people discovered that he had magic powers, and they called him I'nage-utasun'hi (He who grew up wild).

Whenever Kana'ti went into the mountains he always brought back a fat buck or doe, or maybe a couple of turkeys. One day the Wild Boy said to his brother, "I wonder where our father gets all that game; let's follow him next time and find out." A few days afterward Kana'ti took a bow and some feathers in his hand and started off toward the west. The boys waited a little while and went after him, keeping out of sight until they saw him go into a swamp where there were a great many of the small reeds that hunters use to make arrow-shafts. Then the Wild Boy changed himself into a puff of bird's down, which the wind took up and carried until it alighted upon Kana'ti's shoulder just as he entered the swamp, but Kana'ti knew nothing about it. The old man cut reeds, fitted the feathers to them and made some arrows, and the Wild Boy — in his other shape — thought, "I wonder what those things are for?" When Kana'ti had his arrows finished he came out of the swamp and went on again. The wind blew the down from his shoulder, and it fell into the woods, when the Wild Boy took his right shape again and went back and told his brother what he had seen. Keeping out of sight of their father, they followed him up the mountain until he stopped at a certain place and lifted a large rock. At once there ran out a buck, which Kana'ti shot, and then lifting it upon his back he started for home again. "Oho!" exclaimed the boys, "he keeps all the deer shut up in that hole, and whenever he wants meat he just lets one out and kills it with those things he made in the swamp." They hurried and reached home before their father, who had the heavy deer to carry, and he never knew that they had followed.

A few days later the boys went back to the swamp, cut some reeds, and made seven arrows, and then started up the mountain where their father kept the game. When they got to the place, they raised the rock and a deer came running out. Just as they drew back to shoot it, another came out, and then another and another, until the boys got confused and forgot what they were about. In those days all the deer had their tails hanging down like other animals, but as a buck was running past the Wild Boy struck its tail with his arrow so that it pointed upward. The boys thought this good sport, and when the next one ran past the Wild Boy struck its tail so that it stood straight up, and his brother struck the next one so hard with his arrow, that the deer's tail was almost curled over his back. The deer carries his tail this way ever since. The deer came running past until the last one had come out of the hole and escaped into the forest. Then came droves of raccoons, rabbits, and all the other four-footed animals — all but the bear, because there were no bear then. Last came great flocks of turkeys, pigeons, and partridges, that darkened the air like a cloud and made such a noise with their wings that Kana'ti, sitting at home, heard the sound like distant thunder on the mountains and said to himself, "My bad boys have got into trouble; I must go and see what they are doing."

So he went up the mountain, and when he came to the place where he kept the game he found the two boys standing by the rock, and all the birds and animals were gone. Kana'ti was furious, but without saying a word he went down into the cave and kicked the covers off four jars in one corner, when out swarmed bedbugs, fleas, lice, and gnats, and got all over the boys. They screamed with pain and fright and tried to beat off the insects, but the thousands of vermin crawled over them and bit and stung until both dropped down nearly dead. Kana'ti stood looking on until he thought they had been punished enough, when he knocked off the vermin and made the boys a talk. "Now, you rascals," he said, "you have always had plenty to eat and never had to work for it. Whenever you were hungry all I had to do was to come up here and get a deer or a turkey and bring it home for your mother to cook; but now you have let out all the animals, and after this when you want a deer to eat you will have to hunt all over the woods for it, and then maybe not find one. Go home now to your mother, while I see if I can find something to eat for supper."

When the boys got home again they were very tired and hungry and asked their mother for something to eat. "There is no meat," said Selu, "but wait a little while and I will get you something." So she took a basket and started out to the storehouse. This storehouse was built upon poles high up from the ground, to keep it out of the reach of animals, and there was a ladder to climb up by, and one door, but no other opening. Every day when Selu got ready to cook the dinner she would go out to the storehouse with a basket and bring it back full of corn and beans. The boys had never been inside the storehouse, so wondered where all the corn and beans could come from, as the house was not a very large one; so as soon as Selu went out of the door the Wild Boy said to his brother, "Let's go and see what she does." They ran around and climbed up at the back of the storehouse and pulled out a piece of clay from between the logs, so that they could look in. There they saw Selu standing in the middle of the room with the basket in front of her on the floor. Leaning over the basket, she rubbed her stomach — so — and the basket was half full of corn. Then she rubbed under her armpits — so — and the basket was full to the top with beans. The boys looked at each other and said, "This will never do; our mother is a witch. If we eat any of that it will poison us. We must kill her."

When the boys came back into the house, she knew their thoughts before they spoke. "So you are going to kill me?" said Selu. "Yes," said the boys, "you are a witch." "Well," said their mother, "when you have killed me, clear a large piece of ground in front of the house and drag my body seven times around the circle. Then drag me seven times over the ground inside the circle, and stay up all night and watch, and in the morning you will have plenty of corn." The boys killed her with their clubs, and cut off her head and put it upon the roof of the house with her face turned toward the west, and told her to look for her husband. Then they set to work to clear the ground in front of the house, but instead of clearing the whole piece they cleared only seven little spots. This is why corn now grows only in a few places instead of over the whole world. They dragged the body of Selu around the circle, and wherever her blood fell on the ground the corn sprung up. But instead of dragging her body seven times across the ground they dragged it over only twice, which is the reason the Indians still work their crop but twice. The two brothers *sat up and watched their corn all night, and in the morning it was full grown and ripe.*

When Kana'ti came home at last, he looked around, but could not see Selu anywhere, and asked the boys where was their mother. "She was a witch and we killed her," said the boys; "there is her head up there on top of the house." When he saw his wife's head on the road, he was very angry, and said, "I won't stay with you any longer; I am going to the Wolf people." So he started off, but before he had gone far the Wild Boy changed himself again to a tuft of down, which fell on Kana'ti's shoulder. When Kana'ti reached the settlement of the Wolf people, they were holding a council in the townhouse. He went in and sat down with the tuft of bird's down on his shoulder, but he never noticed it. When the Wolf chief asked him his business, he said: "I have two bad boys at home, and I want you to go in seven days from now and play ball against them." Although Kana'ti spoke as though he wanted them to play a game of ball, the Wolves knew that he meant for them to go and kill the two boys. They promised to go. Then the bird's down blew off from Kana'ti's shoulder, and the smoke carried it through the hole in the roof of the townhouse. When it came down on the ground outside, the Wild Boy took his right shape again and went home and told his brother all that he had heard in the townhouse. But when Kana'ti left the Wolf people, he did not return home, but went on farther.

The boys then began to get ready for the Wolves, and the Wild Boy — the magician — told his brother what to do. They ran around the house in a wide circle until they had made a trail all around it excepting on the side from which the Wolves would come, where they left a small open space. Then they made four large bundles of arrows and placed them at four different points on the outside of the circle, after which they hid themselves in the woods and waited for the Wolves. In a day or two a whole party of Wolves came and surrounded the house to kill the boys. The wolves did not notice the trail around the house, because they came in where the boys had left the opening, but the moment they went inside the circle the trail changed to a high brush fence and shut them in. Then the boys on the outside took their arrows and began shooting them down, and as the Wolves could not jump over the fence they were all killed, excepting a few that escaped through the opening into a great swamp close by.

The boys ran around the swamp, and a circle of fire sprang up in their tracks and set fire to the grass and bushes and burned up nearly all the other Wolves. Only two or three got away, and from these have come all the wolves that are now in the world.

Soon afterward some strangers from a distance, who had heard that the brothers had a wonderful grain from which they made bread, came to ask for some, for none but Selu and her family had ever known corn before. The boys gave them seven grains of corn, which they told them to plant the next night on their way home, sitting up all night to watch the corn, which would have seven ripe ears in the morning. These they were to plant the next night and watch in the same way, and so on every night until they reached home, when they would have enough corn to supply the whole people. The strangers lived seven days' journey away. They took the seven grains and watched all through the darkness until morning, when they saw seven tall stalks, each stalk bearing a ripened ear. They gathered the ears and went on their way. The next night they planted all their corn, and guarded it as before until daybreak, when they found an abundant increase. But the way was long and the sun was hot, and the people grew tired. On the last night before reaching home they fell asleep, and in the morning the corn they had planted had not even sprouted. They brought with them to their settlement what corn they had left and planted it, and with care and attention were able to raise a crop. But ever since the corn must be watched and tended through half the year, which before would grow and ripen in a night.

As Kana'ti did not return, the boys at last concluded to go and find him. The Wild Boy took a gaming wheel toward the Darkening land. In a little while the wheel came rolling back, and the boys knew their father was not there. He rolled it to the south and to the north, and each time the wheel came back to him, and they knew their father was not there. Then he rolled it toward the Sunland, and it did not return. "Our father is there," said the Wild Boy, "let us go and find him." So the two brothers set off toward the east, and after traveling a long time they came upon Kana'ti walking along with a little dog by his side. "You bad boys," said their father, "have you come here?" "Yes," they answered, "we always accomplish what we start out to do — we are men." "This dog overtook me four days ago," then said Kana'ti, but the boys knew that the dog was the wheel that they had sent after him to find him. "Well," said Kana'ti, "as you have found me, we may as well travel together, but I shall take the lead."

Soon they came to a swamp, and Kana'ti told them there was something dangerous there and they must keep away from it. He went on ahead, but as soon as he was out of sight the Wild Boy said to his brother, "Come and let us see what is in the swamp." They went in together, and in the middle of the swamp they found a large panther asleep. The Wild Boy got an arrow and shot the panther in the side of the head. The panther turned his head and the other boy shot him on that side. He turned his head away again and the two brothers shot together — tust, tust, tust! But the panther was not hurt by the arrows and paid no attention to the boys. They came out of the swamp and soon overtook Kana'ti, waiting for them. "Did you find it?" asked Kana'ti. "Yes," said the boys, "we found it, but it never hurt us. We are men." Kana'ti was surprised, but said nothing, and they went on again.

After a while he turned to them and said, "Now you must be careful. We are coming to a tribe called the Anada'duntaski (Roasters, i.e., cannibals), and if they get you they will put you into a pot and feast on you." Then he went on ahead. Soon the boys came to a tree that had been struck by lightning, and the Wild Boy directed his brother to gather some of the splinters from the tree and told him what to do with them. In a little while they came to the settlement of the cannibals, who, as soon as they saw the boys, came running out, crying, "Good, here are two nice fat strangers. Now we'll have a grand feast." They caught the boys and dragged them into the townhouse, and sent word to all the people of the settlement to come to the feast. They made up a great fire, put water into a large pot and set it to boiling, and then seized the Wild Boy and put him down into it. His brother was not in the least bit frightened and made no attempts to escape, but quietly knelt down and began putting the splinters into the fire, as if to make it burn better. When the cannibals thought the meat was about ready they lifted the pot from the fire, and that instant a blinding light filled the townhouse, and the lightning began to dart from one side to the other, striking down the cannibals until not one of them was left alive. Then the lightning *went up through the smoke hole, and the next moment there were two boys standing outside the townhouse as though nothing had happened. They went on and soon met Kana'ti, who seemed much surprised to see them, and said, "What! Are you here again?" "O, yes, we never give up. We are great men!" "What did the cannibals do to you?" "We met them and they brought us to their townhouse, but they never hurt us." Kana'ti said nothing more, and they went on.*

He soon got out of sight of the boys, but they kept on until they came to the end of the world, where the sun comes out. The sky was just coming down when they got there, but they waited until it went up again, and then they went through and climbed up on the other side. There they found Kana'ti and Selu sitting together. The old folk received them kindly and were glad to see them, telling them they might stay there a while, but then they must go to live where the sun goes down. The boys stayed with their parents seven days and then went on toward the Darkening land, where they are now. We call them Anisga'ya Tsunsdi' (the Little Men), and when they talk to each other we hear low rolling thunder in the west.

After Kana'ti's boys had let the deer out from the cave where their father used to keep them, the hunters tramped about in the woods for a long time without finding any game, so that the people were very hungry. At last they heard that the Thunder Boys were now living in the far west, beyond the sun door, and that if they were sent for they could bring back the game. So they sent messengers for them, and the boys came and sat down in the middle of the townhouse and began to sing.

At the first song there was a roaring sound like a strong wind in the northwest, and it grew louder and nearer as the boys sang on, until at the seventh song a whole herd of deer, led by a large buck, came out from the woods. The boys had told the people to be ready with their bows and arrows, and when the song was ended and all the deer were close around the townhouse, the hunters shot into them and killed as many as they needed before the herd could get back into the timber.

Then the Thunder Boys went back into the Darkening land, but before they left they taught the people the seven songs with which to call up the deer. It all happened so long go that the songs are now forgotten — all but two, which the hunters still sing whenever they go after deer.

Kana'ti and Selu; The Origin Of Game And Corn — Lynn Lossiah's portrayal of Selu, the Corn Mother, a central figure in Cherokee mythology. Kana'ti, who provides game, is in the background as implied by the deer antlers. Their two troublesome sons, the Thunder Boys, appear also.

KANA'TI AND SELU: THE ORIGIN OF GAME AND CORN

The early stories of creation show animals being created first, then the humans. The first human family story of the Cherokee is tied to life sustenance and yet not far from the animal connections so often seen in most myths. Here the story is told by the story teller citing the authenticity of oral tradition and jumping into the main characters and their family life.

AMPLE EDEN: THE FIRST FAMILY

When I was a boy this is what the old men told me they had heard when they were boys.

Long years ago, soon after the world was made, a hunter and his wife lived at Pilot Knob with their only child, a little boy. The father's name was Kana'ti (the Lucky Hunter), and his wife was called Selu (Corn). No matter when Kana'ti went into the woods, he never failed to bring back a load of game, which his wife would cut up and prepare, washing off the blood from the meat in the river near the house. The little boy used to play down by the river every day, and one morning the old people thought they heard laughing and talking in the bushes as though there were two children there. When the boy came home at night his parents asked him who he had been playing with all day. "He comes out of the water," said the boy, "and he calls himself my elder brother. He says his mother was cruel to him and threw him into the river." Then they knew that the strange boy had sprung from the blood of the game which Selu had washed off at the river's edge.

The creation stories lead into the story of the first family who had ample provisions. The context of the story is Pilot Knob, that mysterious mountain setting of other myths (see Connestee and Tsuwe'nahi). The father, Kana'ti, is the Lucky Hunter who always gets sufficient game for the family no matter when he goes. The mother, Selu, prepares that meat for their use and washes the blood into the nearby river in the preparation process. This little detail seems natural enough. But when their singular child, a son, plays by the river they eventually hear laughter and *two* children playing. The enquiry that follows gives the shocking answer that there is another boy coming out of that water who claims to be the elder brother! Not only that, but he charges that the mother had thrown him into the river as an act of cruelty. The awareness is immediate: he is a product of the blood washed away into the river. This closeness to blood as life force is picked up in other stories, most notably in the Judaculla story later.[1] In this case, the child coming from such a setting is very special and very close to the game.

MISSING CHILD: THE WILD ONE

Every day when the little boy went out to play the other would join him, but as he always went back into the water the old people never had a chance to see him. At last one evening Kana'ti said to his son, "Tomorrow, when the other boy comes to play, get him to wrestle with you, and when you have your arms around him hold on to him and call for us." The boy promised to do as he was told, so the next day as soon as his playmate appeared he challenged him to a wrestling match. The other agreed at once, but as soon as they had their arms around each other, Kana'ti's boy began to scream for his father. The old folks at once came running down, and as soon as the Wild Boy saw them he struggled to free himself and cried out, "Let me go; you threw me away!" but his brother held on until his parents reached the spot, when they seized the Wild Boy and took him home with them. They kept him in the house until they tamed him, but he was always wild and artful in his disposition, and was the leader of his brother in every mischief. It was not long until the old people discovered that he had magic powers, and they called him I'nage-utasun'hi (He who grew up wild).

The "wild boy" or "wild man" is a universal image in most cultures, tying humans close to nature. Woven into art and architecture, especially in the great cathedrals of Europe, this little-observed psychological phenomenon reveals the wilder part of human nature, the untamed and unpredictable part that slips out in even the most sacred or secure settings. Acted out in such settings as the Mardi Gras, the almost universal carnival, or the Basel Fastnacht, in Switzerland, many cultures have the "boogey" man dressed up as the wild man scaring people and especially bringing irreverence into an otherwise serious setting. Interestingly, the Cherokee also have their "wild man" dance and their "booger mask" to do the same.

So early on in this myth, the setting is not just an idealistic Eden, for some tension is felt and the hearer is reminded that there is a wilder presence amongst families and persons that is to be taken seriously. In the story there is the attempt to tame the Wild Boy, which is only partially successful. The Wild Boy does stay, but not without some cost to all. In clinical settings this is close to the difficult situation in which one family member acts out the wilder side of the family in lifestyle or irresponsible deeds. More difficult is when the "wild one" suffers from developmental disability or severe mental illness, and the family works hard to "tame" him, to contain him within the family. This is the caring part of the family; that they do not in fact reject the child, but hold on to try to make him one of the family core.

PARADISE LOST: THE SECRET IS OUT

Whenever Kana'ti went into the mountains he always brought back a fat buck or doe, or maybe a couple of turkeys. One day the Wild Boy said to his brother, "I wonder where our father gets all that game; let's follow him next time and find out." A few days afterward Kana'ti took a bow and some feathers in his hand and started off toward the west. The boys waited a little while and went after him, keeping out of sight until they saw him go into a swamp where there were a great many of the small reeds that hunters use to make arrow shafts. Then the Wild Boy changed himself into a puff of bird's down, which the wind took up and carried until it alighted upon Kana'ti's shoulder just as he entered the swamp, but Kana'ti knew nothing about it. The old man cut reeds, fitted the feathers to them and made some arrows, and the Wild Boy — in his other shape — thought, "I wonder what those things are for?" When Kana'ti had his arrows finished he came out of the swamp and went on again. The wind blew the down from his shoulder, and it fell into the woods, when the Wild Boy took his right shape again and went back and told his brother what he had seen. Keeping out of sight of their father, they followed him up the mountain until he stopped at a certain place and lifted a large rock. At once there ran out a buck, which Kana'ti shot, and then lifting it upon his back he started for home again. "Oho!" exclaimed the boys, "he keeps all the deer shut up in that hole, and whenever he wants meat he just lets one out and kills

it with those things he made in the swamp." They hurried and
reached home before their father, who had the heavy deer to carry,
and he never knew that they had followed.

The curiosity of the boys, driven by the wild boy's initiative, leads
them to seek out the father's secret source of game. One wonders about
the family dynamics; why the father and mother had not taught or
trained them to see and appreciate the abundance of resources. Perhaps they understood the limits of the responsibility the boys could
handle. In any case they follow, and the Wild Boy shape-shifts, a fairly
common event in the tales of most Native American tribes. In psychological terms, the sense of one's "presence" or "knowing" something
when not physically present is fairly common and most often seen in
terms of a strong intuitive function. That "sixth sense" need not be
seen as some magic, but is an observable phenomenon, according to
Jung.

When Kana'ti leaves home he carries only a bow and some feathers but enters the swamp to cut some shafts for arrows while the Wild
Boy rides his shoulder in the form of a tuft of down. Crafting the final
part of his hunting weapon into arrows, he proceeds to the cache of
animals underground. This sense of the animals being shut up in a
hole or cave is, according to Mooney, very widespread among the tribes,
with various stories as to how and why they were released.[2] When the
two boys follow Kana'ti to see how he opens the hole, shoots the deer
and heads home, their discovery becomes an awareness, a kind of
knowledge that excites them and sends them home ahead of the
unknowing father.

Like teenage boys everywhere, the comparison with father in terms
of knowledge, strength and ability runs with the hormones. The desire
to gain his secret is more than the need for meat: it is a search for
power, more power than their father. This is the stuff of legends and
fairy tales, including the myth of Oedipus, in which the son kills the
father to obtain the mother. In many fairy tales the king is fearful that
his sons will take his throne and power.

PARADISE LOST: THE ANIMALS ARE OUT

A few days later the boys went back to the swamp, cut some
reeds, and made seven arrows, and then started up the mountain

where their father kept the game. When they got to the place, they raised the rock and a deer came running out. Just as they drew back to shoot it, another came out, and then another and another, until the boys got confused and forgot what they were about. In those days all the deer had their tails hanging down like other animals, but as a buck was running past the Wild Boy struck its tail with his arrow so that it pointed upward. The boys thought this good sport, and when the next one ran past the Wild Boy struck its tail so that it stood straight up, and his brother struck the next one so hard with his arrow, that the deer's tail was almost curled over his back. The deer carries his tail this way ever since. The deer came running past until the last one had come out of the hole and escaped into the forest. Then came droves of raccoons, rabbits, and all the other four-footed animals — all but the bear, because there were no bear then. Last came great flocks of turkeys, pigeons, and partridges, that darkened the air like a cloud and made such a noise with their wings that Kana'ti, sitting at home, heard the sound like distant thunder on the mountains and said to himself, "My bad boys have got into trouble; I must go and see what they are doing."

So the boys now try their luck at playing adults, at least mimicking the father. They have discovered his secret and they must try on their own, playing like grown men, as if they were capable. They quickly learn that they have not learned it all, that something is missing in their education. They get confused when more and more animals pour out. There seems to be a moment of realization of the seriousness but then when an arrow strikes the deer's tail, forcing it to turn up rather than down, it seems more like a game for boys. It becomes a sport and they play at it so much that the deer's tail is still turned up today. But then all the deer are gone, and the other animals escape also, including game birds, so many birds that the sky darkens and the noise of the wings flapping reach Kana'ti at home. He knows. It is like thunder and the boys are bad.

It is easy to draw direct parallels to struggling teens in family life. Such would be obvious and universal. It is more difficult to see the parallels to adult "teens" who never want to grow up, who keep trying to compete with father or mother, to take the easy way and make short-cuts without the wisdom and experience of the elders. It is like the son who takes over the father's business with new, "modern" ideas, but loses everything because he does not ask the right questions, or thinks he can handle it, or treats it as if it were only a sport. Or it may be like the daughter who does not listen to her mother and marries the alcoholic because she can supposedly handle what she thinks her mother could not. This is not to say that parents are always right, but that the rebellious streak is often acted out by immature boys and girls of any age.

DISCOVERY: PAIN AND PUNISHMENT

So he went up the mountain, and when he came to the place where he kept the game he found the two boys standing by the rock, and all the birds and animals were gone. Kana'ti was furious, but without saying a word he went down into the cave and kicked the covers off four jars in one corner, when out swarmed bedbugs, fleas, lice, and gnats, and got all over the boys. They screamed with pain and fright and tried to beat off the insects, but the thousands of vermin crawled over them and bit and stung until both dropped down nearly dead. Kana'ti stood looking on until he thought they had been punished enough, when he knocked off the vermin and made the boys a talk. "Now, you rascals," he said, "you have always had plenty to eat and never had to work for it. Whenever you were hungry all I had to do was to come up here and get a deer or a turkey and bring it home for your mother to cook; but now you have let out all the animals, and after this when you want a deer to eat you will have to hunt all over the woods for it, and then maybe not find one. Go home now to your mother, while I see if I can find something to eat for supper."

Kana'ti goes straight to the boys and sees the result of their mischief and that all the game for food is lost. Without a word of chastisement, he releases beings that are not game animals, insects of the most irritating kind. They furnish unforgettable pain and punishment upon the boys. They are almost dead from pain and fright when the father stops it. He brushes off the vermin and then talks with them. He calls them "rascals," a term in English for low or unprincipled persons; it comes from old French and has a connection to scratching and scabs. (Since the original story was in Cherokee, the author assumes a close parallel in choice of words.) The irony is not lost, for they faced bedbugs, fleas and other bugs requiring scratching.[3] Kana'ti's lecture reminds them of the consequences of their actions for all and that now, in contrast to having meat easily given, they must hunt for it with no guarantee that it will be found. He sends them away to their mother while he now must hunt. This is only the beginning of their learning and their questionable acts.

SELU'S STOREHOUSE: MISUNDERSTOOD MOTHERHOOD

> *When the boys got home again they were very tired and hungry and asked their mother for something to eat. "There is no meat," said Selu, "but wait a little while and I will get you something." So she took a basket and started out to the storehouse. This storehouse was built upon poles high up from the ground, to keep it out of the reach of animals, and there was a ladder to climb up by, and one door, but no other opening. Every day when Selu got ready to cook the dinner she would go out to the storehouse with a basket and bring it back full of corn and beans. The boys had never been inside the storehouse, so wondered where all the corn and beans could come from, as the house was not a very large one; so as soon as Selu went out of the door the Wild Boy said to his brother, "Let's go and see what she does." They ran around and climbed up at the back of the storehouse and pulled out a piece of clay from between the logs, so that they could look in. There they saw Selu standing in the middle of the room with the basket in front of her on the floor. Leaning over the basket, she rubbed her stomach — so — and the basket was half full of corn. Then she rubbed under her armpits — so — and the basket was full to the top with beans. The boys looked at each other and said, "This will never do; our mother is a witch. If we eat any of that it will poison us. We must kill her."*

Tired and hungry from their ordeal, the boys do as father suggests and go home to mother Selu for something to eat. In the absence of meat she goes, as usual, to the storehouse for corn and beans. The description of the storehouse is detailed, high upon poles to keep out of the reach of animals and vermin. Such a structure is also very common in other cultures; some are even kept as historical structures in developed lands such as Norway and Switzerland to remind people of their heritage of protecting their grain and other food. In the Selu story, however, the storehouse is notably small in light of the many trips she makes there returning with food aplenty. Once again their curiosity takes over and they decide to spy on their mother to see from where this food comes. Climbing up the back side of the storehouse and removing some clay between the logs, they make a second major discovery, more shocking than that of the animals coming from the cave. Mother Selu produces corn by simply rubbing her stomach and produces beans by rubbing her armpits!

The frightened boys draw the quick conclusion that their mother must be a witch and thus they must take action, lest they are poisoned by the food. It is noteworthy that the Cherokee had great fear of witches and witchcraft. Many things were tolerated and forgiven amongst the Cherokee but witchcraft was not; and many ailments, including poisoning, were felt to be from such persons. The story of the Spear-Finger considered later gives one example of this personified evil form. In this story of Selu, the boys' fear blinded them, preventing honest dialogue and drove them to drastic "preventative" action.

In family situations, as in political situations, hasty conclusions may be drawn without dialogue with those affected by decisions. Sometimes there is no serious research or reflection and some dire action is planned without considering the consequences. Consider the father who tosses his teen out of the home due to breaking a rule, without asking why, or the spouse who leaves the family on the basis of false conclusions drawn without any dialogue or adequate information. In this story it is notable that the sons of Kana'ti and Selu must not have considered that they had not yet been poisoned and that they had been eating her food all along. Had they considered that their mother might have had their best interests at heart after all?

SELU'S SACRIFICE: A MARTYR'S NOURISHMENT

> When the boys came back into the house, she knew their thoughts before they spoke. "So you are going to kill me?" said Selu. "Yes," said the boys, "you are a witch." "Well," said their mother, "when you have killed me, clear a large piece of ground in front of the house and drag my body seven times around the circle. Then drag me seven times over the ground inside the circle, and stay up all night and watch, and in the morning you will have plenty of corn."

The boys killed her with their clubs, and cut off her head and put it upon the roof of the house with her face turned toward the west, and told her to look for her husband. Then they set to work to clear the ground in front of the house, but instead of clearing the whole piece they cleared only seven little spots. This is why corn now grows only in a few places instead of over the whole world. They dragged the body of Selu around the circle, and wherever her blood fell on the ground the corn sprung up. But instead of dragging her body seven times across the ground they dragged it over only twice, which is the reason the Indians still work their crop but twice. The two brothers sat up and watched their corn all night, and in the morning it was full grown and ripe.

Mother Selu knows what the boys thought and planned. She also knows she is to be the martyr and still plays the role of mother in seeking to give ongoing nourishment even after she is to be gone. The repulsive nature of this part of the myth startles many who cannot get beyond the horror of the whole idea of children killing parents. Such is the stuff of myths and is not to be seen as any literal issue but rather for the power of the symbolism itself. It is very shocking and thus gets our attention. One Cherokee elder even apologized for the tragedy in this story, feeling it is necessary to do so because of this gory event. But myths, like dreams, have a totally different nature in that they do not fit our conscious world of time, space and morality. There can be a symbolic death of something, or somebody, in order for something new to resurrect. The easiest way to understand this is that dreams often have someone die or be killed. This demonstrates the need, sometimes, for some part of the dreamer to die in order for something better in their personality to be resurrected or come into being. So Selu does not admit she is a witch, seeing they are so convinced, but gives specific instructions to her boys to ensure they have plenty of corn after she is gone. They are to drag her body seven times around the circle but in fact do so only two times, after clearing only seven spots, rather than the whole plot. They watch, and where her blood drops, the corn springs up and grows to ripen overnight as they watch it.

The grotesque image of her severed head on top of the house captures the attention. It can be seen to powerfully symbolize the role of motherhood as being over the house and home, seeing afar ("look for your husband") and looking west, where the sun sets and, in the Eastern

Cherokee setting, where most sustaining rain showers come from. She is the martyr but leaves food that can continue to nourish long after she is gone. One wise Cherokee woman, in discussing this story, noted the old practice of cutting off the corn silks from the corn ears before they are fully mature. The practice is done after pollination in order to remove the larvae that develop into corn worms, which do eat some of the corn kernels. Thus, the preventative action provides more ongoing nourishment, just as with Selu, the Corn-Mother.[4]

In the Cherokee context, the positive role of women, and especially the mother, is captured in this story. The matrilineal society is subtly underlined for the woman was the "head of household." It emphasizes not only the deep Cherokee connection to Selu as symbolic mother figure but also to corn as their basic food for many centuries. Most Native American (and all eastern) tribes have myths of the corn spirit as a woman. Either blood drops or the body of the corn spirit gives the corn. Corn is the survival food and is woven into songs, ceremonies and art. The "three sisters" sometimes mentioned are corn, beans and squash, as they grow well together in the field and are eaten together.[5]

The section ends with the boys watching the corn grow and ripen, implying that there may also be a parallel process going on in their own growth and need to mature; but they are not yet there.

PATERNAL ANGER: THE WOLF CONTRACT

> When Kana'ti came home at last, he looked around, but could not see Selu anywhere, and asked the boys where was their mother. "She was a witch and we killed her," said the boys; "there is her head up there on top of the house." When he saw his wife's head on the roof, he was very angry, and said, "I won't stay with you any longer; I am going to the Wolf people." So he started off, but before he had gone far the Wild Boy changed himself again to a tuft of down, which fell on Kana'ti's shoulder. When Kana'ti reached the settlement of the Wolf people, they were holding a council in the townhouse. He went in and sat down with the tuft of bird's down on his shoulder, but he never noticed it. When the Wolf chief asked him his business, he said: "I have two bad boys at home, and I want you to go in seven days from now and play ball against them." Although

Kana'ti spoke as though he wanted them to play a game of ball, the Wolves knew that he meant for them to go and kill the two boys. They promised to go. Then the bird's down blew off from Kana'ti's shoulder, and the smoke carried it through the hole in the roof of the townhouse. When it came down on the ground outside, the Wild Boy took his right shape again and went home and told his brother all that he had heard in the townhouse. But when Kana'ti left the Wolf people, he did not return home, but went on farther.

Kana'ti reenters the story after some time and asks about Selu. The boys answer, tell what they have done and why, pointing out her head on the roof. He is appropriately angry and announces he will leave them and abandon that place; he even says where he will go: to the Wolf people. Following his anger and departure, the wild son once again shape-shifts into a tuft of down and accompanies his father into the townhouse of the Wolf people. He takes out a contract on the boys, calling it a game of ball. They all know what it means. And the tuft-shaped son blows out the smoke hole to return home with the news. The parallel to the boy's first game or sport of playing with the game is striking, for now the game of ball is far more serious, carrying the anger and murderous rage of the father. As if to avoid the wolves' visit to the boys, Kana'ti does not go home but travels on.

What is strikingly modern is the play on words to avoid what one really means, by using more comfortable terms for some dastardly deeds. Some examples are "final solution," "let go," "terminate," and "expire." In a similar way, in some situations it is easier for persons in power positions, be it family, business, church or military, to hire or order another to do the dirty business while the decision maker leaves town or keeps a distance, not accepting responsibility for the consequences of their own decisions (or anger).

WOLF GAMES: WOLVES 0, BOYS 1

The boys then began to get ready for the Wolves, and the Wild Boy — the magician — told his brother what to do. They ran around the house in a wide circle until they had made a trail all around it excepting on the side from which the Wolves would come, where they left a small open space. Then they made four large bundles of arrows and placed them at four different points on the outside of the circle,

*after which they hid themselves in the woods and waited for the
Wolves. In a day or two a whole party of Wolves came and surrounded the house to kill the boys. The wolves did not notice the trail
around the house, because they came in where the boys had left the
opening, but the moment they went inside the circle the trail changed
to a high brush fence and shut them in. Then the boys on the outside took their arrows and began shooting them down, and as the
Wolves could not jump over the fence they were all killed, excepting
a few that escaped through the opening into a great swamp close by.
The boys ran around the swamp, and a circle of fire sprang up in
their tracks and set fire to the grass and bushes and burned up nearly
all the other Wolves. Only two or three got away, and from these have
come all the wolves that are now in the world.*

Now the boys work together for survival using the Wild Boy's gift
of magic. They set up a trap with an opening for the wolves and, iron-
ically, with a skill learned from the father, make arrows enough to make
their attack. The trail becomes a high brush fence, and the wolves are
trapped with only one exit and the boys hiding outside ready to ambush.
Fire the arrows they do, destroying almost all. They chase the remnant
into the swamp and set fire to burn them out. Only a few wolves survive to be the ancestors of all those that live today.

Some shift is slowly taking place in the story, for now the boys are
facing a serious enemy and planning together for a counterattack on
those who would do them harm. One can see some limited matura-
tion.

The Gift of Corn: Selu's Heritage

*Soon afterward some strangers from a distance, who had heard
that the brothers had a wonderful grain from which they made bread,
came to ask for some, for none but Selu and her family had ever
known corn before. The boys gave them seven grains of corn, which
they told them to plant the next night on their way home, sitting up
all night to watch the corn, which would have seven ripe ears in the
morning. These they were to plant the next night and watch in the
same way, and so on every night until they reached home, when they
would have enough corn to supply the whole people. The strangers
lived seven days' journey away. They took the seven grains and*

watched all through the darkness until morning, when they saw seven tall stalks, each stalk bearing a ripened ear. They gathered the ears and went on their way. The next night they planted all their corn, and guarded it as before until daybreak, when they found an abundant increase. But the way was long and the sun was hot, and the people grew tired. On the last night before reaching home they fell asleep, and in the morning the corn they had planted had not even sprouted. They brought with them to their settlement what corn they had left and planted it, and with care and attention were able to raise a crop. But ever since the corn must be watched and tended through half the year, which before would grow and ripen in a night.

The boys are now faced with a different challenge, the opportunity to help others in need. It is not their own survival, nor a game, but a simple request from other people. They have heard about this Selu grain that makes such wonderful bread, and seek some. The seven grains are given with specific instructions as to watching all night for each of the seven nights of travel with an abundance promised. As earlier with the boys, it all starts well, but with a hot sun and a long, tiring trip they are unable to watch on the last night, and they get no yield. They do come home with some grain but to grow the corn takes half a year rather than overnight. The ideal is lost but the result is not totally bad for they have the corn and simply must work harder for it.

In many ways this story parallels the human experience of getting one's first job and finding how hard it is to work for that money. When the parents or community have fed and clothed one and the time comes to go out and earn one's keep by the sweat of the brow it can be exhausting. In marriage counseling one of the difficult issues is when one spouse feels entitled to be fed and clothed but learns they must really work, and for less results than they expected. They may have expected overnight riches from a job, or the spouse, or even from society, but they must work much longer than they had hoped for that car or house. Early in this story the sons of Kana'ti and Selu had assumed such instant reward but by now in the story they are learning some important lessons in sharing and they share from the bounty of their mother, the life-giving corn.

SWAMP SIDE-STEP: BOYS WILL BE BOYS

As Kana'ti did not return, the boys at last concluded to go and find him. The Wild Boy took a gaming wheel toward the Darkening land. In a little while the wheel came rolling back, and the boys knew their father was not there. He rolled it to the south and to the north, and each time the wheel came back to him, and they knew their father was not there. Then he rolled it toward the Sunland, and it did not return. "Our father is there," said the Wild Boy, "let us go and find him." So the two brothers set off toward the east, and after traveling a long time they came upon Kana'ti walking along with a little dog by his side. "You bad boys," said their father, "have you come here?" "Yes," they answered, "we always accomplish what we start out to do — we are men." "This dog overtook me four days ago," then said Kana'ti, but the boys knew that the dog was the wheel that they had sent after him to find him. "Well," said Kana'ti, "as you have found me, we may as well travel together, but I shall take the lead."

Soon they came to a swamp, and Kana'ti told them there was something dangerous there and they must keep away from it. He went on ahead, but as soon as he was out of sight the Wild Boy said to his brother, "Come and let us see what is in the swamp." They went in together, and in the middle of the swamp they found a large panther asleep. The Wild Boy got an arrow and shot the panther in the side of the head. The panther turned his head and the other boy shot him on that side. He turned his head away again and the two brothers shot together — tust, tust, tust! But the panther was not hurt by the arrows and paid no attention to the boys. They came out of the swamp and soon overtook Kana'ti, waiting for them. "Did you find it?" asked Kana'ti. "Yes," said the boys, "we found it, but it never hurt us. We are men." Kana'ti was surprised, but said nothing, and they went on again.

At this phase in their life pilgrimage the boys decide to find their father and use the gaming wheel, a circular rock or disc used in a popular Cherokee game and described by many early visitors. Most tribes had some form of the game, which also had betting associated with it.[6] In this case, they use the wheel to find their father, somewhat of a gamble in itself. After tries in other directions, the wheel does not return from its trip into the land of the rising sun, the east. There is a reunion. The father calls them "bad boys" and seems to have moderated in his rage for he not only permits them to walk with him, as leader, but he gives them a warning about a danger in the nearby swamp. He tells them not to go near it, but once again their curiosity challenges them.

Or is it really a challenge from Kana'ti? Of course they go.

The boys find a sleeping panther and try to kill it with their arrows, both shooting but to no avail. Their father is surprised by the news that they are not hurt and that they feel they are men. The journey of father and sons continues.

The panther in Appalachian mountain culture and folklore is a mighty animal rarely seen but powerful and, like the bear, notorious for protecting its young. That maternal instinctual element seems to be in contrast to the former acts of the boys, when they did destroy their own mother. In ancient Egypt, pharaohs wore panther skins to be rejuvenated and in most societies the panther was considered a mark of powerful femininity and maternity. Symbolically, this can show that, in spite of their previous acts, the feminine can live on.

There could be many family clinical associations with this phase, for many are in search of the father or have the need to reconnect with him after a serious break. Some fathers are halfhearted in warnings to their children, even to being passive about dangers they may face. It is not just the words but also how the parent communicates the urgency of some dangers in the swamps of growing up. Overly permissive parents who never say no or set clear boundaries for their children create many problems for them. As they try to grow up so that they can also declare, "we are men," they may attempt some foolish things like driving recklessly or drinking and driving. Another example, close in symbolism to the story, is when youth try drugs, like cocaine. They think they are "big" but they are playing with a dangerous animal, like a mighty panther. Symbolically, they are shooting their own heads, dulling their minds. But not all come out as well as the two brothers in the story, for the mighty powerful beast of drug addiction can consume them.

Next in the father-son journey another challenge faces them and the warning from their father seems stronger than before.

CANNIBAL CAPTURE: BOYS IN THE BOILING POT

After a while he turned to them and said, "Now you must be careful. We are coming to a tribe called the Anada'duntaski (Roasters, i.e., cannibals), and if they get you they will put you into a pot and feast on you." Then he went on ahead. Soon the boys came to a tree that had been struck by lightning, and the Wild Boy directed his brother to gather some of the splinters from the tree and told him what to do with them. In a little while they came to the settlement of the cannibals, who, as soon as they saw the boys, came running out, crying, "Good, here are two nice fat strangers. Now we'll have a grand feast." They caught the boys and dragged them into the townhouse, and sent word to all the people of the settlement to come to the feast. They made up a great fire, put water into a large pot and set it to boiling, and then seized the Wild Boy and put him down into it. His brother was not in the least bit frightened and made no attempts to escape, but quietly knelt down and began putting the splinters into the fire, as if to make it burn better. When the cannibals thought the meat was about ready they lifted the pot from the fire, and that instant a blinding light filled the townhouse, and the lightning began to dart from one side to the other, striking down the cannibals until not one of them was left alive. Then the lightning went up through the smoke hole, and the next moment there were two boys standing outside the townhouse as though nothing had happened. They went on and soon met Kana'ti, who seemed much surprised to see them, and said, "What! Are you here again?" "O, yes, we never give up. We are great men!" "What did the cannibals do to you?" "We met them and they brought us to their townhouse, but they never hurt us." Kana'ti said nothing more, and they went on.

This time Kana'ti is very specific about the danger ahead and tells them about the cannibals who would capture them, put them in a pot and eat them. As he goes on ahead, having warned them, they find a tree struck by lightning and get several pieces of wood. In Native American tribes, as in much of Europe, special potency is attached to the wood of a tree struck by lightning. Some healing practices are attached, and conjurers use it for some actions. Some even plant it with corn seed to help it grow. (It should be noted that the boys will themselves be known as the "Thunder Boys," which ties them closely to lightning.)[7]

The boys face the challenge and are captured by the cannibals, with the Wild Boy tossed in the pot to boil while his brother places some of the splinters into the fire. When the time comes to lift the lid, the room is filled with flashes of lightning bouncing in all directions until all of the cannibal tribe are killed. With a grand finale of lightning up the smoke hole, the boys stand outside as if nothing has happened. When they catch up to Kana'ti he is once again surprised to see them, perhaps as much for their diligence of pursuit as for surviving the cannibals. This time he does not call them any negative names and asks what was done to them. The boys can now declare that they never give up and are not just men but great men.

PARENTAL REUNION: THE LITTLE MEN OF THUNDER

He soon got out of sight of the boys, but they kept on until they came to the end of the world, where the sun comes out. The sky was just coming down when they got there, but they waited until it went up again, and then they went through and climbed up on the other side. There they found Kana'ti and Selu sitting together. The old folk received them kindly and were glad to see them, telling them they might stay there a while, but then they must go to live where the sun goes down. The boys stayed with their parents seven days and then went on toward the Darkening land, where they are now. We call them Anisga'ya Tsunsdi' (the Little Men), and when they talk to each other we hear low rolling thunder in the west.

The journey ends at the end of the world where the sun comes out. They follow their father who leads and is out of sight. They wait until the right time and cross over to the other side, finding Kana'ti and Selu together once again. There is a kind, positive reunion and a seven-day visit, but they are told they cannot stay forever. Their place is in the west, where the sun goes down. Now they have a name, the Little Men, recognized when they talk, or thunder, in the west.

The story seems to have come full circle with the reunion of parents and children, but things are different now. They seem to be recognized as being adults now, seen as men not just boys. But the rest of the story is like an epilogue to let the hearer know there is more than a happy ending.

HELP FOR THE HUNTERS: THE THUNDER BOYS IN ACTION

After Kana'ti's boys had let the deer out from the cave where their father used to keep them, the hunters tramped about in the woods for a long time without finding any game, so that the people were very hungry. At last they heard that the Thunder Boys were now living in the far west, beyond the sun door, and that if they were sent for they could bring back the game. So they sent messengers for them, and the boys came and sat down in the middle of the town-house and began to sing.

At the first song there was a roaring sound like a strong wind in the northwest, and it grew louder and nearer as the boys sang on, until at the seventh song a whole herd of deer, led by a large buck, came out from the woods. The boys had told the people to be ready with their bows and arrows, and when the song was ended and all the deer were close around the townhouse, the hunters shot into them and killed as many as they needed before the herd could get back into the timber.

Then the Thunder Boys went back into the Darkening land, but before they left they taught the people the seven songs with which to call up the deer. It all happened so long ago that the songs are now forgotten — all but two, which the hunters still sing whenever they go after deer.

The story revisits the first mistake of the boys and the consequences for all. There is hunger in the land, for game is not available. Upon hearing that the Thunder Boys are in the far west beyond the sun door and that now they are available to help obtain game, the people send for them. Not unlike then in helping the villagers to get the corn given by Selu, the boys now sing the songs that bring the game literally to their doorstep. They are prepared, and the singing of the seven powerful songs provides what is needed. The others return to the woods. The boys now seem to be mature, helpful men and give the seven songs to call up the deer before they return to the west.

The west is the twilight land, Usunhi'yi, the spirit land. Used in many sacred formulas, this is more than a simple geographic term about a direction or place where the sun sets, according to Mooney.[8] So in coming back to the completed family setting where Kana'ti, Selu and the two mature sons reside in a special spiritual place far to the west, they are able to give to others not only the corn, but also the special songs to call up the deer. They have grown from their narcissistic immaturity to sharing and family solidarity. In a sense, the story pictures some sense of hope in the long family pilgrimage filled with tragedy, pain and poor decisions. In light of, and in spite of, the wild actions of youth, there can be growing up and maturity.

THEOLOGICAL COMMENTS

The most obvious parallel to the myth of Kana'ti and Selu is that of Adam and Eve in the Garden of Eden. The sense of the first chapters of Genesis shows where food is in plenty, with heavier emphasis on the plants and their seeds. It is very good. Humans are to keep the Garden of Eden and may eat the fruit of the trees, except for the one tree of knowledge. The great temptation, proposed by the serpent, is that to eat that fruit would not bring the promised death but wisdom, like God.[9] For the Thunder Boys, the temptation in the father's case was quite similar, for they think that they themselves could do what he did. As with Adam and Eve, one boy tempts the other but they both fully participate.

The Wahnenauhi version of the Kana'ti and Selu story is so much closer to the biblical story, even pointing to how "sin" enters the world, that one wonders if there already had been missionary influences upon that tradition. The ending of that version also leaves all people having been cast out to work hard as a result of the sin. Paradise is lost. Appendix B gives the Kana'ti and Selu story from the Wahnenauhi manuscript as provided by Mooney. It is much shorter and has a gentler form. Both parents' secrets of game and corn are discovered, and both parents die as martyrs, leaving the boys to hunt and raise corn by themselves. It is tied more closely to creation and the concept of the origin of sin is seen as the basis for the misdeeds of the sons. There is neither the reunion at the end, nor the role of the Thunder Boys in helping others.[10]

The Thunder Boys, or sons of Kana'ti and Selu, bring up the names Jesus gave to his disciples as he calls them to follow. The sons of Zebidee, James and John, he calls "Bo-aner'ges, that is, sons of thunder."[11]

Some early mystics called Jesus "Rabbi Ben Panther," probably as a play on the words "pan(all) and "theos" (god). Also, it was said that a panther sleeps three days, then awakens to a loud roar heard far and wide, a reference to Jesus' death and resurrection. The panther's breath is said to be sweet and a parallel to the Holy Spirit.[12] In some sense the growth process of this story shows a death and resurrection of the family and of each individual in it, a parallel to what most religions hope to accomplish. The ancient imagery of Christ like a panther could also carry into the story where the boys cannot kill him; he tolerates their antics. And the sweetness of the breath of the Spirit is carried in much Christian music.

4

U'tlun'ta, the Spear-Finger and Nun'yunu'wi, the Stone Man

U'TLUN'TA, THE SPEAR-FINGER: THE MYTH

Long, long ago — hilahi'yu — there dwelt in the mountains a terrible ogress, a woman monster, whose food was human livers. She could take on any shape or appearance to suit her purpose, but in her right form she looked very much like an old woman, excepting that her whole body was covered with skin as hard as a rock that no weapon could wound or penetrate, and that on her right hand she had a long, stony forefinger of bone, like an awl or spearhead, with which she stabbed everyone to whom she could get near enough. On account of this fact she was called U'tlun'ta, "Spear-finger," and on account of her stony skin she was sometimes called Nun'yunu'wi, "Stone-dress." There was another stone-clothed monster that killed people, but that is a different story.

Spear-finger had such powers over stone that she could easily lift and carry immense rocks, and could cement them together by merely striking one against another. To get over the rough country more easily she undertook to build a great rock bridge through the air from Nunyu'-tlu'gun'yi, the "Tree Rock," on Hiwassee, over to Sanigila'gi' (Whiteside Mountain), on the Blue Ridge, and had it well started from the top of the Tree Rock when the lightning struck it and scattered the fragments along the whole ridge, where the pieces can still be seen by those who go there. She used to range all over the mountains about the heads of the streams and in the dark passes of Nantahala, always hungry and looking for victims. Her favorite haunt on the Tennessee side was about the gap on the trail where Chilhowee mountain comes down to the river.

Sometimes an old woman would approach along the trail where the children were picking strawberrries or playing near the village, and would say to them coaxingly, "Come, my grandchildren, come to your granny and let granny dress your hair." When some little girl ran up and laid her head in the old woman's lap to be petted and combed the old witch would gently run her fingers through the child's hair until it went to sleep, when she would stab the little one through the heart or back of the neck with the long awl finger, which she had kept hidden under her robe. Then she would take out the liver and eat it.

She would enter a house by taking the appearance of one of the family who happened to have gone out for a short time, and would watch her chance to stab someone with her long finger and take out his liver. She could stab him without being noticed, and often the victim did not even know it himself at the time — for it left no wound and caused no pain — but went on about his own affairs, until all at once he felt weak and began gradually to pine away, and was always sure to die, because Spear-finger had taken his liver.

When the Cherokee went out in the fall, according to their custom, to burn the leaves off from the mountains in order to get the chestnuts on the ground, they were never safe, for the old witch was always on the lookout, and as soon as she saw the smoke rise she knew there were Indians there and sneaked up to try to surprise one alone. So as well as they could they tried to keep together, and were very cautious of allowing any stranger to approach the camp. But if one went down to the spring for a drink they never knew but it might be the liver eater that came back and sat with them.

Sometimes she took her proper form, and once or twice, when far out from the settlements, a solitary hunter had seen an old woman, with a queer-looking hand, going through the woods singing low to herself:

Uwe'lana'tsiku.' Su' sa' sai'
(Liver, I eat it. Su' sa' sai.')

It was rather a pretty song, but it chilled his blood, for he knew it was the liver eater, and he hurried away, silently, before she might see him.

At last a great council was held to devise some means to get rid of U'tlun'ta before she should destroy everybody. The people came from all around, and after much talk it was decided that the best way would be to trap her in a pitfall where all the warriors could attack her at once. So they dug a deep pitfall across the trail and covered it over with earth and grass as if the ground had never been disturbed. Then they kindled a large fire of brush near the trail and hid themselves in the laurels, because they knew she would come as soon as she saw the smoke.

Sure enough they soon saw an old woman coming along the trail. She looked like an old woman whom they knew well in the village, and although several of the wiser men wanted to shoot at her, the others interfered, because they did not want to hurt one of their own people. The old woman came slowly along the trail, with one hand under her blanket, until she stopped upon the pitfall and tumbled through the brush top into the deep hole below. Then, at once, she showed her true nature, and instead of the feeble old woman there was the terrible U'tlun'ta, with her stony skin, and her sharp awl finger reaching out in every direction for some one to stab.

The hunters rushed out from the thicket and surrounded the pit, but shoot as true and often as they could, their arrows struck the stony mail of the witch only to be broken and fall useless at her feet, while she taunted them and tried to climb out of the pit to get at them. They kept out of her way, but were only wasting their arrows when a small bird, Utsu'gi' the titmouse, perched on a tree overhead and began to sing "un, un, un." They thought it was saying u'nahu', "heart," meaning that they should aim at the heart of the stone witch. They directed their arrows where the heart should be, but the arrows only glanced off with the flint heads broken.

Then they caught the Utsu'gi' and cut off its tongue, so that ever since its tongue is short and everybody knows it is a liar. When the hunters let it go it flew straight up into the sky until it was out of sight and never came back again. The titmouse that we know is only an image of the other.

They kept up the fight without result until another bird, little Tsi-kilili', the chickadee, flew down from a tree and alighted upon the witch's right hand. The warriors took this as a sign that they must aim there, and they were right, for her heart was on the inside of her hand, which she kept doubled into a fist, this same awl hand with which she had stabbed so many people. Now she was frightened in earnest, and began to rush furiously at them with her long awl finger and to jump about in the pit to dodge the arrows, until at last a lucky arrow struck just where the awl joined her wrist and she fell down dead.

Ever since the Tsi'kilili' is known as a truth teller, and when a man is away on a journey, if this bird comes and perches near the house and chirps its song, his friends know he will soon be safe home.

NUN'YUNU'WI, THE STONE MAN: THE MYTH

This is what the old men told me when I was a boy.

Once when all the people of the settlement were out in the mountains on a great hunt, one man who had gone on ahead climbed to the top of a high ridge and found a large river on the other side. While he was looking across he saw an old man walking about on the opposite ridge, with a cane that seemed to be made of some bright, shining rock. The hunter watched and saw that every little while the old man would point his cane in a certain direction, then draw it back and smell the end of it. At last he pointed it in the direction of the hunting camp on the other side of the mountain, and this time when he drew back the staff he sniffed it several times as if it smelled very good, and then started along the ridge straight for the camp. He moved very slowly, with the help of the cane, until he reached the end of the ridge, when he threw the cane out into the air and it became a bridge of shining rock stretching across the river. After he had crossed over upon the bridge it became a cane again, and the old man picked it up and started over the mountain toward the camp.

The hunter was frightened, and felt sure that it meant mischief, so he hurried on down the mountain and took the shortest trail back to the camp to get there before the old man. When he got there and told his story the medicine-man said the old man was a wicked cannibal monster call Nun'yunu'wi, "Dressed in Stone," who lived in that part of the country, and was always going about the mountains looking for some hunter to kill and eat. It was very hard to escape from him, because his stick guided him like a dog, and it was nearly as hard to kill him, because his whole body was covered with a skin of solid rock. If he came he would kill and eat them all,

*and there was only one way to save themselves. He could not bear
to look upon a menstrual woman, and if they could find seven menstrual women to stand in the path as he came along, the sight would
kill him.*

So they asked among all the women, and found seven who were
sick in that way, and with one of them it had just begun. By the order
of the medicine-man they stripped themselves and stood along the
path where the old man would come. Soon they heard Nun'yunu'wi
coming through the woods, feeling his way with his stone cane. He
came along the trail to where the first woman was standing, and as
soon as he saw her he started and cried out: "Yu? my grandchild;
you are in a very bad state!" He hurried past her, but in a moment
he met the next woman, and cried out again: "Yu! my child; you are
in a terrible way," and hurried past her, but now he was vomiting
blood. He hurried on to the third and the fourth and the fifth woman,
but with each one that he saw his step grew weaker until when he
came to the last one, with whom the sickness had just begun, the
blood poured from his mouth and he fell down on the trail.

Then the medicine-man drove seven sourwood stakes through
his body and pinned him to the ground, and when night came they
piled great logs over him and set fire to them, and all the people
gathered around to see. Nun'yunu'wi was a great ada'wehi and knew
many secrets, and now as the fire came close to him he began to talk,
and told them the medicine for all kinds of sickness. At midnight he
began to sing, and sang the hunting songs for calling up the bear
and the deer and all the animals of the woods and mountains. As
the blaze grew hotter his voice sank low and lower, until at last when
daylight came, the logs were a heap of white ashes and the voice was
still.

Then the medicine-man told them to rake off the ashes, and
where the body had lain they found only a large lump of red wa'di
paint and a magic u'lunsuti stone. He kept the stone for himself, and
calling the people around him he painted them, on face and breast,
with the red wa'di, and whatever each person prayed for while the
painting was being done — whether for hunting success, for working skill, or for a long life — that gift was his.

The Spear-Finger and the Stone Man — Portrayal of the deceptive nature of the grandmotherly Spear-finger, along with the trusting child. The masculine counterpart to this evil form is seen in Stone Man nearby, blending into the stone background. By Lynn Lossiah.

INTRODUCTION

These two related mythological figures, Spear-finger and Stone Man, have similar characteristics, and both represent forms of evil, one feminine and one masculine. They are cross-referenced by the story tellers because they are so much alike, thus they will be considered as one myth, or as two-in-one. They symbolize some of the Cherokee fears, including the fear of witches and the power such figures have over others. The stories of Spear-finger and Stone Man, combined as one, could parallel some early stories from Salem, Massachusetts, where the fear of witches paralyzed the European settlers and drove them to action in the same time period. Because the stories of witches and evil power over others are so universal, the assumption is that something more than hysteria over strange behavior is involved. Since a major element of the witch was to obtain "power" from others in order to extend the witch's own life, some who lived longer than usual were thought to have such power and were feared rather than revered. For the Cherokee, the fear of witchcraft was strong and they often worked with the Christian missionaries to eradicate the belief and to protect the innocent who might be accused unfairly. As the Cherokee compiled their laws in written form they outlawed punishing anyone accused of witchcraft, but the fears remain. Interestingly, some seek conjurers even today to offset a suspected spell by some unknown witch.[1] In antiquity, before the priests disappeared, they used rituals to remove the powers cast.[2] In these two stories, the task is not to validate witches, but rather to examine how the community faced the reality of evil in their midst.

THE EVIL OGRESS: SPEARS AND STONES

Long, long ago — hilahi'yu — there dwelt in the mountains a terrible ogress, a woman monster, whose food was human livers. She could take on any shape or appearance to suit her purpose, but in her right form she looked very much like an old woman, excepting that her whole body was covered with skin as hard as a rock that no weapon could wound or penetrate, and that on her right hand she had a long, stony forefinger of bone, like an awl or spearhead, with which she stabbed everyone to whom she could get near enough. On account of this fact she was called U'tlun'ta, *"Spear-finger," and on account of her stony skin she was sometimes called* Nun'yunu'wi, *"Stone-dress." There was another stone-clothed monster that killed people, but that is an different story.*

This picture of an evil monster, an ogress, is painted with some unique features. First, she subsists on human livers, obtained from innocent persons. Second, she can shape-shift, not into animals but into the form of other Cherokee persons or family members with familiar faces. Third, she has skin as hard as rock, and thus is also called "stone-dress." So hard is this skin that no weapon can penetrate it. Fourth, she has on her right hand a vicious weapon or tool in the form of one long, bony finger like an awl or spear. She stabs with it, and removes livers as well. In this introduction the story teller lets the hearer know there is another monster with stone clothing, probably that of Stone Man, the myth that followed this one.

In practical, everyday situations, Spear-finger can be a metaphor for those who feed on others and who draw energy, even life, from those around them. This is a different figure from the dependent person who loafs and lives on others around them, an emotional or literal moocher. (In some sense the later myth of the Lazy Hunter seems to play on this theme.) In daily life, these moochers may come to ask for $5 or $20 as a "loan" but rarely pay it back. One learns to say no. Others in this mild form who are emotionally dependent may "unload," telling long, often detailed, stories to everyone, even strangers, and drain the energy from all who will listen. They do not really seek help, but attention. Spear-finger, however, speaks to extremes. Such persons drain the energy and patience of those who earnestly seek to help them. For those who are captured by such folks on the street it can be difficult, especially when they know the person. Their life may be one of ongoing great tragedy, or their story of needs is so moving one cannot escape and is drawn into an exhausting web of attempting to help.

This story speaks to facing the Spear-fingers of life when they get close enough to hurt people. It is not just that Spear-finger has this terrible weapon, but also that she has a stone skin. She is so hard and insensitive that no pleas, no pain or sorrow can get to her. Her persona is rigid. These are people without without feelings, and when they inflict pain on others they are unmoved. They are called sociopaths or psychopaths. Not all are in jails or hospitals. Some have hardened their "skins" into stone by drugs and other substances or have a history of being abused. Some are even born that way, with some genetic flaw in their nature.

From the viewpoint of depth psychology this ogress figure could also symbolize the devouring, terrible mother, an archetypal image of the negative mother figure, some prehuman form of life. This negative mother figure is opposite of the positive, nurturing, life-giving mother. In that sense Spear-finger is the opposite of Selu. In clinical settings, it has been found that most people have experienced more of the nurturing side of their own mother, but some may have had experiences of being betrayed and devoured by a mother or grandmother figure as in this story. It defies the stereotype that all mothers and grandmothers are loving, nurturing feminine forces. There are opposites, both good and evil forces in feminine form.

STONE POWER: BUILDING AND HAUNTING

Spear-finger had such powers over stone that she could easily lift and carry immense rocks, and could cement them together by merely striking one against another. To get over the rough country more easily she undertook to build a great rock bridge through the air from Nunyu'-tlu'gun'yi, the "Tree Rock," on Hiwassee, over to Sanigila'gi' (Whiteside Mountain), on the Blue Ridge, and had it well started from the top of the Tree Rock when the lightning struck it and scattered the fragments along the whole ridge, where the pieces can still be seen by those who go there. She used to range all over the mountains about the heads of the streams and in the dark passes of Nantahala, always hungry and looking for victims. Her favorite haunt on the Tennessee side was about the gap on the trail where Chilhowee mountain comes down to the river.

Spear-finger has power not only over people, when she can get close enough, but also over stone. She has the strength to carry massive stones and to cement them together. She once began a stone bridge between two prominent mountains for her own convenience in getting across the rough country. But lightning destroyed it, implicitly sent by the Thunder Boys, sons of Selu and Kana'ti. Her favorite haunting places are also noted, including the dark Nantahala, "Land of the Noonday Sun." Her hunger and search is constant.

Psychologically, the power of psychotics, those with a serious mental illness and out of touch with reality, is beyond the grasp of most folks. Their power strikes fear in most people they encounter. They try to build "bridges" with seemingly inhuman might, as if they could lift great stones. Some who suffer with mania can do the same and can initially accomplish great feats, which often tumble down or are struck down. For example, the power of certain big businesses, and even some religious groups, that build great edifices gives this Spear-finger effect. The leaders draw power from the unsuspecting victims, draining their life savings and hope. It seems that these power brokers will stop at nothing to feed their power or fame, even at the sacrifice of others. But while such a business or religious group can seemingly build great "bridges," they sometimes are destroyed, leaving only remnants.

GRANNY POWER: CARESSING AND BETRAYING

Sometimes an old woman would approach along the trail where the children were picking strawberries or playing near the village, and would say to them coaxingly, "Come, my grandchildren, come to your granny and let granny dress your hair." When some little girl ran up and laid her head in the old woman's lap to be petted and combed the old witch would gently run her fingers through the child's hair until it went to sleep, when she would stab the little one through the heart or back of the neck with the long awl finger, which she had kept hidden under her robe. Then she would take out the liver and eat it.

Here is the evil core of the story, in that Spear-finger appears to be a sweet little old grandmother. She seduces children into her lap under the guise of loving, caressing and caring for them. She relaxes them to sleep in her lap, only to go for their liver when they are asleep. The children go looking for the sweetness of strawberries and end up in losing their own lives to this witch because she offers sweet comfort. They are betrayed.

From a clinical and a Jungian perspective, this underscores the powerful destruction when children are betrayed by a mother or grandmother figure. The "caring" caress and the offer to "love" or "pet" the child is only a cover to lure the unsuspecting little one. The hair often symbolizes the thoughts, and as she combs the hair she is rearranging their thoughts, perhaps removing the parents' warnings. She also puts them to sleep, a sign of children being unconscious, i.e., not consciously aware of what is going on. Young children are particularly vulnerable to such abuse. The Spear-finger symbolizes more than a tool to gain the liver; it also captures sexual abuse in the crudest way. Some children die from such abuse, if not literally right away, after their "livers" (or life forces) are taken by the abuser. Later in life they cannot cope with what has happened. Death, both physical and emotional, can be slow.

SPEAR-FINGER STEALTH: DECEIVED AND DE-LIVERED

She would enter a house by taking the appearance of one of the family who happened to have gone out for a short time, and would watch her chance to stab someone with her long finger and take out his liver. She could stab him without being noticed, and often the victim did not even know it himself at the time — for it left no wound and caused no pain — but went on about his own affairs, until all at once he felt weak and began gradually to pine away, and was always sure to die, because Spear-finger had taken his liver.

A similar betrayal is in the second example of her acts, in that she is able to take on the identity of a family member who is away. This action she can take unnoticed by the victims who only realize later when they pine away and die. Liver not only secretes bile but also filters the blood; it is a vital organ and without it or its function one dies. Even before modern medicine, attempts to help or heal the liver were central in many cultures when sickness hit.

Also, the "stealth" entrance into a family in the guise of someone close captures the unknown power of evil that takes a toll over the long term. Clinically, it may be a long lost family member or old friend who comes for a friendly visit and leaves, after which one or two family members become very depressed without knowing why. At the surface level it seems to be a normal, nice visit, but something is taken and life energy is drained. The irony is that the "grandmother" visitor may have gone away energized, feeling renewed, and planning for the next trip. In therapy it is not easy to find out just how this visit from "Spear-finger" stabbed or hurt them, for there is no wound. But often a dream, or other message from the unconscious, will reveal just when "she" tapped the liver. Often it is some long lost family secret or family pain that was forgotten or suppressed. In therapy when the discovery is made, one familiar with this myth may declare with relief and humor, "Spear-finger lives still!" And they are prepared not to expose their back the next time. It is important to remember that Spear-finger is not limited to women, for the negative feminine can also be in a man who relates in the same friendly, "grandmotherly" way.

CHEROKEE FEARS: FRIEND OR FOE?

When the Cherokee went out in the fall, according to their custom, to burn the leaves off from the mountains in order to get the chestnuts on the ground, they were never safe, for the old witch was always on the lookout, and as soon as she saw the smoke rise she knew there were Indians there and sneaked up to try to surprise one alone. So as well as they could they tried to keep together, and were very cautious of allowing any stranger to approach the camp. But if one went down to the spring for a drink they never knew but it might be the liver eater that came back and sat with them.

Sometimes she took her proper form, and once or twice, when far out from the settlements, a solitary hunter had seen an old woman, with a queer-looking hand, going through the woods singing low to herself:

Uwe'lana'tsiku.' Su' sa' sai.'
(Liver, I eat it. Su' sa' sai.')

It was rather a pretty song, but it chilled his blood, for he knew it was the liver eater, and he hurried away, silently, before she might see him.

The community dilemma is clear. They try to stay together, knowing how she stalks, but it is not always possible. For the Cherokee the burning of the leaves to get chestnuts was a major source of food for the winter yet they knew that the smoke meant she would come. She would go for any person alone. Worse yet, they begin to fear strangers, not knowing if one might be Spear-finger. This would have been most difficult for the Cherokee, who were known for their hospitality. Even a break for water at the spring might invite her to sit alongside. On rare occasions someone would see or hear her in her real form, or at least as an old woman singing the eerie song about eating liver, and, most of all, revealing the strange looking hand with the long, destructive spear-finger. Noting that the song is pretty, the hunter's very blood is chilled. He escapes without discovery.

Although the community at large can be cautious about danger from known evil forces in society, the fear also calls individuals to be diligent. One is not to be naive about those who would seek to destroy life for their own evil pleasures. Sometimes it is not easy to discern where the danger lies for it may be sitting next to one. But evil may also be obvious when one listens to the song carefully, and watches carefully. Over the long term, it is not healthy to keep looking everywhere for such evil, lest one become paranoid. Thus community action may be required.

Of C.G. Jung's contributions to psychology, one of the most misunderstood and yet vital was his assertion of the reality of evil, both individually and collectively. He declared its existence to be an empirical fact, not just some philosophical topic. As a psychiatrist in clinical work he worked with the power of evil in personality and saw it as the opposite of good. The shadow of persons could be part of this negative dynamic in each person. Evil is more than ethics, although it involves ethics. There is something behind, something greater in the nature of being. Evil cannot be relativized or rationalized.[3] These Cherokee stories underline the pragmatic acceptance of evil as a force in life, as Jung did.

FACING THE FEAR: TRAPPED AND TURNED

At last a great council was held to devise some means to get rid of U'tlun'ta before she should destroy everybody. The people came from all around, and after much talk it was decided that the best way would be to trap her in a pitfall where all the warriors could attack her at once. So they dug a deep pitfall across the trail and covered it over with earth and grass as if the ground had never been disturbed. Then they kindled a large fire of brush near the trail and hid themselves in the laurels, because they knew she would come as soon as she saw the smoke.

Sure enough they soon saw an old woman coming along the trail. She looked like an old woman whom they knew well in the village, and although several of the wiser men wanted to shoot at her,

the others interfered, because they did not want to hurt one of their
own people. The old woman came slowly along the trail, with one
hand under her blanket, until she stopped upon the pitfall and tum-
bled through the brush top into the deep hole below. Then, at once,
she showed her true nature, and instead of the feeble old woman
there was a terrible U'tlun'ta, with her stony skin, and her sharp awl
finger reaching out in every direction for some one to stab.

The community acts for its survival and processes it in long dis-
cussions at council, a traditional Cherokee means of making decisions.
The outcome affects all and all must cooperate for it to work. Their chosen method is a pitfall, covered with brush and dirt so she cannot see
it. They build a fire, as if they are looking for chestnuts, to lure her. It
works and she comes. Then some difference in the community comes
up for some of the older, "wiser" ones want to shoot her right away,
but one learns later that it would not have worked. The others fear that
in fact it might not be Spear-finger for the little old lady looks just like
one of their own. They wisely wait to see and sure enough, when she
falls into the trap she shows her true, stony self, leaping and scream-
ing, stabbing wildly with her finger. But contained as she is, it is not
over. Adversity can bring out the true character of a person.

Perhaps no better example of how a community can deal with the
criminally insane or severely mentally ill is captured in this part. It
takes full community dialogue, discussion and decision, not just a few
who "know how." The few who would shoot first and ask questions
later are acting in haste, before a good diagnosis is made or a correct
judgment is made. The pit can be symbolic of the containment society needs for those who are harmful to others or themselves. Taking
seriously the evil and severe illness in human society means that there
will need to be penitentiaries and mental hospitals, places where they
are no harm to others, as pitiful as they may appear. The goal is always
healing from their suffering, but in the "Spear-finger" situations, there
is no healing, only containment.

WINGED MESSENGERS: HEART AND HAND

The hunters rushed out from the thicket and surrounded the
pit, but shoot as true and often as they could, their arrows struck
the stony mail of the witch only to be broken and fall useless at her

feet, while she taunted them and tried to climb out of the pit to get at them. They kept out of her way, but were only wasting their arrows when a small bird, Utsu'gi the titmouse, perched on a tree overhead and began to sing "un, un, un." They thought it was saying u'nahu', "heart," meaning that they should aim at the "heart" of the stone witch. They directed their arrows where the heart should be, but the arrows only glanced off with the flint heads broken.

Then they caught the Utsu'gi' and cut off its tongue, so that ever since its tongue is short and everybody knows it is a liar. When the hunters let it go it flew straight up into the sky until it was out of sight and never came back again. The titmouse that we know is only an image of the other.

They kept up the fight without result until another bird, little Tsi-kilili', the chickadee, flew down from a tree and alighted upon the witch's right hand. The warriors took this as a sign that they must aim there, and they were right, for her heart was on the inside of her hand, which she kept doubled into a fist, this same awl hand with which she had stabbed so many people. Now she was frightened in earnest, and began to rush furiously at them with her long awl finger and to jump about in the pit to dodge the arrows, until at last a lucky arrow struck just where the awl joined her wrist and she fell down dead.

Ever since the Tsi'kilili' is known as a truth teller, and when a man is away on a journey, if this bird comes and perches near the house and chirps its song, his friends know he will soon be safe home.

The fearful witch is captured but the hunters are not at all successful in finishing her. She still has the upper hand due to the stony protection that repels all their arrows. She threatens and taunts; she tries to get out of the pit to get them. The scene is tense and a seemingly hopeless standoff until a small bird, the titmouse, seems to tell them to aim at her heart. This has no effect so they cut off the bird's tongue as punishment. Another small bird, the chickadee, reveals the witch's secret; a lucky arrow finally hits the part of her hand that in fact holds her heart. She falls and dies. They all feel now that they can return safely since the great, destructive Spear-finger is finished with the help of this tiny winged messenger. The chickadee becomes known as the truth-teller.

At this final stage in the story the listener learns another, heretofore unknown, characteristic about the witch: her heart is not in her chest where normal people have a heart. They learn that it is very near that evil awl or spear. The major final psychological point is made in the location of the heart so near the destructive weapon. Those who are essentially evil do not have a normal heart. Their morals and values are their own and they live to feed their own sick needs. Persons without a conscience are a danger to those around them and yet try to hide their values or their different heart "location." They take on many different forms to accomplish their destructive work. Perhaps no better example of this would be the sociopath or serial killer who lives a seemingly normal life in front of neighbors and family, yet eventually is captured while doing their evil deeds. In much Native American thinking, as in Jungian work, the bird is a spirit creature. So the first bird, the titmouse, seems to be either an unlucky creature to be so misunderstood or is perhaps not telling the truth. In fact, to shoot the heart is correct, but the heart is not where it should be. As the chickadee locates it for them, the right spirit, that spirit of truth, prevails and victory over evil is theirs. In this story the form of evil is a woman, but the Cherokee also have an evil man, the Stone Man, with many similarities.

NUN'YUNU'WI, THE STONE MAN

The next story also begins with the authority of oral tradition; in other words, it came from the old traditions and was not just made up by the story teller. It jumps right into the problem.

THE PROBLEM: A CANNIBAL HARD AS STONE

This is what the old men told me when I was a boy.

Once when all the people of the settlement were out in the mountains on a great hunt, one man who had gone on ahead climbed to the top of a high ridge and found a large river on the other side. While he was looking across he saw an old man walking about on the opposite ridge, with a cane that seemed to be made of some bright, shining rock. The hunter watched and saw that every little while the old man would point his cane in a certain direction, then draw it back and smell the end of it. At last he pointed it in the direction of the hunting camp on the other side of the mountain, and this time when he drew back the staff he sniffed it several times as if it smelled very good, and then started along the ridge straight for the camp. He moved very slowly, with the help of the cane, until he reached the end of the ridge, when he threw the cane out into the air and it became a bridge of shining rock stretching across the river. After he had crossed over upon the bridge it became a cane again, and the old man picked it up and started over the mountain toward the camp.

The hunter was frightened, and felt sure that it meant mischief, so he hurried on down the mountain and took the shortest trail back to the camp to get there before the old man. When he got there and told his story the medicine-man said the old man was a wicked cannibal monster call Nun'yunu'wi, "Dressed in Stone," who lived in that part of the country, and was always going about the mountains looking for some hunter to kill and eat. It was very hard to escape from him, because his stick guided him like a dog, and it was nearly as hard to kill him, because his whole body was covered with a skin of solid rock. If he came he would kill and eat them all, and there was only one way to save themselves. He could not bear to look upon a menstrual woman, and if they could find seven menstrual women to stand in the path as he came along, the sight would kill him.

The story reports the observation of a lone hunter who sees an old man with a stone walking stick that is magic. With it he sniffs out humans in nearby camps, using the cane for a bridge over the river. The hunter's intuition registers something is wrong and pushes him to a visit with the medicine-man. There he learns of the wicked cannibal monster, one dressed in stone who hunts hunters to kill and eat.

Mooney notes that the Iroquois had very close parallels to this story. One focuses on a race of cannibals also known as Stonish Giants who had once been normal humans but, living in the harsh wilderness, became accustomed to eating human flesh and rolling themselves in sand until their skin was hardened. One variation has a man with a stone finger showing him the way to go. Several similar concepts found in this and the Spear-finger stories are pointed out.[4] As noted, this story is similar in many ways to that of Spear-finger. The hardness of his skin protects him from any potential enemies and their arrows. Spear-finger uses her awl finger to kill or maim; he has a magic stone cane to lead him to his prey. He also uses it to cross rivers, whereas

Spear-finger's bridge-building efforts failed. She can shape-shift to look like a family member and he simply appears as a harmless old man. But he can hone in quickly on his prey. Whereas her secret is hard to find and found only after much effort, his vulnerability is already known by the medicine man. The singular solution is to find seven menstrual women, a sight the old man cannot bear.

In a parallel to the Spear-finger story, the stone skin seems to symbolize the insensitive nature and hardened protection of many people. Many are so hardened in life, so hardened in their actions, and tell of having grown up "in the school of hard knocks." They take pride in their ability to not feel other people's pain and take joy in not being "soft" or "wimpy." They can destroy life without guilt or remorse. The cane made of a shining, white rock can symbolize any weapon, and in the modern day, technology pushes that idea to the extreme. The ability to take another's life is easy with more and more powerful and technical weapons. Perhaps these pathological persons do not literally eat others, but they are cannibals in some symbolic sense. Information technology, by way of computers, can be used also as a weapon to cannibalize others, to take their identity, their money and property. Victims of such theft often express their helplessness, woundedness and frustration for the years it takes to recover, if they ever can. Much of that sense of frustration is that another human can be so insensitive.

The solution to attacking Stone Man's vulnerability is so simple, yet unexpected. He cannot face menstruating women. From a symbolic perspective, the blood has to do with life and the ability to give life, quite the opposite of the taking of life to which he was accustomed. Historically, in most Indian groups menstrual women were separated from the men during their period and the "menstrual lodge" was common institution; there women worked, ate and slept during their period. There were various taboos. In looking at this from a depth perspective, the meaning of the blood is important. As noted in other myths, blood is the life force and not to be thrown away carelessly. (See the Judaculla story following.)

THE ACTION: BLOOD, STAKES AND FIRE

So they asked among all the women, and found seven who were sick in that way, and with one of them it had just begun. By the order of the medicine-man they stripped themselves and stood along the path where the old man would come. Soon they heard Nun'yunu'wi coming through the woods, feeling his way with his stone cane. He came along the trail to where the first woman was standing, and as soon as he saw her he started and cried out: "Yu? my grandchild; you are in a very bad state!" He hurried past her, but in a moment he met the next woman, and cried out again: "Yu! my child; you are in a terrible way," and hurried past her, but now he was vomiting blood. He hurried on to the third and the fourth and the fifth woman, but with each one that he saw his step grew weaker until when he came to the last one, with whom the sickness had just begun, the blood poured from his mouth and he fell down on the trail.

Then the medicine-man drove seven sourwood stakes through his body and pinned him to the ground, and when night came they piled great logs over him and set fire to them, and all the people gathered around to see. Nun'yunu'wi was a great ada'wehi *and knew many secrets, and now as the fire came close to him he began to talk, and told them the medicine for all kinds of sickness. At midnight he began to sing, and sang the hunting songs for calling up the bear and the deer and all the animals of the woods and mountains. As the blaze grew hotter his voice sank low and lower, until at last when daylight came, the logs were a heap of white ashes and the voice was still.*

The community takes action in finding seven menstruating women, called "sick in that way." They strip down so it is obvious what is happening. The Stone Man rushes past each woman. He vomits blood and becomes weaker with each passing until he falls down with blood pouring from his mouth. They stake him down and pile wood to burn him. With crowds gathering, he shares many secrets for hunting and medicine until he dies.

Perhaps the most important part of this story is the role of women in Native American cultures, especially around childbearing issues. Perdue notes that many rituals around menstruation and childbirth, events that had spiritual power, were exclusive to women.[5] She notes that "menstruating women, in particular, had great power, and men regarded them as dangerous; consequently, they kept their distance and knew nothing about rites women performed to control and channel that power."[6]

Nothing could speak more clearly to Stone Man's anxiety and fear of these women. He is protected against the arrows and weapon blows of men and women. However, his stone protection is only on the outside. His inner world, his psyche, is not ready for this blood onslaught. It is significant that as they are showing the blood from their life-producing femininity, his somatic response is his own blood vomiting from his death-producing cannibal mouth.

To drive stakes through the body of a witch is very common in myths. Sourwood is used for cooking meat and medicinal purposes. It also was thought to counter witches' spells.[7] With the crowd coming to watch the consuming fire, they learn that he is also a great *ada'wehi*, a magician, with many secrets about medicine and hunting which he reveals in his dying. Thus in a symbolic sense, by using the "medicine" stakes of sourwood to hold him down, they force him to reveal secrets of other medicine as well as for provision of food.

THE RESULT: MAGIC IN PAINT AND STONE

Then the medicine-man told them to rake off the ashes, and where the body had lain they found only a large lump of red wa'di *paint and a magic* u'lunsuti *stone. He kept the stone for himself, and calling the people around him he painted them, on face and breast, with the red* wa'di, *and whatever each person prayed for while the painting was being done — whether for hunting success, for working skill, or for a long life — that gift was his.*

The rite of painting the body while praying a prayer was a special religious ritual, Mooney notes.[8] The cannibal is gone and the remnant of ashes, red paint and a magic stone is theirs. The shift is from the terror of being eaten, to finding food, to working and to healing. In both of these stories, the opposites are noteworthy: forces of evil versus forces of good, death and sickness versus life and healing. Noteworthy is the fact that it takes community action to face evil this powerful. Most single individuals are helpless against forces this powerful.

THEOLOGICAL COMMENTS

The scriptures often warn against hardening the heart or mind.[9] Both figures in these stories also remind one to face the reality of evil in one's midst. The history of Jewish, Christian and other traditions is filled with the tension of caring for the community and being hospitable to strangers, yet there is awareness of the reality that it will be abused and that there are dangers in being naive. Even Jesus' words of warning were clear and couched in symbolic, metaphorical language: "Behold I send you out as sheep in the midst of wolves; so be wise as serpents and innocent as doves."[10] The Jewish and Christian scriptures list numerous warnings about evil, including the natural existence of evil.[11] The dangerous finger of Spear-finger stands in contrast to the several references to the positive finger of God, which wrote in stone to give the commandments and which cast out demons.[12] With his finger Jesus wrote some mysterious message on the ground, and he challenged the doubting Thomas to test his wound with his finger.[13]

In these two stories, perhaps the most powerful point is that of the healing power of blood, or at least the power of the blood in counteracting evil. In many Christian traditions the blood of Christ takes on ritual and theological forms. At the core of the Holy Eucharist, Holy Communion, Lord's Supper, or whatever term is used, the sharing of the wine symbolizes Christ's sharing of his blood.[14] That also carried something of the early covenant of Christians, and had healing, cleansing power in its meaning. Many historical divisions of the Christian church have occurred over the interpretation or meaning of the blood. Religious songs of all traditions communicate the power of the blood. Also, in Jewish tradition the blood on the doorpost meant the plague would pass over that faithful house.[15]

This is not to compare these women to Jesus in a theological sense. Rather, in a deeper, symbolic parallel, these seven women do expose themselves and their life-giving blood to save their people. The blood is not on the doorpost as in Passover, but on their legs. They defeat the "death angel" or cannibal by their action. And there are seven women, that holy number again. The mystery of the feminine is brought forth to heal and rid the community of an evil presence.

5

Tsul'Kalu', or Judaculla, the Slant-Eyed Giant

THE MYTH

A long time ago a widow lived with her one daughter at the old town of Kanuga on Pigeon River. The girl was of age to marry, and her mother used to talk with her a good deal, and tell her she must be sure to take no one but a good hunter for a husband, so that they would have some one to take care of them and would always have plenty of meat in the house. The girl said such a man was hard to find, but her mother advised her not to be in a hurry, and to wait until the right one came.

Now the mother slept in the house while the girl slept outside in the asi. One dark night a stranger came to the asi wanting to court the girl, but she told him her mother would let her marry no one but a good hunter. "Well," said the stranger, "I am a great hunter," so she let him come in, and he stayed all night. Just before day he said he must go back now to his own place, but that he had brought some meat for her mother, and she would find it outside. Then he went away and the girl had not seen him. When day came she went out and found there a deer, which she brought into the house to her mother, and told her it was a present from her new sweetheart. Her mother was pleased, and they had deer steaks for breakfast.

He came again the next night, but again went away before daylight, and this time he left two deer outside. The mother was more pleased this time, but said to her daughter, "I wish your sweetheart would bring us some wood." Now wherever he might be, the stranger

108

knew their thoughts, so when he came the next time he said to the girl, "Tell your mother I have brought the wood"; and when she looked out in the morning there were several great trees lying in front of the door, roots and branches and all. The old woman was angry, and said, "He might have brought us some wood that we could use instead of whole trees that we can't split, to litter the road with brush." The hunter knew what she said, and the next time he came he brought nothing, and when they looked out in the morning the trees were gone and there was no wood at all, so the old woman had to go after some herself.

Almost every night he came to see the girl, and each time he brought a deer or some other game, but still he always left before daylight. At last her mother said to her, "Your husband always leaves before daylight. Why doesn't he wait? I want to see what kind of a son-in-law I have." When the girl told this to her husband he said he could not let the old woman see him, because the sight would frighten her. "She wants to see you, anyhow," said the girl, and began to cry, until at last he had to consent, but warned her that her mother must not say that he looked frightful (usga' se ti'yu).

The next morning he did not leave so early, but stayed in the asi, and when it was daylight the girl went out and told her mother. The old woman came and looked in, and there she saw a great giant, with long slanting eyes (tsul'kalu') lying doubled up on the floor, with his head against the rafters, in the left-hand corner at the back, and his toes scraping the roof in the right-hand corner by the door. She gave only one look and ran back to the house, crying, "Usga' se ti'yu! Usga' se ti'yu!" Tsul'Kalu' was terribly angry. He untwisted himself and came out of the asi, and said good-bye to the girl, telling her that he would never let her mother see him again, but would go back to his own country. Then he went off in the direction of Tsune-gun'yi.

Soon after he left, the girl had her monthly period. There was a very great flow of blood, and the mother threw it all into the river. One night after the girl had gone to bed in the asi her husband came again to the door and said to her, "It seems you are alone," and asked where was the child. She said there had been none. Then he asked where was the blood, and she said that her mother had thrown it into the river. She told just where the place was, and he went there and found a small worm in the water. He took it up and carried it back to the asi, *and as he walked it took form and began to grow, until, when he reached the* asi, *it was a baby girl that he was carrying. He gave it to his wife and said, "Your mother does not like me and abuses our child, so come and let us go to my home." The girl wanted to be with her husband, so, after telling her mother goodbye, she took up the child and they went off together to Tsunegun'yi.*

Now, the girl had an older brother, who lived with his own wife in another settlement, and when he heard that his sister was married he came to pay a visit to her and her new husband, but when he arrived at Kanuga his mother told him his sister had taken her child and had gone away with her husband, nobody knew where. He was sorry to see his mother so lonely, so he said he would go after his sister and try to find her and bring her back. It was easy to follow the footprints of the giant, and the young man went along the trail until he came to a place where they had rested, and there were tracks on the ground where a child had been lying and other marks as if a baby had been born there. He went on along the trail and came to another place where they had rested, and there were tracks of a baby crawling about and another lying on the ground. He went on and came to where they had rested again, and there were tracks of a child walking and another crawling about. He went on until he came where they had rested again, and there were tracks of one child running and another walking. Still he followed the trail along the stream into the mountains, and came to the place where they had rested again, and this time there were footprints of two children running all about, and the footprints can still be seen in the rock at that place.

Twice again he found where they had rested, and then the trail led up the slope of Tsunegun'yi, and he heard the sound of a drum and voices, as if people were dancing inside the mountain. Soon he came to a cave like a doorway in the side of the mountain, but the rock was so steep and smooth that he could not climb up to it, but could only just look over the edge and see the heads and shoulders of a great many people dancing inside. He saw his sister dancing among them and called to her to come out. She turned when she heard his voice, and as soon as the drumming stopped for a while she came out to him, finding no trouble to climb down the rock, and leading her two little children by the hand. She was very glad to meet her brother and talked with him a long time, but did not ask him to come inside, and at last he went away without having seen her husband.

Several other times her brother came to the mountain, but always his sister met him outside, and he could never see her husband. After four years had passed she came one day to her mother's house and said her husband had been hunting in the woods near by, and they were getting ready to start home tomorrow, and if her mother and brother would come early in the morning they could see her husband. If they came too late for that, she said, they would find plenty of meat to take home. She went back into the woods, and the mother ran to tell her son. They came to the place early the next morning, but Tsul'Kalu' and his family were already gone. On the drying poles they found the bodies of freshly killed deer hanging, as the girl had promised, and there were so many that they went back and told all their friends to come for them, and there were enough for the whole settlement.

Still the brother wanted to see his sister and her husband, so he went again to the mountain, and she came out to meet him. He asked to see her husband, and this time she told him to come inside with her. They went in as through a doorway and inside he found it like a great townhouse. They seemed to be alone, but his sister called aloud, "He wants to gee you," and from the air came a voice, "You can not see me until you put on a new dress, and then you can see me." "I am willing," said the young man, speaking to the unseen spirit, and from the air came the voice again, "Go back, then, and tell your people that to see me they must go into the townhouse and fast seven days, and in all that time they must not come out from the townhouse or raise the war whoop, and on the seventh day I shall come with new dresses for you to put on so that you can all see me."

The young man went back to Kanuga and told the people. They all wanted to see Tsul'Kalu', who owned all the game in the mountains, so they went into the townhouse and began the fast. They fasted the first day and the second and every day until the seventh — all but one man from another settlement, who slipped out very night when it was dark to get something to eat and slipped in again when no one was watching. On the morning of the seventh day the sun was just coming up in the east when they heard a great noise like the thunder of rocks rolling down the side of Tsunegun'yi. They were frightened and drew near together in the townhouse, and no one whispered.

Nearer and louder came the sound until it grew into an awful roar, and everyone trembled and held his breath — all but one man, the stranger from the other settlement, who lost his senses from fear and ran out of the townhouse and shouted the war cry. At once the roar stopped and for some time there was silence. Then they heard it again, but as if it were going farther away, and the farther and farther, until at last it died away in the direction of Tsunigun'yi, and then all was still again. The people came out from the townhouse, but there was silence, and they could see nothing but what had been seven days before.

Still the brother was not disheartened, but came again to see his sister, and she brought him into the mountain. He asked why Tsul'Kalu' had not brought the new dresses, as he had promised, and the voice from the air said, I came with them, but you did not obey my word, but broke the fast and raised the war cry." The young man answered, "It was not done by our people, but by a stranger. If you will come again, we will surely do as you say." But the voice answered, "Now you can never see me." Then the young man could not say more, and he went back to Kanuga.

THE SETTING

The geographic setting for this, and the third, story is Kanuga, one of the oldest Cherokee settlements on the Pigeon River, in the current Haywood County. Though abandoned many years ago, Mooney located it near the forks of the river, a few miles east of Waynesville, and theorizes it was abandoned due to its vulnerability to the coming invaders. The significant point, however, is that the Pigeon River has its main headwaters at the mythological home of Judaculla, also not far from Pilot Knob and Connestee on the other side of today's Blue Ridge Parkway. As noted, flowing water was very important in early Cherokee life.

The word Kanuga itself is probably related to the "scratcher" or

Tsul'Kalu', or Judaculla, the Slant-Eyed Giant — The mystical giant Judaculla
with his family, including the mother-in-law. Both Judaculla Rock and Looking Glass Rock are integrated into the setting by Cherokee artist Lynn Lossiah.

kind of comb used for scratching ball players and part of the rite of
"going to water," so central to Cherokee life.[1] Whether preparing for a
wedding, ball game or any important event this spiritual occasion was
very important. Those who would avoid the often painful scratching
were not looked upon favorably. One such boy, De'tsata, ran away to
avoid scratching and became a "Little Person," trying to keep himself
invisible ever since. He hunts birds with blowgun and arrows and sometimes scares birds into flight when others are hunting. He will hide a
lost hunting arrow but if the hunter says, "De'tsata, you have my arrow,
and if you don't give it up I'll scratch you," when the hunter looks again
he will find it.[2]

    The older, historical purification rite of going to water was dis-
cussed in the first myth. Psychologically it meant one became more
conscious, or in other words, was not just thrown about by unknown,
unconscious impulses. Also, one hears in everyday talk about someone

who is naive or not quite with it, that that person has "not having been to water yet." Water symbolizes the source of life in all cultures.

The Cast of Characters

The story is a powerful drama with seven characters: the widow, the young girl, the husband hero son-in-law, the girl child, the older brother, the second child and the stranger. The number seven is a special number for the Cherokee, who have seven clans and see the number, as do many other cultures, as powerfully symbolic. Here is an archetypal pattern with three plus four, even a family of four indicating balance moving toward completion. But the number seven only develops throughout the plot as it moves toward resolution of the problem.

The Stated Problem: A Single Mother and Her Daughter

A long time ago a widow lived with her one daughter at the old town of Kanuga on Pigeon River. The girl was of age to marry, and her mother used to talk with her a good deal, and tell her she must be sure to take no one but a good hunter for a husband, so that they would have some one to take care of them and would always have plenty of meat in the house. The girl said such a man was hard to find, but her mother advised her not to be in a hurry, and to wait until the right one came.

The initial characters include a dominant, widowed mother and her unmarried daughter. There is the absence of a father; one does not know his name or what happened to him. The mother rules, makes decisions and, like a queen in a fairy tale, can represent also those things in society that dominate such as issues in the collective world that seem to determine one's existence. Stating the problem at the start emphasizes a massive problem of most modern families: the absence of the masculine. Whether the cause is a tragic death, a painful divorce or any other reason, how does one satisfy the need for the healthy masculine in the family? The unnamed, unknown father could also simply be so passive as to not count, as if he were dead. In many problem marriages there are husbands who do not communicate, are not intimate or are not able to even make basic decisions or express feelings. Many a man has seemingly "married his mother" and assumes the wife will take care of him without any effort on his part. In any case, there seems to be in the Cherokee myth a single mother apparently concerned for her daughter. In this drama the absent father is replaced by an archetypal hero as a masculine figure. The spirit of the masculine survives in archetypal form in every person and can assert itself when needed.

The problem seems to focus on the young maiden but it is soon obvious that the single mother has her own self-survival in mind as well. Mother's advice is good: to wait for the right one who should also be a good provider. Even the fact that he should take care of them, and not just the daughter, is quite solid Cherokee community thinking with its matrilineal connections. From a cultural and anthropological perspective this would not seem strange, given the strong sense of tribal or community support and need for harmony and family support, as well as the harsh environment. But a little clue to another coming problem slips in early in the story: the mother wants *plenty* of meat, not just enough.

This universal human desire to have "plenty," or more than is necessary, is the bane of many families and marriages. He or she wants more and more, bigger and better, rather than basics or necessities. Greed raises its ugly head. Sometimes parents project their deepest inner needs onto their children, not just physical ones; children have great difficulty escaping the power of those parental needs, and feel guilty when they try to move on. The father who wanted to become a doctor and pushes his son to become one, or the mother who pushes her daughter to be a movie star are two of many examples. In this Cherokee story the daughter knows that such a person is hard to find and mother gives seemingly sound advice to wait until the right man comes along, but had her agenda apparently still in mind. Does the daughter also represent the passively dependent child so evident in some families? Is she somehow still an extension of her mother, unable to stand on her own? In any case mother sends a double message: "Go, but not too far. You are free to marry, but here are the conditions."

HOPE ARRIVES: A STRANGER IN THE NIGHT

Now the mother slept in the house while the girl slept outside in the asi. *One dark night a stranger came to the* asi *wanting to*

court the girl, but she told him her mother would let her marry no
one but a good hunter. "Well," said the stranger, "I am a great
hunter," so she let him come in, and he stayed all night. Just before
day he said he must go back now to his own place, but that he had
brought some meat for her mother, and she would find it outside.
Then he went away and the girl had not seen him. When day came
she went out and found there a deer, which she brought into the
house to her mother, and told her it was a present from her new
sweetheart. Her mother was pleased, and they had deer steaks for
breakfast.

So the partial separation begins with daughter sleeping in the *asi*,
the separate, low building used for a sweat house at times, for rituals,
and for winter protection from the cold. Built lower, partially into the
ground, it was often but not always round. The term *asi* came from
not only a sweat house, according to linguist and tribal elder Robert
Bushyhead, but also from "holy place" and a related word for "good."[3]
What a context for a courtship and marriage, for something holy and
hopeful. Built into mother earth with more protection, in a holy circle, the womblike room is a perfect symbolic setting for the beginning
steps of a difficult separation from the mother and the bonds of home.

The man who comes into her life seems to meet the test: he is an
excellent provider and passes daughter's screening test, so well coached
by mother. He leaves a generous gift for mother and daughter, providing them with deer steaks for breakfast, quite a luxury. Mother is
pleased. In this first visit, he is not seen by his sweetheart. So it is with
most courtships; neither person is really "seen" in the first excitement
of contact, of projecting hopeful dreams on the other. In this courtship
phase he returns to his home and she to her mother to share in the nourishment left in the new encounter. She is still tied to mom, he to his
home.

Sleep opens up the inner world, that of dreams, hopes, and access
to the depths of the unconscious. But this can also bring fearful
thoughts, feelings and worries.

PLEASURE TO ANGER: THE STRUGGLE BEGINS

He came again the next night, but again went away before day-
light, and this time he left two deer outside. The mother was more

pleased this time, but said to her daughter, "I wish your sweetheart would bring us some wood." Now wherever he might be, the stranger knew their thoughts, so when he came the next time he said to the girl, "Tell your mother I have brought the wood"; and when she looked out in the morning there were several great trees lying in front of the door, roots and branches and all. The old woman was angry, and said, "He might have brought us some wood that we could use instead of whole trees that we can't split, to litter the road with brush." The hunter knew what she said, and the next time he came he brought nothing, and when they looked out in the morning the trees were gone and there was no wood at all, so the old woman had to go after some herself.

It appears that more than need is met; double the deer, twice the amount of food, is given the next night by this still unseen stranger. The mother expresses an added desire: some wood for her fire. The stranger brings "the wood," but in the form of great trees! She had not specified that it should be cut, split, ready for the cook fire and the yard cleaned up. Unspoken assumptions arise. Greed shows up as well as anger that her desires are not met. And then she loses the opportunity and has to forage for herself.

But there is much deep, inner wisdom beginning to show in the story, which is also a story of a young girl beginning to grow and develop, to individuate and to separate from her mother. The stranger is the hero who will help her in that process. That hero image is the universal symbol used in all cultures. It is used by the unconscious on individuals and groups to connect the deepest core of one's being, the Self, with the Ego in facing the outer world. The hero helps one get the development started. Little kids need heroes, models to look up to inspire them and give them something bigger and stronger to hold on to. People watch John Wayne movies or *Star Wars* battles to help them overcome forces and fears that are really archetypal within each.

So the young girl gets in touch with some new parts of herself through this encounter with her own inner hero and starts out on her own journey. Mother is a powerful force in her life, in both her physical and inner survival. Mother still controls, even through her requests. Up to this part of the story the gifts play important symbolic roles as well, for they are spiritual gifts from her hero.

The deer in Cherokee lore is more than just food; it is a spiritual animal, one that can see in the darkness (the inner world) and that moves with nimbleness and is gentle in nature. Some South American Indians once felt that the souls of deceased humans resided in the deer and thus did not eat them.[4] For some, the deer carries the sun. In many ancient societies the deer had not only a special place with humans, but were special spiritual creatures. In ancient Europe, deer, often with glowing horns or candles in the horns, led people to special spiritual places, as in the myth about Charlemagne's granddaughters being led to the spot of the place of martyrdom of the first Christian missionaries in Zurich, where the granddaughters founded a convent.

The tree is one of the oldest and most powerful archetypal symbols in all cultures. It carries many ancient images: mother, wisdom, life itself, love, eternity. The tree connects the past, present and future; the underworld, the earth and the upper world. Sometimes the tree was a symbol of regeneration, especially deciduous trees, which lose leaves and then renew in the spring. Perhaps the most universal role of the tree is as a symbol of the bridge between heaven and earth, as well as the underworld. Many creatures reside around the roots and in the bark and shade. Those high in the limbs capture the essence of the loftiest spiritual creature, the bird. Many volumes have been written about the tree and its many meanings, so universal is its symbolism. When people speak of their "family tree" they are really using more than just a metaphor for the family relationships, past and present; they are at a deeper, purely unconscious level reaching for ancient connectedness. So strong is this in some cultures that a "holy tree" or a "mother tree" is sacred at some level. And how does one honor a historical place? Sometimes a monument is set or a tree is planted. How many old trees in the world are protected to remember the founding of a country, a battle won or other special event?

Back to the story: Just as the mother does not want to work to process the raw wood-energy for her fire, it seems she can not process the raw spiritual possibilities and loses the opportunity. Perhaps the girl is beginning her slow process of differentiation from her outer and inner mother at this point. The process of separation from mother is not always easy and the powerful, controlling mother can not only bring havoc for the dependant child but also miss crucial spiritual gifts at their doorstep. This girl's mother seems greedy and lazy, unrefined in her thinking. She prefers the easy way out.

CONFRONTATION: CURIOSITY AND CAUTION

> *Almost every night he came to see the girl, and each time he brought a deer or some other game, but still he always left before daylight. At last her mother said to her, "Your husband always leaves before daylight. Why doesn't he wait? I want to see what kind of a son-in-law I have." When the girl told this to her husband he said he could not let the old woman see him, because the sight would frighten her. "She wants to see you, anyhow," said the girl, and began to cry, until at last he had to consent, but warned her that her mother must not say that he looked frightful (usga' se ti'yu).*

Tension is increased. The pattern is continuing with gifts of food and his leaving before daylight. He is now clearly identified as her husband and thus the mother claims some rights as mother-in-law. She demands to see him and puts pressure on her daughter. The husband, no longer fully a stranger although he had not been seen fully, does not want to be seen by the mother-in-law, and with reason: she would find his countenance frightful. The classic "Beauty and the Beast" setting is presented. There is no indication that the bride found anything fearful or frightening about her groom. Yet she yields to the pressure of her mother and puts tearful pressure on him to allow her mother to meet him in person. In counseling or home conflict, women and men may use tears to force a partner to go against their will or wisdom to change their mind or to stop a change of mind. Is the bride manipulating him? Or is the pressure from her mother so heavy that the tears show the pain of her conflict between her attachment to her husband and her family of origin? In any case he yields, but with a major caution; that the mother must agree not to declare that he looked frightful.

In terms of normal outward events, one can understand the man's reluctance: his experience in life is that people are frightened by his size and looks. His shyness and fear are well founded. His response to the former request had been honest, knowing it would frighten her; he fears rejection and humiliation. But also, as the story evolves, he may be aware of the larger threat not only his appearance but his very being may pose. Persons who possess some form of power or natural authority may create fear and awe in others, making life most awkward for them as different beings. Or sometimes it is simply being different in skin color or culture.

THE MEETING: A PROMISE BROKEN AND A NAME GIVEN

The next morning he did not leave so early, but stayed in the
asi, *and when it was daylight the girl went out and told her mother.*
The old woman came and looked in, and there she saw a great giant,
with long slanting eyes (tsul'kalu') *lying doubled up on the floor,*
with his head against the rafters, in the left-hand corner at the back,
and his toes scraping the roof in the right-hand corner by the door.
She gave only one look and ran back to the house, crying, "Usga' se
ti'yu! Usga' se ti'yu!" Tsul'Kalu' was terribly angry. He untwisted
himself and came out of the asi, *and said good-bye to the girl, telling*
her that he would never let her mother see him again, but would go
back to his own country. Then he went off in the direction of Tsune-
gun'yi.

The groom is seen in daylight for the first time, with no response
from the bride, who has accepted him. When mother looks into the *asi*,
however, she discovers a giant, filling the space of the tiny sweat house.
Even doubled up, his head push the rafters and his toes hit the roof by
the door. Not only is he a massive giant but his eyes also are slanted,
giving him the name Tsul'Kalu', or Judaculla, the Slant-Eyed Giant.

When the meeting comes, the mother does exactly what she promised not to do and cries out that he is frightful! Twice she cries out the
forbidden words, and he is very angry. She flees and he extracts himself from the *asi*, taking leave of his wife and declaring that he would
not let mother-in-law see him again. He heads toward his home in
Tsunegun'yi.

There is no pain like family pain. No mother-in-law jokes here:
these are the tragedies of painful separation, of hurt feelings, of fear
and hurtful words spoken, of promises broken. This is the archetypal,
universal experience of family pain. It may mean temporary or permanent separation, even divorce or not speaking for years. No idealized
family harmony is played out. The story also captures the struggle of
parents whose children do not meet their expectations. Perhaps the
new spouse is of another racial origin, another land, another socioe-
conomic level, or another religious persuasion. Or perhaps a simple
misunderstanding in communication has triggered a basic fear in one
party so that an overreaction occurs, and a breach comes in the relationship, not intended but very real and very painful.

There is no more powerful motivation than fear. The central nervous system responds to fear with fight or flight. One learns early to fear abandonment by a parent, to fear unknown creatures or things outside one's experience. That is part of human survival. But when one is unable to grow up sufficiently, to individuate and become mature, one tends to carry fear into all of life or at least into areas not meriting such fear. One may equate loss of face or embarrassment with falling off a cliff, or a raging animal. In the Cherokee story, the daughter-bride has a secure experience with her husband. He has also provided many tangible benefits to both mother and daughter in the form of nourishment and security. But the mother sees in his size and looks some danger, and she reacts in basic fear, fleeing danger as she perceives it. Tsul'Kalu', or Judaculla, is introduced to the listener far along in the story. He would be known to the Cherokee as the one who owned all the game, that mysterious superhuman giant living high in the mountains, farming his place on the top of Tsunegun'yi or sitting on his judgment seat on the next mountain top, later misnamed the Devil's Courthouse. It is he who could look at his reflection on the nearby wet or icy granite outcropping now called Looking Glass Rock.

Tsul'Kalu' was transliterated by early European settlers as "Judaculla," still the preferred name by modern Cherokee. His home mountain top called Tsunegun'yi was called Tanasee Bald or Tanasee Old Fields and is at the point where the counties of Haywood, Jackson and Transylvania now merge (see map on page 32). The modern day Blue Ridge Parkway runs close by both the so-called Devil's Courthouse and Tanasee Old Fields, with a parking lot near each. Not far away in the Pisgah Ranger District of Pisgah National Forest are seen other special places for the traditional Cherokee including the Looking Glass Rock, Looking Glass Falls, Pilot Knob, Cold Mountain and Shining Rock.

One unique and mysterious phenomenon is the Judaculla Rock located on Caney Fork, not so far from Tsunegun'yi as the crow flies. Long lost in antiquity are the meanings of the petroglyphs or figure carvings on this rock. There are a few others in Cherokee territory and many others in the western part of America. The Cherokee response recorded by Mooney at the end of the nineteenth century and still used today is that these marks are where Tsul'Kalu', Judaculla, would jump down and land in the valley from high in his mountain land above. The petroglyphs have been dated from 3000 to 1000 years B.C., the Late

Archaic Period, according to University of North Carolina archeologists.[5] (See page 12, a photograph of Judaculla Rock with the figures
chalked in.)

What's in a name? Often judgment and misinformation are based
on fear. The Blue Ridge Parkway was finished in this writer's lifetime;
signs were put up giving stories about places and traditions. Unfortunately, those writers picked up a quote by early travelers from the north
in describing the so-called Devil's Courthouse. It was called that by
some, but many local mountain people and most Cherokee knew that
it had nothing to do with the devil or a satanic figure of any kind. It
was a place in Cherokee mythology where Judaculla would consider
how persons dealt with game. Did they take only what they needed?
Did they do the right ritual before taking down an animal, with apol-
ogy and thanksgiving? Some diseases were felt to be the result of vio-
lating such principles.[6]

The idea of a giant is also universal and captures both fear and
fascination. Humans make their heroes, be they sport figures, political
leaders, or historical ancestors such as Lincoln or Washington, into
giants. Rarely are the monuments built to remember them life-sized.
The collective thinking of society demands a giant size. One team of
scholars in symbols noted that "the myth of the giants is summons to
human heroism. Giants stand for all those things which the individual must overcome to allow full freedom and the development of personality."[7] Certainly the essence of the story of Judaculla is captured
in this statement.

What does one make of the slanting eyes, those organs on the body
with which one sees? The eyes are also universal symbols of intellectual perception as well as visual. Not just sight but also insight. The
eye is seen by many to be the window to the soul. In some societies,
the concept of an evil eye is important, producing fear in facing some
looks or appearances. In the story certainly the appearance is significant,
perhaps due to the great size and the look of the eyes. Is there more
fear because mother is really feeling guilty for her own motives? Or does
she fear that with those perceptive, slanting eyes he has real insight into
her soul? What does it say when someone cannot look another in the
eyes? In many cultures, on the other hand, it is considered impolite or
offensive and improper to look another directly in the eyes.

The Final Break: Abuse and Loss

Soon after he left, the girl had her monthly period. There was a very great flow of blood, and the mother threw it all into the river. One night after the girl had gone to bed in the asi *her husband came again to the door and said to her, "It seems you are alone," and asked where was the child. She said there had been none. Then he asked where was the blood, and she said that her mother had thrown it into the river. She told just where the place was, and he went there and found a small worm in the water. He took it up and carried it back to the* asi, *and as he walked it took form and began to grow, until, when he reached the* asi, *it was a baby girl that he was carrying. He gave it to his wife and said, "Your mother does not like me and abuses our child, so come and let us go to my home." The girl wanted to be with her husband, so, after telling her mother goodbye, she took up the child and they went off together to Tsunegun'yi.*

While Judaculla is away for some unknown period of time a great secret drama takes place: his bride has what she thinks is her menstrual period but it is described as a very great flow of blood that her mother throws into the river. Judaculla comes to see her, noting she is alone, i.e., the mother is not present. He asks for their child and she thinks there was not one. Finding the place where the mother threw away everything, he discovers a small worm, an embryonic form of human life. He saves the child and takes control of its life and development. He intervenes in the family situation. With a sense of protracted time it grows as he returns to the *asi*, the former temporary home. He arrives with a baby girl and hands it over to its mother, his wife. He declares a truth he has known or suspected all along: her mother does not like him and now has abused their child. He declares it is time for a complete break and to go to their own home, away from the control and abuse of the needy mother. Finally, with clear proof in hand, literally in her arms, she decides to make to break completely in terms of living with her husband and not with her mother. She makes a geographic separation, not a complete fracture, for she does go to tell her mother good-bye, to inform her that they are gone. She is not abusive or vindictive to her mother in return. The two finally begin the pilgrimage away from the childhood home to their own home and future.

This is the toughest part of the story, for it describes child abuse, something universal and yet denied until recently. Abuse can also be neglect or refusal to love an unwanted child. It can be beating a child or loving only conditionally. It can be sexual abuse, also by a parent or grandparent. It can mean many things. In this case the child's grandmother is the abuser and, like most abusers, she tries to get rid of the evidence, or deny the existence of the baby. The child is but a "lowly worm" in her treatment. Not worthy of keeping. Perhaps it is also a reminder of her dislike of, or fear of, the father. Perhaps the grandmother knows that if her daughter keeps the child she would leave her alone and without support. In any case it is a threat to her and she tries to rid herself of such a threat. It might mean she no longer controls the world of her daughter. A new feminine form comes into being and challenges the old.

In clinical situations where mothers or grandmothers have been abusive to their daughters or granddaughters, the pain and power is very frightening, for they are supposed to be the major source of nourishment, of loving care and of modeling what mothering is about. They should have held, loved and protected the daughter, the granddaughter. The sense of betrayal is profound, often taking years to get over, to work through with the help of an inner hero like Judaculla.

This is thus the story of an inner journey of the feminine, of a young lady growing up, getting in touch with inner forces, especially her own masculine side, which allows her to stand up, not only to the outer mother, but also to the inner mother she has carried all her life. The old inner mother tries to stop development, to stop a new femininity, and holds to the inertia of the "old collective pattern of femininity."[8] The protecting, nurturing love of the inner hero holds it together; by the time he gets back to the *asi*—the womb—there is a baby girl, symbolizing the birth of her new personal feminine identity. She is an adult, making adult decisions on her own (without mother) and she is now free enough to leave and go with her husband.

Blood itself symbolizes the medium of life itself, as well as the connection between kinship groups. The universal "blood oath" is, in many forms, the way of making a tie between two persons as powerful as between family members or even stronger, as it is chosen. In our story, however, the blood is tossed away (perhaps capturing a rite of cleanliness) but it contained more than the daughter knew. It really carried life itself, literally.

Now the couple is together and headed for the great mountain homeland on Tsunigun'yi, Tannasee Old Fields, making their way slowly up the long path into their own family setting, starting anew.

OLD FAMILY AND NEW: A BROTHER AND ANOTHER BABY

Now, the girl had an older brother, who lived with his own wife in another settlement, and when he heard that his sister was married he came to pay a visit to her and her new husband, but when he arrived at Kanuga his mother told him his sister had taken her child and had gone away with her husband, nobody knew where. He was sorry to see his mother so lonely, so he said he would go after his sister and try to find her and bring her back. It was easy to follow the footprints of the giant, and the young man went along the trail until he came to a place where they had rested, and there were tracks on the ground where a child had been lying and other marks as if a baby had been born there. He went on along the trail and came to another place where they had rested, and there were tracks of a baby crawling about and another lying on the ground. He went on and came to where they had rested again, and there were tracks of a child walking and another crawling about. He went on until he came where they had rested again, and there were tracks of one child running and another walking. Still he followed the trail along the stream into the mountains, and came to the place where they had rested again, and this time there were footprints of two children running all about, and the footprints can still be seen in the rock at that place.

Now the hearer learns of another family member who enters the drama, a married brother from another settlement. He comes to visit his sister and her new husband on the basis of news that has reached him, but the later news of the break he has not yet heard. It does not say he also came to visit his mother, although that might be assumed. The mother's report is interesting in its wording and in what it does not tell. She only tells him that his sister had taken *her* child and gone with *her* husband to some unknown place. For the mother, the frame of reference seems to be her own daughter, with the husband and child somehow being possessed by her. This is implied by the possessive pronoun. This would match her own sense of possession of, and control of, her daughter previously. She makes no claim to Judaculla as her own son-in-law or as the father of her own grandchild.

The mother's loneliness moves the brother to try to find his sister to bring her back; one does not know if only for a visit or for longer. That is open. His task is not so hard, in that the giant's tracks are easy to follow. But then the resting places along this pathway and pilgrimage reveal powerful messages. He finds a series of resting places along the way, the first revealing where his niece had been lying as well as signs that another baby had been born. The second resting place shows that the one baby had grown so much that she was crawling; the other infant that had been born had been lying on the earth. One is not told if it was a boy or girl. He moves on to find a third resting place where the older child was walking and the infant was crawling. At the fourth resting place he sees that the older child was running and the younger walking. At the fifth place along the stream starting into the higher mountains, he sees that the two children have both been running about and footprints are left in solid rock. Mooney locates the footprints at Datsu'nalasgunyi, "where their tracks are this way."[9] These are reported either at Shining Rock or Cold Mountain, both on the way from Kanuga to Tsunigun'yi.

The entry of the brother seems to symbolize the entry into the story of a more balanced and mature member of the family. The outer pilgrimage of the sister moves rapidly once she has left home, joined to her husband and now making her own family. The brother tracks them, representing the community left behind. Whenever one leaves home to make his or her way in life, the community and family always follow, both the good and bad elements.

The family development seems to capture symbolically the parts of her personality (and those of her family) that are rapidly moving. The stages of birthing, being carried, crawling, walking and running are universal, archetypal understandings, not only for each person but also for different parts of the personality. Once she is freed from demands of home, from mother's personality and needs, once she is "birthed" from the *asi* and launched into the world, she can grow into her own person. The solid footprints left capture the truth that healthy human development lays down a solid foundation for human personality that can weather time and generations. These footprints are imprinted in each person in each family and are permanent as if etched in stone.

The break for the woman of the story, now a mother herself, means a break from an all-powerful mother and development for coming generations. The cycle of the dysfunctional family is broken when she can experience inner freedom and then see different parts of her own person come to birth and grow. With the birth of a daughter comes the potential for a new healthy feminine self-identity. Her family is now a balanced foursome, a symbol of totality. There are to be seven stops along the pathway to her new home, seven being not only the holy number amongst the Cherokee but also in many religions of the world. It signifies wholeness and completion.

THE GOAL REACHED: AFTER SEVEN STOPS, TSUNIGUN'YI

Twice again he found where they had rested, and then the trail led up the slope of Tsunegun'yi, and he heard the sound of a drum and voices, as if people were dancing inside the mountain. Soon he came to a cave like a doorway in the side of the mountain, but the rock was so steep and smooth that he could not climb up to it, but could only just look over the edge and see the heads and shoulders of a great many people dancing inside. He saw his sister dancing among them and called to her to come out. She turned when she heard his voice, and as soon as the drumming stopped for a while she came out to him, finding no trouble to climb down the rock, and leading her two little children by the hand. She was very glad to meet her brother and talked with him a long time, but did not ask him to come inside, and at last he went away without having seen her husband.

Brother's goal is reached in finding not only the mountain home but also his sister. After the seven steps along the way he is complete in his path but there is another obstacle: no actual entry into the cave-like doorway into the mountain. It is too steep and smooth, so it is not to be traversed. There is a drum to be heard as well as voices and even dancing. The drum and dancing are important Cherokee elements of celebration, of thanksgiving, of communication in community and spiritually. Something special is happening and he can only see the heads of those celebrating. He is not in the party but he does recognize his own sister as she dances.

She hears his call, recognizes his voice and easily walks down to meet him with her two children. The reunion occurs; she is very glad and spends quality time, but does not invite him inside nor does he meet her husband.

In the outer world of fractured families it is often a long process on the part of one or another before reconciliation or reunion is achieved. And after a time apart, or after painful history, it is never the same. Just as she has changed, each person changes independently from the family. Distance does that. Sometimes a more neutral member who has not been a part of whatever happened tries to mediate and is only partially successful. Here she accepts, welcomes and honors her brother, but she does not let him into her inner world inside the mountain.

One could think of the sister as finding and celebrating her own inner freedom, dancing to a different drummer and rejoicing with her new family and community. She has made a difficult pilgrimage and can cross the hard places because she knows how. She can show her own children the way across the rocks and steep cliff. Symbolically she can cross from the inner world to the outer. She can bridge from the inner, spiritual world, captured in the mountain cave, to the outer world of mundane existence. She can dance to celebrate her newfound spiritual freedom and joy.

A NEAR-REUNION: A MESSAGE AND MORE MEAT

Several other times her brother came to the mountain, but always his sister met him outside, and he could never see her husband. After four years had passed she came one day to her mother's house and said her husband had been hunting in the woods near by, and they were getting ready to start home tomorrow, and if her mother and brother would come early in the morning they could see her husband. If they came too late for that, she said, they would find plenty of meat to take home. She went back into the woods, and the mother ran to tell her son. They came to the place early the next morning, but Tsul'Kalu' and his family were already gone. On the drying poles they found the bodies of freshly killed deer hanging, as the girl had promised, and there were so many that they went back and told all their friends to come for them, and there were enough for the whole settlement.

Contact continues between brother and sister, outside the mountain. After four years, a balanced period of time, the daughter, now a fully grown woman in her own right, gives a surprise visit to her mother. Finally it appears they would meet Judaculla. Mother goes to get her son. One senses the enthusiasm as she runs to tell him, but, alas, the next morning they arrive too late and miss the couple.

Once the girl has developed a proper, balanced length of time she can reenter her former world, but on her own conditions. She is willing to introduce Judaculla but they must to be there very early. One does not know why they do not make it or why the family had to leave so early, but the very generous gift of meat is not only for her family of origin but also for the entire community, an honor for all. She remembers her people.

One can think of this developing feminine person as having developed or individuated so far that she could not only make contact with her past in a mature way but also nourish them in a symbolic way. Often persons who have been seriously abused as children and who work for years to get beyond those deep injuries and to find healing, do so when they can develop either their feminine or masculine side to be more balanced, and especially to develop their spiritual, inner world to such a place that they can go home again to help give some spiritual nourishment to others. They do not change them, or seek revenge, or punish, just feed them.

Persistence Pays: Preparation and Provision

Still the brother wanted to see his sister and her husband, so he went again to the mountain, and she came out to meet him. He asked to see her husband, and this time she told him to come inside with her. They went in as through a doorway and inside he found it like a great townhouse. They seemed to be alone, but his sister called aloud, "He wants to gee you," and from the air came a voice, "You can not see me until you put on a new dress, and then you can see me." "I am willing," said the young man, speaking to the unseen spirit, and from the air came the voice again. "Go back, then, and tell your people that to see me they must go into the townhouse and fast seven days, and in all that time they must not come out from the townhouse or raise the war whoop, and on the seventh day I shall come with new dresses for you to put on so that you can all see me."

Still the brother takes the initiative, not giving up on seeing his sister and famous brother-in-law. When he requests to meet Judaculla she invites him inside the mountain. He lands in a space like a townhouse, the main gathering place for the Cherokee community, though this one is much larger. Sister announces to her husband that her brother wants to see him and the response is from high above, from the air. The spirit nature of Judaculla is noted here as he says that the brother-in-law cannot see him until he puts on a new dress, new clothing. He is of course willing to do this seemingly minor act, but there is more required to prepare.

The invitation is given not only to him but to all who would see him, who would meet this famous being. The voice from above makes clear that there are definite requirements that he is to carry back to the community. The call for the community to gather in the townhouse calls for harmony and communication, for some togetherness for a serious fast, a period of developing both individual and community spirit. The way one faces the outer world is directly related to how one faces the inner world. Outer reality and inner spirit are to be matched, balanced. A healthy ego helps one face the outer world, but one becomes healthy only with a cleansed inner spirit.

In this challenge of Judaculla they are not to sound the war cry. The war cry gives chaotic power over order and it brings war and aggression into the peace process. To pray for peace means reducing one's own personal aggression first, and then reducing community aggression collectively; it is a spiritual exercise.

OPPORTUNITY MISSED: FAME AND FEARS

The young man went back to Kanuga and told the people. They all wanted to see Tsul'Kalu', who owned all the game in the mountains, so they went into the townhouse and began the fast. They fasted the first day and the second and every day until the seventh — all but one man from another settlement, who slipped out every night when it was dark to get something to eat and slipped in again when no one was watching. On the morning of the seventh day the sun was just coming up in the east when they heard a great noise like the thunder of rocks rolling down the side of Tsunegun'yi. They were frightened and drew near together in the townhouse, and no one whispered.

Nearer and louder came the sound until it grew into an awful roar, and everyone trembled and held his breath — all but one man, the stranger from the other settlement, who lost his senses from fear and ran out of the townhouse and shouted the war cry. At once the roar stopped and for some time there was silence. Then they heard it again, but as if it were going farther away, and the farther and farther, until at last it died away in the direction of Tsunigun'yi, and then all was still again. The people came out from the townhouse, but there was silence, and they could see nothing but what had been seven days before.

The brother has brought back good news, which they gladly accept for they gather together in the townhouse and begin the fast. But one notable item pops up: their motivation seems to be mostly to see the famous Judaculla, "who owned all the game in the mountains." Is this in hopes of good favor? Of more free food? Of the power felt or assumed in the presence of a powerful personage? Are they "star struck," having learned that one of their own has connections to this mighty person? The little phrase seems innocent enough, yet does it betray a lot about their motives? They let down their guard in letting a stranger in, and not noticing that the same stranger is slipping out each night to feed his hungry body, breaking the fast. He is playing the game at a superficial level but not really doing the spiritual preparation needed for the journey they could all make.

On the seventh day they are greeted with terrifying noise. They huddle in silence, but not everyone holds his breath, for the same stranger who had broken the fast now runs outside and shouts the war cry: his fear overcomes him. Silence. Then slowly the noises depart back up the mountain.

Fear causes one to lose perspective. It distorts one's senses. In this story there is an irony: they had paid a price to look into the face of fear itself, to integrate this awesome, yet friendly, caring, providing giant who was, in fact, part of their own inner strength; yet they took for granted their own process and their own privacy. There was a stranger in their midst, some unprepared, insecure part of themselves. A glimpse of paradise is lost. Access to great inner strength is missed, not found or integrated.

A FINAL TRY: A HOPE AND A PLEA

Still the brother was not disheartened, but came again to see his sister, and she brought him into the mountain. He asked why Tsul'Kalu' had not brought the new dresses, as he had promised, and the voice from the air said, "I came with them, but you did not obey my word, but broke the fast and raised the war cry." The young man answered, "It was not done by our people, but by a stranger. If you will come again, we will surely do as you say." But the voice answered, " Now you can never see me." Then the young man could not say more, and he went back to Kanuga.

Persistent and hopeful, the brother tries again. He captures that spirit in each person who needs to not lose heart when all seems lost, that part of everyone who keeps going back to the holy mountain, the Jacob who wrestles with the angel waiting for a blessing. His connection is still by way of his sister, his healthy feminine side. When he asks why the promised encounter has failed, the voice from above makes it clear: the contract is broken as they have broken the fast and raised the war cry. A nonspiritual attitude is present in not fasting and in the aggressive spirit shown by the whoop. The young man gives a clear defense that the stranger, not their people, has done these terrible things; he is sure that another attempt can be successful. It is not to be, however. They have missed their chance and will not ever see the gentle giant with slanted eyes who owns all the game in the mountains. The answer is final, so the young man goes home to Kanuga where it all started.

The story does not have a happy ending like that of Connestee, or Kana'sta, the Lost Settlement, and some other Cherokee stories. But the ancient wisdom therein speaks to many life issues both modern and as old as human existence. Some parts of the story do touch on important matters of Cherokee life that the average modern American or Western European would not fully grasp. One is the emphasis on the crucial role of family and community solidarity, rather than on individualism. The story shows the balance of individual in community, the role of solid growing up by the girl, and the sense of responsibility to her own family and community remains. The Jungian concept of individuation captures this in that it does not call for one to become so individualistic as to "do one's own thing" at the expense of others.

Rather it calls for growth and maturity through one's own inner, spiritual growth, not determined by what others say, and then for reentering that collective world as a mature person, bringing one's unique gifts and contributions. It is a great story of the creative tension between the individual and the community.

One needs to understand this harmony in the community to understand what would appear to be unfair in the final decision. They had to be in harmony, as one people, for this community spiritual rebirth. Aggression has no place in true community, whatever the source. It takes time (seven days) to make inner and community peace, to process personal differences and to discover when one among them breaks the "fast." Many outsiders misunderstand what is going on in Cherokee and many other mountain families when they must make decisions. It is not just some simple democratic vote. It takes time to work matters through, to process disagreements and to find common grounds. Often decisions are not made, or are made by default, because of not wanting to offend others. What appears to be inefficiency is really a search for harmony.

Another unique point from the Cherokee perspective that might be missed by the average reader is the significant role played by women in all of life. Some early English visitors complained of the influence that women had in Cherokee life and could not comprehend that women could or should have such power. Family and clan connections were matrilineal, that is traced through the mother. Unfortunately European writers did not know what to do with these women. Some mistakenly described influential women as "princesses" although there were no such persons. Some names became well known, such as Nancy Dragging Canoe. Although there is no known record of a woman being a war chief, some think there may have been a peace chief or two; they definitely played a role in tribal councils. In modern history women have been chiefs among the Cherokee. The wise woman also played a crucial role in Cherokee life, exemplifying the universal, archetypal need for the wise old woman in every society and for each human. Where are the grandmothers who share their love and the wisdom of the years?

The Judaculla story is given in the context of the positive, significant role of mothers and of women in general. This is of course true, with many variations, in all societies. Perhaps nothing is more universal, more archetypal, than the mother, the source of all life. All humans (and animals) have mothers and experience their first nourishment, their earliest life lessons, at the breast of their mothers. Those lessons are both good and bad for they contain both the nourishing love and the personal needs of the mother. Can she love and let go? Can she help that child launch into the world with a healthy, mature attitude? One should not be too hard on the mother in the Judaculla story, for one does not know her story of the loss of her husband, of needed support in her old age, of any maladies or fears that might be very real for her. But the focal lesson of the story is the growth and separation from the mother, the hard task of leaving home.

So in this ancient, yet modern, story one meets more than a Beauty and a Beast, more than a Cherokee hero figure, for here also is in the struggle to grow up, as well as the struggle for a spiritual life. The outer story starts with the girl and her individuation or growth out of a dysfunctional family. It does not appear too bad at the beginning of the story, when the family seems "normal" enough. The story carries the girl in her own courtship, marriage, and leaving home in the midst of pain, and eventually shifts to the brother and the community. The real hero is Judaculla, who is like an inner figure, a guiding figure from the Self, the core of her being. The girl is connected with both the inner and outer world, once she is growing and moving on. She changes from a passive, dependent, weak person to a strong, assertive, self-assured and balanced feminine person in her own right. She comes to grips with powerful forces within. She seems to love Judaculla early on and is not frightened by his looks or overwhelmed by his power. Fear is overcome by love. Others are so afraid that they can not see the loving side of Judaculla. They see mostly the results of his loving kindness (food, presents, fuel-energy, and spiritual directions) but can not experience direct love, in part because of the blockage of fear.

JUDACULLA PRINCIPLES

Each person who hears and responds to this story with all four functions, thinking and feeling, sensing and intuiting, will hear the message that fulfills their needs at that time. Some ancient wisdom coming in the form of modern lessons can be summarized as follows.

1. Parents, even with the best of intentions for their children,

often make mistakes, perhaps as a result of their own family hardships but more often because of their own unconscious (unknown) inner motives and needs. Who wants to admit that greed is a force within? Or who can admit that uncertainty about the future scares them into "frightful" acts?

2. Many children struggle to leave home, to move from dependence to independence. This may be a fight for balance, a struggle to find one's own way, to make one's own life pilgrimage. Yet, like the girl, how can one still take one's family seriously and be responsible in appropriate support of them while on that personal growth pilgrimage?

3. Many also struggle to learn to be free from the complicated inner mother or father and thus to find inner balance in one's own masculinity and femininity.

4. One need not be not naive about the "stranger in our midst," the evil one or shadow deep down inside everyone, that aggressive side that can thwart one's best intentions by "raising the war cry." People often lose their temper because they were caught unawares. If one tries to put on new clothes for facing the world with integrity and authenticity, one may need to do some fasting, literally or symbolically. Does one risk seeking an inner spiritual direction?

5. One can be born into a dysfunctional family and still find their own unique life as well as break the cycle of generations to create their own balanced, more functional family. One is not cursed by one's past.

6. One can also discover the hero within oneself, the symbolic Judaculla that will give enough direction, guidance and sustenance for the journey. For some this may be a guardian angel, a saint or other spiritual being.

7. One may identify with the brother who wants to reach for his sister's new freedom and peace but who is still underway, torn between loyalty to family and an inner search, trying to bridge the inner and outer worlds. One can use what Jung calls active imagination in thinking he is still seeking, still in pilgrimage, that he will return to the mountain again and again. His journey is still open, like everyone's life journey. Every person has an inner hero of their own, available to lead, to energize and direct.

THEOLOGICAL COMMENTS

The overarching story is that of a pilgrimage, a journey of life in one sense, of a young woman, who symbolizes every person. Everyone leaves family, struggles, grows through pain, finds their way and spiritual home, their connection to the divine. Not all can find their way in the same way. This story carries many parallels to the Christian story, and those who have a background in scripture and the biblical traditions will recognize many similar ones. Only a few are noted here in the hope they will stimulate the reader to appreciate how early Cherokee may have heard the missionary message, limited as it was by those bearing the message.

It is striking to observe how close the "going to water" is to the Christian baptism by immersion where one not only went through a rite of initiation, but experienced more than a formality, a really powerful symbolic act underlining death and burial and resurrection to a new life with courage and deeper appreciation for spiritual things.

When the mother wants the best for her daughter and herself, it is reminiscent of the special favor-seeking mother of the sons of Zebidee to whom Jesus said, "You do not know what you ask."[10]

The historical naming of the Judaculla's judgement seat next to Pilot Knob as Devil's Courthouse by sensational journalists and then by the National Park Service was not universally accepted by locals including the Cherokee. There was no Satan in their thinking, although there were evil forms or forces, expressed in other ways. One could understand that either the early sensational writers or even some well-intentioned missionary to the Cherokee or to the early mountain European settlers could have heard of Judaculla and could have equated him with the devil on a very superficial hearing. Mission history, and church history itself, is replete with unsophisticated, unreflected equivocation: it is easier to name any cultural difference, as being "demonic." History's greatest travesties have usually been justified by such rationale.

Here also is the universal tension spoken to in the scriptures regarding finding a balance between the call for children to honor father and mother, and the need for parents to avoid provoking their children and to let them go. How does one leave parents and cling to the one loved, while still honoring them?[11]

Not all would agree that the mother's problem was greed. Greed is one of the Christian church's traditional cardinal sins. At one workshop on this myth one woman, a single mother, protested that she identified with the mother, who was a survivor who had to fight for her existence. One wise Cherokee friend who gave input to the comments on this myth pointed out that in the very close structure of Cherokee families, this mother's expectations would have been normal; that the family takes care of its own, especially the mother. Daily visits by adult children to their mothers are not uncommon. Taking care of the children of family, kin and neighbors is the norm, also true in the traditional Anglo Appalachian culture. This is very close to the strong biblical admonition in Timothy about caring for widows and orphans. In fact some of the strongest words in the Christian scriptures are in that context: "If any one does not provide for his relatives, and especially for his own family, he has disowned the faith and is worse than an unbeliever."[12]

Further, the wise Cherokee friend underlined that the girl's brother was really looking for her children, and that as their uncle his responsibilities for her children were a high Cherokee value. In some traditional Cherokee weddings the brother has also a part; this demonstrates his role in caring for her future children, not unlike the tradition of God-parents in some Christian traditions. The brother's pursuit, then, was in order to see that someone cared for the children. One is reminded also of older Hebrew laws and traditions that a brother cares for his brother's (sibling's) offspring. In Cherokee society today one sees how close the extended family is: does not need to be blood kin to fill the role of parents to Indian children. Female friends on the Boundary who refer to "my kids" or "the young-uns I raised" are not limiting that to their birth children. There is a lot of nurture in the small community and there are many families where children can go to find "home" during difficult times. This is also why many Cherokee strongly resist outsiders adopting Indians outside their own culture.

There is a deep psychological and theological tension found in the Judaculla story; namely, how hard it is to feel so closely tied to one's family and yet to launch out and provide for one's own family of the next generation as well. How can one honor father and mother and still launch your own? How can that twofold desire be held in a creative tension? In the story the daughter does come back to provide for her family of birth after she has established her immediate, newer family.

In the massive cultural changes today the family is being challenged tremendously, and this Cherokee-Appalachian value offers some hope for those who grasp it.

As for giants, the biblical concerns for giants is brought to mind, not only the fear when "there were giants in the earth in those days,"[13] but especially in the story of the small David slaying the giant Goliath. The almost universal fear of giants makes Judaculla's demand that the mother-in-law not cry out that he looks frightful understandable. The amazing and oft-avoided reference to giants or Nephilim in Genesis 6 says that they were descendants of human women and supernatural beings! They were even declared to be the great heroes and famous men of long ago. This is remarkably close to a picture of the hero of the Cherokee, the slant-eyed giant, keeper of the game and provider for many.

The role of the eye, not only in reference to God but also to humans, is captured in biblical references in far too many places to enumerate. A few come to mind that would speak to this story in some way: The eye is the "lamp of the body."[14] "I have made a covenant with my eyes."[15] "I will lift up my eyes unto the hills, from whence cometh my help."[16] The healing of the blind man by Jesus, and especially the protective eye of God, are powerful roles the metaphor of the eye has in biblical language.

Likewise, blood is a major biblical concept, especially in the understandings of sacrifice in both the Hebrew and Christian texts. The role of Christ's spilling of his blood for all can be understood as a love offering and speaks to overcoming evil. A parallel can be seen in the saving of the blood by Judaculla for the life of the new born. In similar form, the sharing of communion (the Lord's Supper or Eucharist) is symbolic of sharing in that sacrifice of life's blood.

The role of dancing in the biblical record is twofold: both as a joyous celebration and as a grave concern. Clearly the call to praise the Lord's name in dance is given, and it is proclaimed that there is a time to dance in celebration.[17] But the abuse and misuse of dance, usually with drinking, is also noted in the negative examples. Perhaps the most moving biblical parable told by Jesus could have been really grasped by the Cherokee who first heard the parable of the celebration in the context of their own dances: that of the prodigal son, which really is a story of the loving, forgiving nature of God. The final return of the wandering, penitent son who expects and deserves nothing gets that wonderful response from the father:

"Bring quickly the best robe, and put it on him; and put a ring on his hand and shoes on his feet; and bring the fatted calf and kill it, and let us eat and make merry; for this my son was dead and is alive again; he was lost and is found. And they began to make merry."[18]

The early missionaries were greatly influenced by not only the Puritan and other religious movements but also by the excesses of the American frontier. Certainly those influences were part of the many waves of religious revivals, which most often were outspoken against the "evils" of dance in any form. They and those major denominations that grew so rapidly on the American frontier, namely Baptists, Presbyterians, Methodists and Pentecostals, for many years preached against any form of dance as evil.

The spiritual nature of the story, not to be separated from emotional development, family dynamics, or any other part of normal life, is crucial. Something very special had happened to the girl in her development. The spiritual life is not segmented or split from outer life. Entering the deep, inner world is not only getting in touch with one's own depths, psychologically speaking, but also with the soul or with spiritual things. Somewhat similar to the Pauline passage to "put on the whole armor of God," the people are to get new clothing.[19] Perhaps this is very close to the powerful metaphor used by Jesus about being anxious about clothing, noting how God clothes the grass of the field, and even more so "will clothe you, o men of little faith."[20] Speaking directly to the human tendency to worry and be driven by anxiety, the offer of being "clothed by God" speaks to spiritual needs for inner and outer consistency, to facing a kind of inner peace that brings a different countenance.

Inwardly most people long for and are even enthusiastic about spiritual opportunity, and they easily overlook the evil that creeps in to thwart their best desires. They are betrayed because they do not take evil seriously. Like a thief in the night, some unconscious content trips them up. It may be seen as "a thorn in the flesh." Perhaps also it shows how naive optimism can become destructive simply because many do not take their own dark side or shadow seriously. None is without sin and to admit it is the human task. Jung called strongly to all to take their own inner dark side seriously and not to project it on to others.

The principle applies both to individuals and groups, to every person, including families or larger groups.

Some may know the way to "fast," literally or symbolically, to prepare themselves for great things. In caring for oneself, one learns to love oneself better, to love others and to be loved. "Perfect love does cast out fear."[21] But fear can and does creep in easily, assuming danger is present when it is really a great blessing on the way. Fear is at the core of most of the neuroses and psychoses, even collective ones. Everyone is most vulnerable at their fear points, their places of uncertainty and deep-seated anxieties. When the Evil One, or evil ones, can make one constantly fearful, there is much power over people.

Perhaps no better expression of a call to loving relationships is captured in the old story of Judaculla, for his loving acts not only to his wife and children but also to the community underline the contrast to fear. She never calls out in fear because she loves him. Others are fearful and cannot get the love message. But perfect love is sometimes tough love and calls for discipline, for fasting, for spiritual sacrifice. It is not just doing what others want or need; it demands responsibility. But love is possible, it is nourishing, it is rejoicing, it is balancing, it is harmony.

6

Kana'sta, or Connestee, the Lost Settlement

THE MYTH

Long ago, while people still lived in the old town of Kana'sta, on the French Broad, two strangers, who looked in no way different from other Cherokee, came into the settlement one day and made their way into the chief's house. After the first greetings were over the chief asked them from what town they had come, thinking them from one of the western settlements, but they said, "We are of your people and our town is close at hand, but you have never seen it. Here you have wars and sickness, with enemies on every side, and after a while a stronger enemy will come to take your country from you. We are always happy, and we have come to invite you to live with us in our town over there," and they pointed toward Tsuwa'tel'da (Pilot Knob). "We do not live forever, and do not always find game when we go for it, for the game belongs to Tsul'Kalu', who lives in Tsunegun'yi, but we have peace always and need not think of danger. We go now, but if your people will live with us let them fast seven days, and we shall come then to take them." Then they went away toward the west.

The chief called his people together into the townhouse and they held a council over the matter and decided at last to go with the strangers. They got all their property ready for moving, and then went again into the townhouse and began their fast. They fasted six days, and on the morning of the seventh, before yet the sun was high, they saw a great company coming along the trail from the west, led by the two men who had stopped with the chief. They seemed just

141

like Cherokee from another settlement, and after a friendly meet-
ing they took up a part of the goods to be carried, and the two par-
ties started back together for Tsuwa'tel'da. There was one man from
another town visiting at Kana'sta, and he went along with the rest.

When they came to the mountain, the two guides led the way
into a cave, which opened out like a great door in the side of the rock.
Inside they found an open country and a town, with houses ranged
in two long rows from east to west. The mountain people lived in
the houses on the south side, and they had made ready the other
houses for the newcomers, but even after all the people of Kana'sta,
with their children and belongings, had moved in, there were still a
large number of houses waiting ready for the next who might come.
The mountain people told them that there was another town, of a
different people, above them in the same mountain, and still farther
above, at the very top, lived the Ani'-Hyuntikwala'ski (the Thun-
ders).

Now all the people of Kana'sta were settled in their new homes,
but the man who had only been visiting with them wanted to go back
to his own friends. Some of the mountain people wanted to prevent
this, but the chief said, "No; let him go if he will, and when he tells
his friends they may want to come, too. There is plenty of room for
all." Then he said to the man, "Go back and tell your friends that
if they want to come and live with us and be always happy, there is
a place here ready and waiting for them. Others of us live in Dat-
su'nalasgunyi and in the high mountains all around, and if they
would rather go to any of them it is all the same. We see you wher-
ever you go and are with you in all your dances, but you cannot see
us unless you fast. If you want to see us, fast four days, and we will
come and talk with you; and then if you want to live with us, fast
again seven days, and we will come and take you." Then the chief
led the man through the cave to the outside of the mountain and
left him there, but when the man looked back he saw no cave, but
only the solid rock.

The people of the lost settlement were never seen again, and they
are still living in Tsuwa'tel'da. Strange things happen there, so that
the Cherokee know the mountain is haunted and do not like to go
near it. Only a few years ago a party of hunters camped there, and
as they sat around their fire at supper time they talked of the story

and made rough jokes about the people of old Kana'sta. That night they were aroused from sleep by a noise as of stones thrown at them from among the trees, but when they searched they could find nobody, and were so frightened that they gathered up their guns and pouches, and left the place.

Introduction: What's in a Name?

Apparently more than one settlement carried the name Kana'sta, usually transliterated as Connestee. Ethnologists, historians, archeologists and others have long debated whether Mooney had located the correct Connestee setting for the myth in current Transylvania County, N.C. Some had assumed that there was only one such Cherokee settlement with that name, it being the one reported in the "Travels of Col.

Kana'sta or Connestee, the Lost Settlement — Artist Lynn Lossiah's portrayal of the departure of the Connestee community toward Pilot Knob with the help of the visitors. Special attention is given to detailing an authentic setting in the 1700s.

George Chicken" on his way to a treaty conference with his British troops in 1725 where such warm hospitality was recorded. However, in a 1777 visit by others, the village had "disappeared." The village visited by Col. Chicken was probably one on the Hiwassee river, which could have met the travel times and directions in the journal of his travels. That village still appeared on a map of 1781 and was listed as "Conostee" in early official South Carolina documents.[1]

Many settlements disappeared quickly after visits by European settlers, traders, trappers, soldiers and explorers. Smallpox and many other diseases brought in by such foreigners wiped out great numbers of Native American Indians all across the continent, both intentionally and unintentionally. In the year 1738 alone, smallpox reduced the Cherokee people to about 11,000, one half their previous number. With the British campaigns in 1760 and later, and the North Carolina Militia's famous Rutherford campaign in 1776, three-fourths of the 72 identified Cherokee towns were totally annihilated. By the end of the American Revolution they had lost half of the territory that they occupied.

For this myth the location on the French Broad River in current Transylvania County, N.C., given by Mooney is used, due to its affinity to the other nearby mythological sites and due to the fact that it actually was the site of an ancient Cherokee settlement long disappeared. Mooney's source also uses other nearby locations in the story itself. Some folks who have farmed the rich Connestee bottom lands for generations, finding shards, arrowheads and other items, have known that there were those who went before them. There is no clear archeological evidence of a village during the 1700s but there is a lot of evidence of hunters, travelers and others all through the area. Early travelers noted that the closer they got to the Middle Towns along the Tuckaseegee and Little Tennessee rivers going west, the more permanent villages they found. Many of those were known during the military campaigns and removal programs as well. However, because the mythological Connestee area was a hunting ground on the Eastatoe trade route to Charles-Town, the early Euro-American settlers had very great anxiety about the potential return of some not-so-friendly Cherokee and built John Carson's fort at the Transylvania Connestee site in about 1800. It was never used and fell into decay.[2]

Transylvania County was established as such only in 1861. The

Connestee community under consideration for the myth has a fascinating political history. It was included in the following counties: Burke (1777), Rutherford (1779), Buncombe (1792), and Henderson (1838). It was also in the center of the Orphan Strip claimed at the same time by the states of South Carolina, Georgia and North Carolina. The Walton War in 1803 was a brief skirmish fought between North Carolina and Georgia with one fatality and some injuries. A temporary compromise was made in favor of North Carolina in 1819 and as late as 2003 some disagreements still remained as to the exact border. Those struggles were in the heart of the Connestee community, from the Wilson bridge on U.S. 276 outside Brevard to the Selica community on the other side of Connestee, on the way to Pilot Knob as geography goes.[3]

One of the earliest archeological surveys done in North Carolina was carried out at this Connestee site in 1934 by a Brevard College student named Joffre Coe, who came to be one of the best-known pioneer archeologists in the southeastern United States. During those difficult depression days he led students and faculty on the ten-mile round trip by foot for the dig in Connestee. In his letter to the people of Transylvania County thanking them for their help in the survey Coe stated, "It is just as important to study the history of America before the coming of our ancestors as it is to study it afterwards. The only means we have of studying prehistory is the Indian remains that are left to us. Indian remains are documents; they should be studied as such."[4]

Coe became one of the dominant driving forces in North Carolina and southeastern archeology until his retirement from the University of North Carolina in Chapel Hill in 1982. His students played key roles in research and field studies as well in the development of typology to help classify pottery in the southeastern United States. One such student was native Transylvanian Pat Holden, who surveyed Transylvania County in 1966. She developed a ceramic typology providing the basic framework for pre-Cherokee pottery, which was further refined by others.[5]

The various archeological phases include, among others, the Woodland Period, which is further broken down into the Early (700–300 B.C.), the Middle (300 B.C.–A.D. 800) and the Late Woodland (A.D. 800–1000.) The Middle Woodland period is further subdivided into the Pigeon phase (300 B.C.–A.D. 200) and Connestee phase (A.D. 200–800). Subsequent work shows carbon-14 dating for Connestee ceramics in western North Carolina ranging from ca. A.D. 280–1000. The Late Woodland phase is not so clearly defined, according to Transylvania archeologist Ruth Wetmore. Holden describes Connestee as an early pottery that is simple but well made and durable, resistant to weathering. Some are plain and some are cord-marked or fabric impressed.[6]

So the term "Connestee" has come to be descriptive of a type of pottery for archeologists, and is named after the Connestee community, honoring the early work there by Coe. Holden notes the unique pleasure he had in that first collection of shards from the Connestee site.[7] Today's archeologists use the term for peoples of that era as "Connestee people." So the Connestee community is the setting for what was once a community of prehistoric peoples, possibly some of the ancestors of the present day Cherokee. Recent carbon-dating gives a date of about A.D. 500 for the Connestee phase of that settlement. It was also occupied during the Pisgah phase. Other archeological surveys and written records also show that Cherokee did hunt and live in the area during the historical period (after 1540).

The Cherokee name Connestee, or Kana'sta, according to Bushyhead comes from one of the three words for stick, in this case for "hard stick." His theory is that at some time it was a place good for gathering hard sticks used for different purposes.[8] There is no evidence for the popular and universal story of a so-called princess who had that name and threw herself off Connestee Falls after the loss of a loved one. That story is found in most countries in one form or another associated with either a high waterfall or cliff. Psychologically it may speak to a universal, deep-seated death-wish when one is near a dangerous place, projected into such a story. Lost love is an archetypal motif, a painful personal experience tapping one's deepest sense of loss and fear of abandonment as a child.

WHAT'S IN A STORY?

This little drama has a cast made up of a village chief, the people of Connestee, two mysterious strangers, a visitor from elsewhere, and a party of helpers from afar related to the two strangers. The opening of the story is the arrival in Connestee of the two strangers and their appealing message in a time of trouble.

AN APPEALING OFFER: PEACE AND PROSPERITY

Long ago, while people still lived in the old town of Kana'sta, on the French Broad, two strangers, who looked in no way different from other Cherokee, came into the settlement one day and made their way into the chief's house. After the first greetings were over the chief asked them from what town they had come, thinking them from one of the western settlements, but they said, "We are of your people and our town is close at hand, but you have never seen it. Here you have wars and sickness, with enemies on every side, and after a while a stronger enemy will come to take your country from you. We are always happy, and we have come to invite you to live with us in our town over there," and they pointed toward Tsuwa'tel'da (Pilot Knob). "We do not live forever, and do not always find game when we go for it, for the game belongs to Tsul'Kalu', who lives in Tsunegun'yi, but we have peace always and need not think of danger. We go now, but if your people will live with us let them fast seven days, and we shall come then to take them." Then they went away toward the west.

The story teller lets the listener know right away that this was long ago and that the village no longer had people living in it at the time of the hearing. He, or she, immediately introduces to the hearer the two strangers who appear to be just like other Cherokee and who do the proper thing in seeking out the leader, the chief. Greetings are exchanged and he asks from whence they came to check out the assumption that they are from a nearby settlement.

Those greetings were crucial then and still are in many cultures, certainly still in Appalachian mountain culture. Not only among the Cherokee and other tribal heritages, but also among our pioneer forefathers and all the way back to Scots-Irish, Scots, Germans, English and other ancestors, the role of greetings, and of mutual identification is a crucial way of asking to be trusted, of proclaiming oneself not as an enemy but a friend. This is like the use of biblical language as a shibboleth, or the most ancient use of the handshake to show one did not hide a weapon, all of which was far more than mere cordiality or social gesture. In hostile environments one had to check out one's dialogue partner.[9]

Introductions in Appalachia are more than formalities. They put one in context. Anxieties decrease and trust increases when they can identify one not as a total stranger. Often joked about by outsiders, those few minutes leaning on a pickup or a tractor in the field and talking about other things such as the weather, crops or fishing is a vital part of these initial greetings. The main point of a visit is saved for the right time and right moment when both know it has arrived. Efficiency of time is not the rule, but the building of trust. This remnant of Appalachian history is not limited to this area but is more universal than one realizes. It seems prevalent where people have been isolated or have been through heavy struggles. Until fairly recently in "civilized" western Europe any visitors checking into a hotel had to yield their passports to be registered with the police. This practice goes back to the middle ages, when upon entering a walled city one had to enroll to ask for asylum for the night. Certainly in earlier Communist bloc lands one had to register with the police to visit or stay. The point is that this is an ancient form of protection against perceived enemies and not just arbitrary control.

In the Connestee story itself, the two strangers answer the chief's question about their home by telling that they are kinsmen and their village is quite close, but is never seen. Then they get down to stating the problem of which they all were keenly aware: the chief's Connestee village is surrounded by enemies, war and sickness. In fact, they are told that a stronger enemy will come and take their country from them. They indicate that they, the visitors and their kin, are always happy and have come to invite them to come and live with them at Pilot Knob (Tsuwa'tel'da). Careful not to lay claim to immortality or to claim that their hunts for game are always successful, they do announce that they always have peace and do not even think of danger.

As the story progresses, having announced their departure, the two messengers tell the chief how to go about the task of preparing to live with them, should they so decide: first fast seven days and then they will come to take them back. The strangers go away westward from Connestee toward Pilot Knob.

Mooney sees Tsuwa'tel'da as a contraction of Tsuwa'teldunyi, for which the meaning has been lost. He identifies it with Pilot Knob, which he describes as a "high mountain in Transylvania County, about eight miles north of Brevard." Mooney also notes that "because of the peculiar stratified appearance of the rocks, the faces of the cliffs are said frequently to present a peculiar appearance under the sun's rays, as of shining walls with doors, windows, and shingled roofs."[10] Pilot Knob is a singular pointed peak seen from many directions and had on that peak a fire lookout tower for many years. There are only very small cliffs on Pilot Knob itself, although it is very steep on most sides. The above description by Mooney fits closely the mountain next to Pilot Knob, called Cedar Rock, with its many cliffs seen from many directions and from great distances. In addition, John Rock and Looking Glass Rock nearby have massive granite faces. Any mountain in this group would certainly be appropriate for the myths associated with Tsuwa'tel'da, for they carry in their own way a certain mystique. In fact, all throughout the ancient Appalachian Cherokee territory mountain rock cliff faces capture one's attention and are subject to mental projections of images all sorts. Due to local tradition and its closeness to the other mythological settings, the most likely site is Pilot Knob. Also, Pilot Knob is the home of Kana'ti and Selu, the hunter and corn mother, or first parents like Adam and Eve (see chapter 3).

Psychologically, or for the inner story caught by this Connestee tale, the chief may represent the ego, that vital, organizing, rational function in everyone. The ego helps one face the outer world and makes decisions on the basis of information taken in by the proper functions. A healthy ego is a crucial part of keeping balance between the inner and outer worlds, between the spiritual and the mundane realities. In European myths and fairy tales that ego function is often portrayed by the king. The two strangers who bring such good news are like angels unaware, messengers of hope letting him know there is an alternative to what they face, a spiritual one. They also represent inner impulses from deep within one's soul, those times one hears the still, small voice of the divine with a call to be something other than what one is. It is a call to deeper things beyond the mundane in life. It is that deep, inner call to peace.

These two come from the unconscious and its potential for spiritual peace; they give some hope to the conscious world of rational thinking and cruel outer reality. They head west where the sun sets when day is dying, even as the village seems to be dying. The west also captures the left side of the body, the more creative, spontaneous part that is less restricted by fears and cognitive realities.

COMMUNITY COUNCIL: DECISION AND DEPARTURE

The chief called his people together into the townhouse and they held a council over the matter and decided at last to go with the strangers. They got all their property ready for moving, and then went again into the townhouse and began their fast. They fasted six days, and on the morning of the seventh, before yet the sun was high, they saw a great company coming along the trail from the west, led by the two men who had stopped with the chief. They seemed just like Cherokee from another settlement, and after a friendly meeting they took up a part of the goods to be carried, and the two parties started back together for Tsuwa'tel'da. There was one man from another town visiting at Kana'sta, and he went along with the rest.

A council meeting in the townhouse is called for the crucial discussion and community decision. It must have been a lengthy process, for the story says "at last" they decided to go with the strangers. The decision is not made by the chief alone or in haste. In human terms, this reminds one to take time for major life decisions and to use ones healthy ego (symbolized by the chief) to allow for all parts of their inner and outer world to speak to major life issues. Before one decides to move, change jobs, change relationships or even enter into serious spiritual directions, this calls one to communicate carefully with all who are affected. It takes serious, rational thought and deliberation before one enters a journey. It also involves one's community and family.

However, the major issue in the story is not just making that decision and gathering their belongings; it is the more difficult task of inner, spiritual preparation needed to even qualify for this new opportunity. For most people, the first half of life is spent in this kind of outer preparation such as getting an education, finding a job, having a family, and so on. Some never get beyond that stage and spend their whole lives preoccupied with worldly goods, money, prestige or power. Others choose the road less traveled, looking for meaning in their lives they run the risks involved in the symbolic fast, or spiritual preparation. The people of Connestee reenter the townhouse to prepare themselves by fasting. As noted previously, the fast is a vital part of the Indian way of seeking inner answers, of finding the vision from the Great Spirit or of preparing the inner spirit for whatever faces them. In the story itself, after the people prepare earnestly, they see the strangers returning but with a large group of folks with them. They too seem like their own Cherokee kinsmen, and they help them to carry their load of goods.

Symbolically, the helping crowd of people implies a totality, a sense of completion in a superior way. They are helpers, a friendly crowd, not an unruly mob of people out of control and destructive. They cooperate and help and rescue. They assist in carrying the baggage of their new colleagues. They are like energy from the inner world helping preserve the past and the meaningful memories. Many people struggle for years with the emotional baggage that they have accumulated through the years both as individuals and as families. Sometimes one needs some help from the inner world to carry and to dispose of it in a proper place. Also one leaves a lot of it behind in the old painful places from whence one came, so one can move onto a much better place emotionally.

THE ARRIVAL: A MASSIVE MOUNTAIN HOMELAND

When they came to the mountain, the two guides led the way into a cave, which opened out like a great door in the side of the rock. Inside they found an open country and a town, with houses ranged in two long rows from east to west. The mountain people lived in the houses on the south side, and they had made ready the other houses for the newcomers, but even after all the people of Kana'sta, with their children and belongings, had moved in, there were still a large number of houses waiting ready for the next who might come. The mountain people told them that there was another town, of a different people, above them in the same mountain, and still farther above, at the very top, lived the Ani'-Hyuntikwala'ski (the Thunders).

The Connestee folks are led safely into the mountain of Pilot Knob by way of a cave created in solid rock. They find themselves in a paradise, protected from the outer world by the rock. Like a return to the womb of mother earth, the image is one of birth, death and burial, of resurrection and hope, all in one symbol. The cave is one of the oldest and deepest archetypal symbols. The earliest humans were cave dwellers; ancient cave paintings keep being discovered and reveal a lot about religious portrayals of human ancestors. Caves hold both fascination and fear. They often have to do with transformation of the soul, especially when they occur in one's dreams. In many cultures caves are tied to mother earth, the eternal womb, to birth and rebirth and spiritual pilgrimages. Perhaps one of the most widely used cave images is that used by Plato: his cave is a metaphor for humankind's place in the world. The cave person sees a shadow or image reflected on the cave wall, implying a sun not seen. The image is not the real thing and one must search back to find the source. The search is for the soul to make that differentiation, to "find the sun" or the real world and not be satisfied with the reflection alone.

Caves are usually associated with mountains, with places closer to the heavens, to spiritual things. The sense of birth and rebirth is captured. Many American Indians feel that humankind was first born in caves. Entering a cave is like revisiting one's beginnings. In most cultures the cave is a place of entering the "world" but is also a way to heaven. Some of that drift is caught in this Connestee story.

Jung often spoke of how hard it is to access the unconscious world, which is like solid rock. It is seemingly impregnable, especially in dreams. The people of Connestee find their place on the south side, where warmth is found. They are oriented in their new, inner world. The heights and depths are like a multitiered universe. The unconscious also is unlimited, as in the underworld of this mountain. Not only is there more than abundant room for them and others but also different people are above them. This acceptance of differences is true to their tradition. It is nonjudgmental. When one enters a deeper spiritual place, one also discovers that many other people are like one is, that differences in the outer world are not so important. This is quite a commentary in light of the historical racial prejudice against all native peoples of the Americas.

A brief reference is made to the nearby Thunders who, like the Slant-Eyed Giant Judaculla, owner of all the game, play a key role in Cherokee myths. The Thunder boys are the sons of the original parents, Kana'ti (Lucky Hunter) and Selu (Corn Mother), who live at Pilot Knob. The misadventures of these two wild boys capture a kind of fall from Eden of the Cherokee (see chapter 4).

In the Connestee story, entering the cave is for both the individual and the community a unique opportunity to individuate and develop as persons in light of, and in spite of, the surrounding outer world's values. Such a pilgrimage is not without risks but is essential in order to face the uncertainty of an ever-changing world.

THE RETURNING MESSENGER: INFORMATION AND INVITATION

Now all the people of Kana'sta were settled in their new homes, but the man who had only been visiting with them wanted to go back to his own friends. Some of the mountain people wanted to prevent this, but the chief said, "No; let him go if he will, and when he tells his friends they may want to come, too. There is plenty of room for all." Then he said to the man, "Go back and tell your friends that if they want to come and live with us and be always happy, there is a place here ready and waiting for them. Others of us live in Dat-su'nalasgunyi and in the high mountains all around, and if they would rather go to any of them it is all the same. We see you wherever you go and are with you in all your dances, but you cannot see us unless you fast. If you want to see us, fast four days, and we will come and talk with you; and then if you want to live with us, fast again seven days, and we will come and take you." Then the chief led the man through the cave to the outside of the mountain and left him there, but when the man looked back he saw no cave, but only the solid rock.

The conclusion of this story is a contrast to the conclusion of the Judaculla story in terms of the role of the stranger. In the former the stranger broke the fast, let out a war whoop and ruined the potential visit; here the visitor is received, and peacefully asks to return to his friends on the outside. The Connestee people are anxious and want to stop him, but the wise chief pleads for him to go, giving solid reasons for doing so. In that sense of openness and plenty, of welcome to come and share in the peace and happiness they have, the chief sends him with blessings and instructions, noting that they would be able to see him and his friends from their lofty new homes and that they would be with them in the joyous times of their dances. But he and his friend on the outside would not see them in return unless then fasted. After four days of fast they would come and talk. Should they decide to come and live there, they would come for them after another seven days of fasting, repeating essentially the procedure that they had just experienced.

In the midst of this invitation they are told of the great inside expanse of this mountain and of other such holy places mentioning Datsu'nalasgunyi or Shining Rock Mountain. "Where their tracks are" is the meaning of the Cherokee name, referring to the tracks in solid rock mentioned in the Judaculla myth.

The first psychological truism this part of the story is that, having reached their paradise-like abode, the people want to protect it at all costs and to keep it for themselves exclusively. There does not seem to be a survival risk in this situation; it is not a "life boat" situation in which the boat would sink if more came aboard. Rather, it seems to speak to a fear in each person. One cannot always tell if one's fears are justified when others are seemingly crowding one. In most areas, it is found in the resistance to newcomers.

At a deeper level, so often when some folks have a meaningful psychological, social or spiritual experience and develop a close fellowship with fellow travelers in that common experience, they unwittingly close ranks and functionally prevent others from joining them in their experience of peace and happiness. It is rarely intentional, among church folks, but their exclusive language or strict teaching often says to others that they are not welcome. The wise leader (chief), the good ego functioning for individuals and groups, will send the words out the others are welcome: Welcome to the party.

A Cautioning Postscript: Jokes and Stones

> The people of the lost settlement were never seen again, and they are still living in Tsuwa'tel'da. Strange things happen there, so that the Cherokee know the mountain is haunted and do not like to go near it. Only a few years ago a party of hunters camped there, and as they sat around their fire at supper time they talked of the story and made rough jokes about the people of old Kana'sta. That night they were aroused from sleep by a noise as of stones thrown at them from among the trees, but when they searched they could find nobody, and were so frightened that they gathered up their guns and pouches, and left the place.

Not all versions of this myth recorded by Mooney have a postscript such as this, but it seems very appropriate to the spirit of the story.

Most Cherokee would assume that these stones were thrown by

the Little People who were believed to fling stones as punishment, or cause rock slides. Of course, they are also known for being hospitable.

In modern day Pisgah National Forest where Pilot Knob is located, two popular camping places are close to, in a sense "under," the purview of this steep mountain. For the years that the fire lookout tower was perched atop the mountain, it gave a great view far and wide. There is something special about Pilot Knob with its view of the Courthouse, Tanasee Old Fields, Looking Glass Rock and far to the southwest where other mountains carry other Cherokee myths. One can only stand in awe of the beauty and feel some respect for peoples who have gone before them. One can learn to respect those who preceded in this place, even if one does not understand what happened. For anyone who is sensitive to other times, other peoples and other cultures, walking or working the lands of old Connestee gives a deep appreciation for the past and an appreciation for all the predecessors. One does not joke about them, and certainly not about spiritual matters.

Conclusion: Connestee Principles

What can one learn from these "shards" found in the archeology of these ancient psyches? There are many ways to look at the story, of course. Some will simply write it off as an explanation, after the fact, about the disappearance of a village, however old. Some assume falsely that these ancient remnants of a prehistoric people are more recent settlements and created an explanation. In any case, this type of story is common around the world in most societies. Peoples have come and gone since the beginning of time. However the story came to be in the first instance, it has its own power in the hearts and minds of people, as most of these older stories and fairy tales do. Following are some possibilities for bits of wisdom for modern persons which can be called "Connestee Principles."

1. All persons have relationships. They live as individuals but also are related to families and to communities that are like extended families. As individuals, one needs healthy, wise egos; as communities and families one needs healthy, wise leaders.

2. Everyone faces serious problems. Some are seemingly insurmountable ones like sickness, impending death or the loss of all one has. Those issues will be very individual for each person, but will raise

issues about the meaning of life, questions such as "Who am I?" and "Where am I going with my life?" For some, the real issue is one of motivation, of taking seriously the journey, perhaps in resistance to deep-seated fears.

3. Everyone receives deep, intuitive messages from within, whether they recognize them or not. These messengers speak in the language of one's heritage and religious tradition. They speak to the common fears, worries and problems that beset folks. They are friends. They often come during dreams and meditation. They may come in a church or other religious worship service or outside, high on a mountain.

4. All who must make a journey must prepare. One can really only prepare for the journey by some form of fasting, literal or symbolic. It costs something. No pain, no gain. This is not a prescription for a type of fasting or prayer, but a call to silence to listen to the still small voice, to pause and get in touch with other messages that may not be just words. They may be heard or experienced by way of music or visual art or a walk in the woods.

5. One can listen to the inner world. There can be some peace, some warmth and some perspective on life and death.

    A. For the extraverts this may be a call to listen to the deep inner possibilities, to listen to one's soul for direction (not just the outer world).

    B. For the introverts this may not mean to crawl further into their own inner world in isolation, but rather to meet the visiting messenger that is called to go back into the outer world, to communicate more with outer reality.

6. One can experience hope. It comes with learning that deep down inside, one can belong; one does have a home, a resting place.

7. Finally, folks need to heed the warning of the postscript: do not make fun of spiritual matters or of those people who have chosen the road less traveled. This warning is for those who do not appreciate their own heritage and show disrespect for the ancient, archetypal impulses, for deeper matters. The warnings (stones) come from the trees, above, from the heavens. It happens when they sleep and dream. The unconscious is not mocked. One's soul is not mocked. Truth comes from above. They flee with their guns, their "powerless power" in the face of spiritual forces. Even those who not go on an inner journey to find

their own personal peace need to show respect for those who do choose their Connestee pilgrimage.

STORY PARALLELS

There are similar stories, such as the one titled "The Removed Townhouses," with some variation in details. In one case, the entire townhouse, with its occupants and the mound upon which it was built, is transported by the Nunnehi to the Lone Peak near the head of the Cheowa. That mountain is solid rock and the people are now invisible and immortal. In another case the Nunnehi take the people way down under the water on the Hiwassee. In still another variation along the Tennessee river an entire townhouse slides into the river with dancing occupants. Sounds of dance and drum are heard there.

Of most interest is the account of the disappeared town of Austoghe as reported to Alexander Long and written down in 1725. Bearing close parallels to the Kana'sta story, this is one of the earliest extant descriptions of Cherokee life and beliefs, recorded by one who lived with them for over a decade (1714–1724). Long's account is entitled "A Small Postscript on the ways and manners of the Nashon of Indians called Charikees, the contents of the whole so that you may find everything from the pages."[11] Long's text reveals his attempts to verify topics and documents as best he can for his day, but he works very much with the "Ten Tribe" theory, as did most people of his day, namely that the early Americans were really descendants of the lost ten tribes of Israel. This topic was discussed in chapter 1.

Appendix E gives the more readable version of the Long account of the Austoghe story as prepared by David H. Corkran. Corkran comments that the notes of Long are very much like the John Howard Payne papers collected from Cherokee informants a century later. He says, "While both are dominated by Ten tribism, the error of that theory does not necessarily mean that the items of evidence are false, merely that they have been misinterpreted."[12]

THEOLOGICAL COMMENTS

The Connestee story has to do with universal human suffering and how it is faced, one of the oldest themes known to humankind.

The book of Job, perhaps one of the oldest in Hebrew scripture, struggles with this ancient question. Here the issue of facing it as a spiritual battle is proposed, rather than the question of why suffering exists. The theme is faced in different ways in Jewish, Christian, Buddhist, Hindu and other traditions. From a predominantly Christian setting, the most obvious parallel is a kind of heaven as a spiritual refuge. With the right preparation, the Connestee folks can find peace and no more sickness, find escape from the very things that were decimating them. This promised land does not provide immortality, but freedom from fear and suffering. The strange visitors are like "angels unawares" who bring good tidings.

The time of discussion, prayer, fasting and deep deliberation reminds one of Jesus' words in Luke on counting the cost before undertaking the path of following Him.[13] It takes serious rational thought to undertake such a journey. It is a decision of both head and heart. The fast is an ancient practice whereby one prepares for life's difficult tasks. In biblical passages the fast prepared one for God's message, for a hard task, or for deeper insight into a problem. Some examples are when Paul and Barnabas were sent out,[14] and when Anna the Prophetess at 84 years of age fasted and prayed, revealing the news that God would send a child to set Jerusalem free.[15]

What is striking about those helping kinsfolk from Pilot Knob is that they are witnesses to the final decision and then help them in making the trip, not unlike in the challenge from Paul to the Hebrews, "Therefore since we are surrounded by so great a cloud of witnesses, let us lay aside the sin which clings so closely and run with perseverance the race that is set before us."[16] In the same chapter similar issues are raised, as in the Connestee story, in calling for strength for the journey, healing the lame and striving for peace. The spiritual principle behind fasting is touched upon in the passage in Hebrews that Esau sold his birthright for a single meal.[17] There a reminder in given about the extremes to which some will go to avoid the personal sacrifice made in fasting.

The ancient belief that caves are passageways from earth to heaven is certainly implied. In some stories about the life of Jesus, he is born in a stable carved in a cave. The passing reference to the Thunder brothers brings up the image that Jesus gave two of his disciples, the brothers James and John, the surname Bo-aner'ges, Sons of Thunder. Also, when in the Connestee story the chief sends out word that others are welcome, many images of the universal welcome to the Kingdom of Heaven come to mind, but most of all the powerful parable Jesus told about the prodigal son who repented and returned to a forgiving father and where the elder son was protective of his hard-earned place.[18]

One of the most powerful and universal symbols in the Connestee story is the use of the cave in the rock as the place of salvation. The Hebrew and Christian scriptures use the rock as refuge many times, usually referring to God or Jesus as a rock: "The Lord is my Rock,"[19] "O Lord, my rock and my redeemer,"[20] "Be thou a rock of refuge for me,"[21] "The Lord is an everlasting rock,"[22] "And the rock was Christ,"[23] and many more. Many of these rock themes are carried in hymns and gospel songs so cherished in all Appalachian mountain traditions, including the Cherokee. "In Thy cleft o Rock of Ages hide Thou me," is a line from one song that comes very close to this Connestee spiritual refuge story, as does an old American frontier gospel classic, "Rock of Ages hide Thou me."[24]

The theme of moving into a cave for refuge, thus implying not only safety but also new life, captures a powerful process parallel to the sense of going to water and baptism in Cherokee and Christian traditions. The theme of death is followed by resurrection. Baptism captures death to the old and rising to new life in the new. Jesus' tomb was one that Joseph of Arimathea had "hewn in the rock."[25] That sense of dying or entering an underground tomb in order to reach a "resurrected" happier life is one not to be overlooked, and carries much hope for surviving great hardships. Also when one locates the Connestee story in the ancient prehistoric village in Transylvania County on the French Broad River, to head for Pilot Knob meant crossing that river. This is a close parallel to the biblical crossing over the River Jordan, that symbolic move to a higher plane, a life transition to follow God's will, also the stuff of many gospel songs.

In contrast to the Connestee story's focus on community harmony, decisions and a move to another place, the next story is that of an individual not in harmony, making decisions by default, and yet still moving in a pilgrimage to that special Pilot Knob place of spiritual refuge.

7

Tsuwe'nahi: A Legend
of Pilot Knob

The Myth

In the old town of Kanuga, on Pigeon River, there was a lazy fellow named Tsuwe'nahi, who lived from house to house among his relatives and never brought home any game, although he used to spend nearly all his time in the woods. At last his friends got very tired of keeping him, so he told them to get some parched corn ready for him and he would go and bring back a deer or else would never trouble them again. They filled his pouch with parched corn, enough for a long trip, and he started off for the mountains. Day after day passed until they thought they had seen the last of him, but before the month was half gone he was back again at Kanuga, with no deer, but with a wonderful story to tell.

He said that he had hardly turned away from the trail to go up the ridge when he met a stranger, who asked him where he was going. Tsuwe'nahi answered that his friends in the settlement had driven him out because he was not a good hunter, and that if he did not find a deer this time that he would never go back again. "Why not come with me?" said the stranger. "My town is not far from here, and you have relatives there." Tsuwe'nahi was very glad of the chance, because he was ashamed to go back to his own town; so he went with the stranger, who took him to Tsuwa'tel'da (Pilot Knob). They came to a cave and the other said, "Let us go in there"; but the cave ran clear to the heart of the mountain, and when they were inside the hunter found there an open country like a wide bottomland, with a great settlement and hundreds of people. They were all glad to see him and brought him to their chief, who took him to his own house and showed him a seat near the fire. Tsuwe'nahi sat down, but he felt it move under him, and when he looked again he saw that it was a turtle, with its head sticking out from the shell. He jumped up, but the chief said, "It won't hurt you; it only wants to see who you are." So he sat down very carefully, and the turtle drew in its head again. They brought food, of the same kind that he had been accustomed to at home, and when he had eaten the chief took him through the settlement until he had seen all the houses and talked with most of the people. When he had seen everything and rested some days, he was anxious to get back to his home, so the chief himself brought him to the mouth of the cave and showed him the trail that led down to the river. Then he said, "You are going back to the settlement, but you will never be satisfied there any more. Whenever you want to come to us, you know the way." The chief left him and Tsuwe'nahi went down the mountain and along the river until he came to Kanuga.

He told his story, but no one believed it and the people only laughed at him. After that he would go away very often and be gone for several days at a time, and when he came back to the settlement he would say he had been with the mountain people. At last one man said he believed the story and would go with him to see. They went off together to the woods, where they made a camp, and then Tsuwe'-nahi went on ahead, saying he would be back soon. The other waited for him, doing a little hunting near the camp, and two nights afterwards Tsuwe'nahi was back again. He seemed to be alone, but was talking as he came, and the other hunter heard girls' voices, although he could see no one. When he came up to the fire, he said, "I have two friends with me, and they say there is to be a dance in their town in two nights, and if you want to go they will come for you." The hunter agreed at once, and Tsuwe'nahi called out, as if to someone close by, "He says he will go." Then he said, "Our sisters have come for some venison." The hunter had killed a deer and had the meat drying over the fire, so he said, "What kind do they want?" The voices answered, "Our mother told us to ask for some of the ribs," but he still could see nothing. He took down some rib pieces and gave them to Tsuwe'nahi, who took them and said, "In two days we shall come again for you." Then he started off, and the other heard the voices going through the woods until all was still again.

*In two days Tsuwe'nahi came, and this time he had two girls
with him. As they stood near the fire, the hunter noticed that their
feet were short and round, almost like dogs' paws, but as soon as they
saw him looking they sat down so that he could not see their feet.
After supper the whole party left the camp and went up along the
creek to Tsuwa'tel'da. They went in through the cave door until they
got to the farther end and could see houses beyond, when all at once
the hunter's legs felt as if they were dead and he staggered and fell
to the ground. The others lifted him up, but still he could not stand,
until the medicine-man brought some "old tobacco" and rubbed it
on his legs and made him smell it until he sneezed. Then he was able
to stand again and went in with the others. He could not stand at
first because he had not prepared himself by fasting before he started.*

*The dance had not yet begun and Tsuwe'nahi took the hunter
into the townhouse and showed him a seat near the fire, but it had long
thorns of honey locust sticking out from it and he was afraid to sit
down. Tsuwe'nahi told him not to be afraid, so he sat down and found
that the thorns were as soft as down feathers. Now the drummer came
in and the dancers and the dance began. One man followed at the end
of the line, crying "Ku! Ku!" all the time but not dancing. The hunter
wondered, and they told him, "This man was lost in the mountains
and had been calling all through the woods for his friends until he was
only able to pant "Ku! Ku!" And then we found him and took him in."*

*When it was over, Tsuwe'nahi and the hunter went back to the
settlement. At the next dance in Kanuga they told all they had seen
at Tsuwa'tel'da, what a large town was there and how kind everybody was, and this time — because there were two of them — the
people believed it. Now others wanted to go, but Tsuwe'nahi told
them that they must first fast seven days, while he went ahead and
prepared everything, and then he would come and bring them. He
went away and the others fasted, until at the end of seven days he
came for them and they went with him to Tsuwa'tel'da, and their
friends in the settlement never saw them again.*

INTRODUCTION

The last in this selection of Cherokee myths is located in the same
geographic area involving the old town of Kanuga and that special

Tsuwe'nahi; A Legend of Pilot Knob — The Lazy Hunter (left center, with feather) and his companion (far left), as well as the women who lead them and a central figure of the wise chief from Pilot Knob. By Lynn Lossiah.

mountain, Pilot Knob. It introduces some interesting people, both usual and unusual. In fact, the story posits some ancient archetypal issues both for communities and individuals. Every family is touched by questions of accepting and meeting life responsibilities. But how do people judge which ones are most important and how do they set priorities? Are the most commonly held values always ultimate for everyone?

Previously, the village of Kanuga was identified as being at the forks of the Pigeon River. This story has to do with several trips from Kanuga to Pilot Knob; not far away, as the crow flies, but quite a journey on human foot, past Cold Mountain, Shining Rock and the awesome home and judgment seat of Judaculla, the Slant-Eyed giant who owns all the game. This geography is important and would have been known to the hearer. This is an implied fact about the setting to say that the stages in this pilgrimage were not just casual walks in the fields.

SETTING THE STAGE: A PROBLEM

> *In the old town of Kanuga, on Pigeon River, there was a lazy*
> *fellow named Tsuwe'nahi, who lived from house to house among his*
> *relatives and never brought home any game, although he used to*
> *spend nearly all his time in the woods. At last his friends got very*
> *tired of keeping him, so he told them to get some parched corn ready*
> *for him and he would go and bring back a deer or else would never*
> *trouble them again. They filled his pouch with parched corn, enough*
> *for a long trip, and he started off for the mountains. Day after day*
> *passed until they thought they had seen the last of him, but before*
> *the month was half gone he was back again at Kanuga, with no deer,*
> *but with a wonderful story to tell.*

This introduction to the story sets the stage and focuses on a social problem in almost every community, that of what to do with those who will not earn their keep, who are takers and not givers. It is an ancient problem and the stuff of many myths and ethical debates.

The name of the "lazy fellow" is mentioned immediately and seems to have a bit of irony in that, according to Mooney, it may have something to do with success; "He has them in abundance."[1] In that sense it means he has riches, like the English equivalent when translated: Richard, "one who has riches." Is this a sign of things to come, things that may not be apparent at first glance? Why would he have such a name when he is a moocher, perhaps a burden to all? His friends are tired of him and he himself takes the initiative to resolve the problem. He leaves to get his contribution to the family or community table.

His request is to have food for the journey, parched corn, a standard diet for warriors or Cherokee on the road, probably for all the native tribes east of the Mississippi River. Corn eating, corn growing, harvest, the green corn dance, and other issues related to corn were vital to their survival historically. Selu, the Corn Mother, is a key figure in their mythology, the equivalent to Eve in the biblical story. Usually the Cherokee boiled the corn, parched it in hot ashes, sifted it and ground it into a powder that they carried easily in their pouch. Adding a pint of water to a handful of corn made a hearty drink for quick consumption.[2] It is interesting that they give him enough "for a long trip." Are they hoping he would take a very long one and not come back to bother them? Or is it still more generosity? In context, it seems the former is their motivation, for they think they have seen the last of him until he shows up about two weeks after leaving, with no deer but with a story.

How does one face such people who abuse hospitality, who mooch again and again, who know how to work the system to get all they can? How do groups discern when someone is abusing them and their hospitality?

HIS STORY: PART ONE, THE ENCOUNTER

He said that he had hardly turned away from the trail to go up the ridge when he met a stranger, who asked him where he was going. Tsuwe'nahi answered that his friends in the settlement had driven him out because he was not a good hunter, and that if he did not find a deer this time that he would never go back again. "Why not come with me?" said the stranger. "My town is not far from here, and you have relatives there." Tsuwe'nahi was very glad of the chance, because he was ashamed to go back to his own town; so he went with the stranger, who took him to Tsuwa'tel'da (Pilot Knob). They came to a cave and the other said, "Let us go in there"; but the cave ran clear to the heart of the mountain, and when they were inside the hunter found there an open country like a wide bottom-land, with a great settlement and hundreds of people. They were all glad to see him and brought him to their chief, who took him to his own house and showed him a seat near the fire. Tsuwe'nahi sat down, but he felt it move under him, and when he looked again he saw that it was a turtle, with its head sticking out from the shell. He jumped up, but the chief said, "It won't hurt you; it only wants to see who you are." So he sat down very carefully, and the turtle drew in its head again. They brought food, of the same kind that he had been accustomed to at home, and when he had eaten the chief took him through the settlement until he had seen all the houses and talked with most of the people. When he had seen everything and rested some days, he was anxious to get back to his home, so the chief himself brought him to the mouth of the cave and showed him the trail that led down to the river. Then he said, "You are going back to the settlement, but you will never be satisfied there any more. Whenever you want to come to us, you know the way." The chief left him and Tsuwe'nahi went down the mountain and along the river until he came to Kanuga.

This "rich" hunter, who is not a hunter in the traditional way and is thus declared to be poor, meets a stranger along the trail and tells his sad story. He does not get questions about his abilities or contribution to the local economy, but gets an invitation to another town that even has some of his own kin. There is no mention of his family in Kanuga but here the offer of new hospitality and reunion with kin is appealing and promising. As in the Connestee story, he is led to Pilot Knob, through a cave into the heart of the mountain. He discovers not only great expanses of land but also a vast settlement with people who warmly welcome him. And for people of the steep mountains, bottom land is precious, especially for growing corn, that vital food. Hunting is easier as well. Also, Pilot Knob is close to Tsunegun'yi, the home of Judaculla, owner of all the game.

He is welcomed by the leader, the chief, who grants him hospitality in his own home, not in some formal functional place or the town-house where major business and other decisions are made. He sits near the source of heat and energy, the fire. No greater honor could be his than to be there at the chief's fire. In antiquity the fire was the source of warmth and welcome, the place of the holy and the spirit that led, as in the pillar of fire in the Exodus story. In ancient Greece it was the place of the household gods, the holiest of places. In Mooney's collection, the story of creation is followed by the obtaining of fire by the little water spider after many failures of other animals. Fire for warming the body and soul was not taken for granted. Fire was also crucial for healing and warming the hands of the healer before touching a sufferer.[3]

Fire had far deeper meaning for the Cherokee than warmth and cooking. Part of the powerful symbolic meaning of the family fire, the community fire, food for the soul. Not only at the "going to water" ceremony were the family fires rekindled in antiquity but also at the reading of the law (before they changed from a clan system to a court system modeled after the white government). That original law was known by all, but its annual ritual reading was done by a priest with raven wings in his hair. Crimes that were committed during the previous year were named, and the orator asked the sacred fire to forgive those who had committed them.[4] Based on the belief that "the heart cannot be weighed down with all the sorrows of past years," this ceremony was a kind of yearly purge of sins. All sins except murder could be forgiven.[5] Historian Haywood noted:

Here it is that all injuries are forgiven, which have been done to one another. Vengeance and cruelty in the sacrifice made to friendship. No one who has been guilty of unpardonable offenses, can partake of this feast; and all who partake of it must be forgiven, no matter what may be the nature of the offence. The feast assigns to oblivion and extinguishes all vengeance, and forever vanishes from the mind all sentiments of displeasure which before separated them from a close and friendly intercourse with each other.[6]

For untold generations the Cherokee lived in hundreds of small villages and were governed by public consensus and harmony within the group; this puts the renewal of relationships high among their spiritual values. They were not based on confrontation and dispute, but on spiritual laws. Early records indicate that the orator or "beloved man" who told these laws from the wampum belts not only called them to look into the fire and repent, but also could list the sins.

With the mention of such men it should be noted that the Cherokee had a most important title of "beloved woman," bestowed rarely upon a few exceptional women. Three known women in the recent years in the Eastern Band included the naming of Louise Bigmeat Maney, who was a master potter, meticulous historian and teacher of Cherokee traditions to children. Her impact on generations of modern Cherokee was exceptional. Nancy Ward (1738–1822) was noted for great wisdom and valor. Maggie Wachacha, who died in 1993, was widely known for her dedication to the Cherokee, living with her husband Jarrett in the Snowbird district some 60 miles from tribal offices. She was clerk of the tribe and walked the distance with her husband to meetings of the tribe as well as serving as midwife and herbal medicine healer. The key accomplishment of these three women is that they served their people selflessly.[7]

For modern Cherokee, east and west, the Eternal Flame, kept over a century, also captures something of the spirit of forgiveness, even with the loss of the ritual. At the June 29, 2001, rededication of the Eternal Flame in Cherokee, N.C. Principal Chief Leon Jones said: "This fire will burn forever as a symbol of friendship eternal between the white man and the red man. And I hope that's always true. Eternal friendship should be between all mankind."[8]

Back to the poor yet "rich" hunter, does this fireside seat underline not only the new friendships he faced? Does it imply forgiveness for past offenses? Not only is he seated in the place of honor by the fire but upon a strange seat, a turtle that moves, startling him. What a pow-erful ancient image for him to encounter: he sits on a symbol of safety, a being that carries its own house and protection. The turtle captures both heaven and earth, the round on top and the flat on the bottom, a metaphor for the Cherokee story that the flat earth is suspended from the sky arch or vault (the round top) by four cords. The turtle stands for longevity and endurance. The turtle is slow but steadfast and can endure to the end. Jung felt that in many cases the turtle was a sym-bol of the Self, that center of our being. In many Native American tra-ditions, the earth itself is "turtle island." Iroquois and Algonquin traditions tell that the grandmother of humankind fell from the sky when there was no earth. She was rescued by the turtle on its back, and the muskrat covered the back with mud from the bottom of the sea. The island that was formed first on the turtle's back grew eventually into the entire earth. (Perhaps if this very brief appearance in the Cherokee story is also a reference to their ancient connection to the Iroquois.)

So our hunter stumbles on something very deep and very spiri-tual, something about his own inner world and possibilities for trans-formation and value. He is fed and nourished with familiar food. That nourishment would also be spiritual food for his soul that strengthens him for meeting all the people, getting acquainted with people of this inner settlement. As he departs, being shown the way by the chief him-self, he gets prophetic word that he will never be satisfied back at Kanuga anymore, having had this deep experience.

So it is with those who have had a deeply moving, numinous expe-rience and who have felt the presence of higher, more spiritual power. They are not the same in their old former world. When Jung advised the founder of Alcoholics Anonymous (AA) that psychoanalysis was not what he needed for his addiction, but that he needed to go back to America and be with others. Making several points now part of the AA program, Jung emphasized that an experience with a higher power was crucial to facing the addiction.

HIS STORY: PART TWO, HUMILIATION AND RECONNECTION

He told his story, but no one believed it and the people only
laughed at him. After that he would go away very often and be gone

*for several days at a time, and when he came back to the settlement
he would say he had been with the mountain people. At last one man
said he believed the story and would go with him to see. They went
off together to the woods, where they made a camp, and then Tsuwe'-
nahi went on ahead, saying he would be back soon. The other waited
for him, doing a little hunting near the camp, and two nights afterwards Tsuwe'nahi was back again. He seemed to be alone, but was
talking as he came, and the other hunter heard girls' voices, although
he could see no one. When he came up to the fire, he said, "I have
two friends with me, and they say there is to be a dance in their town
in two nights, and if you want to go they will come for you." The
hunter agreed at once, and Tsuwe'nahi called out, as if to someone
close by, "He says he will go." Then he said, "Our sisters have come
for some venison." The hunter had killed a deer and had the meat
drying over the fire, so he said, "What kind do they want?" The
voices answered, "Our mother told us to ask for some of the ribs,"
but he still could see nothing. He took down some rib pieces and
gave them to Tsuwe'nahi, who took them and said, "In two days we
shall come again for you." Then he started off, and the other heard
the voices going through the woods until all was still again.*

A basic humiliation occurs as the friends laugh at him; what a
cock-and-bull story they feel he is sharing with them, probably as an
excuse for not having produced meat for their tables. He comes back
not with what they expect or need, or so they think. But like the turtle he had sat upon, he is persistent and continues his visits to this
unknown place, only reporting that he had been with those mountain
people. One colleague, a hunter, finally believes him and asks to go with
him. How difficult it is to return to normal life when you have been to
the mountain top. Many who have had a deep religious experience,
perhaps as a result of a near-death event, a trip to another culture, or
a powerful numinous dream, find out that they can't really go home
again emotionally. In this case, the prejudice against him within the
community probably does not help: he is just a lazy fellow, they think,
telling stories that no one believes.

Sometimes a singular person, a close friend, will listen and want
to believe. Tsuwe'nahi now has a companion who begins the journey
with him, camping along the way. He goes on ahead to prepare the way
for this new friend, who hunts for a couple of days while waiting. His

return brings a surprise in the form of feminine voices coming from out of sight. These creatures seem to be the Nunnehi, those angel-like creatures, the invisible people who help and guide. Other stories tell of beautiful Nunnehi women showing up at social occasions and dances, daring young suitors to go with them to their underground homes.[8]

In making a spiritual journey like this the hunter has Tsuwe'nahi for a guide, but there seems to be a period of preparation, of waiting and wondering. The presence of the feminine in the process is important for these two men; it gives them balance and sensitivity. Not only in fairy tales and myths but especially in men's dreams, the feminine part of the psyche shows up as the leader, the one who invites and guides. Jung called this the anima. For many persons, the inner dream image may be in the form of an angel, a saint or a wise female elder from the past. In therapy there are people who experience a long lost grandmother or aunt who "converses" with them in a dream. This is not some hocus-pocus but rather a deep connection within their own psyches to a wise old woman part of themselves, a deep archetypal wisdom giving guidance during a crucial time in their lives. As in the story, one often makes a contract to pay for the journey. In this story the payment is for the mother of the girls, implying some form of marriage since gifts were given to the parents as part of a wedding contract. But it is not specific.

His Story: Part Three, Grounding

In two days Tsuwe'nahi came, and this time he had two girls with him. As they stood near the fire, the hunter noticed that their feet were short and round, almost like dogs' paws, but as soon as they saw him looking they sat down so that he could not see their feet. After supper the whole party left the camp and went up along the creek to Tsuwa'tel'da. They went in through the cave door until they got to the farther end and could see houses beyond, when all at once the hunter's legs felt as if they were dead and he staggered and fell to the ground. The others lifted him up, but still he could not stand, until the medicine-man brought some "old tobacco" and rubbed it on his legs and made him smell it until he sneezed. Then he was able to stand again and went in with the others. He could not stand at first because he had not prepared himself by fasting before he started.

The hunter not only meets the girls again but is led to the inner world of Pilot Knob. A strange parallel process is going on: something is strange about the feet and legs. Their feet are most unusual and his own legs are unable to hold him up when he arrives. Feet give one direct contact with mother earth, with reality. Jung felt the feet had a generative and phallic significance, perhaps like some Old Testament uses where feet are referring to the genitals.[9] The main thing that can be seen in this context is that they are very different; their contact to this world is quite different from normal. Comparing them to dog's feet in form seems to capture the primitive, mammalian contact with where they are. Like that lower, mammalian part of the brain, it implies that the priority is a level of primitiveness and simplicity not so complicated by the outer neocortex. These feminine spirit-like beings might in another context be called angels and are not just like regular humans. There is something special. Sometimes the Western, rationally oriented religions with their dogmatic, well-thought-out formulas and "objective truth" miss some of the more basic, subjective dimensions of faith. Also, in the very steep, rocky terrain the girls' "grounding" is more appropriate, symbolically speaking.

After the girls modestly hide their feet, the party eats and breaks camp, heading for Tsuwa'tel'da, Pilot Knob. As soon as the hunter enters this special place and sees it for the first time, he is overcome in such a way that his legs are paralyzed, bringing him to the earth. He must be supported by the others. Is it spiritual shock? Overwhelming beauty? Incomprehensible potential? Amazing awe? It is one of those facts in the psychology of religion that folks are overcome by a religious experience. The manifestations of this in the history of the religions of the world are many and often embarrassing to the more staid, mind-oriented formal groups or churches. They, and many psychologists, would call it hysteria or a psychosomatic reaction. Human bodies tell much more that one wants to admit, even when the event is very special and deeply religious. Sometimes one wants to jump for joy, or one becomes weak in the knees. Sometimes one simply feels good in the heart area. The stories of revivals on the American frontier are filled with descriptions of emotional reactions to religious experiences and, in fact, the famous outbreak of the Ghost Dance among American Indians leading to the infamous Wounded Knee episode is a form of religious ecstasy.[10] The second hunter, the new initiate to Tsuwa'tel'da, to the inner spirit world of a deeper existence, cannot stand on the legs he uses in the outer world; they are not adequate for the new place to which he has come. In light of the crucial role that the legs played for survival for ancient peoples everywhere, including the Cherokee, the loss of leg control must have been shocking for him.

Old Tobacco was literally "ancient tobacco" (*tsal-agayunli*), which was sacred among all the Eastern tribes.[11] Both medicinal and religious in its multiple uses, Old Tobacco was carried in a medicine pouch by most. An entire myth about how the Cherokee got the first tobacco is in their treasure house of stories. For the hunter, the healing works; the ritual of applying old tobacco to his legs brings him to his feet, and sniffing it into his nose causes him to sneeze. There is more to this than just triggering his sneeze reflex. The Cherokee feel that the breath is so related to the spirit and thus to the Great Spirit that what goes in and out of each person is part of their being. One elder, "Mama Gene" Jackson, a longtime nurse, said that when a baby takes its first breath is the holiest of times, for that is when life begins, when the spirit enters the child.[12]

This part ends with the clarification that the hunter's inability to stand is because he had not fasted before entering this place, underlining the spiritual role of this journey.

HIS STORY: PART FOUR, THE THORNY SEAT

> The dance had not yet begun and Tsuwe'nahi took the hunter *into the townhouse and showed him a seat near the fire, but it had long thorns of honey locust sticking out from it and he was afraid to sit down. Tsuwe'nahi told him not to be afraid, so he sat down and found that the thorns were as soft as down feathers. Now the drummer came in and the dancers and the dance began. One man followed at the end of the line, crying "Ku! Ku!" all the time but not dancing. The hunter wondered, and they told him, "This man was lost in the mountains and had been calling all through the woods for his friends until he was only able to pant 'Ku! Ku!' And then we found him and took him in."*

Now it is the other hunter's turn to go into the townhouse and sit by the fire, the source of community energy and place of honor. But his seat this time is a seat of long honey locust thorns. In another myth about a gambler, a boy covered with terrible sores sought out his father, Thunder, who was reputed to be a doctor. He also sat on the long, sharp thorns of the honey locust, passing the identity test. The special place of the honey locust in Western myths, as well as Native American myths, is a connection to lightning and to healing. Mountain ash has similar associations with healing. What appears to be hurtful or painful is not that at all, once the hunter's fear is removed: it is soft as down. So it is when one is fearful of what appears to be sharp and painful about the spiritual way. Biblical references to thorns are bountiful, with both negative and positive meanings. The most basic fact is that thorns represent a defense for a plant, like horns, teeth and hooves for an animal; they are mechanisms to protect, barriers to prevent potential injury. What appears to be hurtful is in fact the opposite for the colleague of the "poor-rich" hunter.

With the arrival of the drummer and dancers, the dance begins, a time of joy and celebration, but with some dissonance: a man is walking at the end of the dance line, crying out some strange, unknown words. They tell of finding this lost soul and taking him in, his having been reduced in communication to those simple sounds. The beautiful thing in this story is the total acceptance of this simple, limited man. No matter that he cannot dance or talk normally. He is rescued and has become one of them. What a powerful lesson for today. In the field of mental health one must deal with many who have lost their family and friends, who have lost their way and who can no longer be normal as far as society is concerned. They cannot really talk but they have something to say, they have a need to belong to a loving community and to take active part as far as they can and not be judged. (Compare this with the derisive laughter Tsuwen'ahi got from Kanuga folks when he first returned.)

In earlier, traditional Appalachian communities, as with the Cherokee, it was assumed that mentally or emotionally limited folks were cared for and accepted, not just tolerated. Some homes were built, food and clothes shared and when many came to church they were accepted even if they sometimes disturbed the worship. The advent of state social systems helped change that, along with changing lifestyles and work requirements.

There is another possible explanation for the presence of this person since it is not said that he is a Cherokee: perhaps he was of another tribe, a stranger lost to his friends and his world. This certainly speaks to diversity, to peoples of other nations and races in any community who may not really be able to speak the language or dance to local tunes, but who want to be accepted. The loving acceptance by the Cherokee of others is well documented, but they, like most Native Americans, have not always been accepted. Their language was not acceptable, as defined by government policy and that of most schools and missions. They were to become more "civilized," that is, more like the European settlers. Many Americans of European origins carry years of prejudice but vehemently deny it because it has become so completely unconscious. Because it is so unconscious it pops up at the strangest times and in the most remarkable ways.

THE STORY'S END

When it was over, Tsuwe'nahi and the hunter went back to the settlement. At the next dance in Kanuga they told all they had seen at Tsuwa'tel'da, what a large town was there and how kind everybody was, and this time — because there were two of them — the people believed it. Now others wanted to go, but Tsuwe'nahi told them that they must first fast seven days, while he went ahead and prepared everything, and then he would come and bring them. He went away and the others fasted, until at the end of seven days he came for them and they went with him to Tsuwa'tel'da, and their friends in the settlement never saw them again.

Tsuwe'nahi is finally vindicated in his own community, now having a witness to the truth of his story. Others are not only willing to believe but also want to make the journey. Some, not all, choose to follow him. The lazy one is now the spiritual leader and is taking them to a better place. Tsuwe'nahi had become a rich hunter after all.

THEOLOGICAL COMMENTS

The setting of the story raises similar issues captured in the Pauline command regarding the struggle of early Christians with those who were living in idleness and not earning their own living: "If anyone will not work, let him not eat."[13] There are references to each carrying his or her own load. In the history of the church, especially in Protestantism, the work ethic is held very high. So at the start of the story, most would be in agreement with the village ethic and send him on his way. Today we use the negative catch words "co-dependent" and "enabling" when families continue to support persons who do not stand on their own at the right time, who stay dependent too long.

The story is as up to date as possible, and an eternal problem. How does society face such people who abuse hospitality, who mooch again and again, who know how to work the system to get all they can? How do groups discern when someone is abusing them and their hospitality? The early Christian church had to struggle with abuses when word got around that they loved people, cared for the sick and hungry and took in strangers. One of the earliest Christian writings that did not make it into the biblical canon was the Didache, the Teachings; it addressed such mundane human problems. They were advised to welcome the strangers, but if after three days the people wanted to stay, they were false prophets, i.e., abusing the hospitality. Records of many early travelers among the Cherokee tell of their warm hospitality. It was part of their belief system and unfortunately cost them dearly. So it is understandable that this lazy character might capture the attention of the people of Kanuga or any settlement or any church or synagogue or temple.

As in many of Jesus' parables, the story presents a real problem with which one may identify, but then it heads in an unexpected direction and one begins to wonder if the main character is a villain or hero or if a judgment has been made in haste. His pilgrimage is out of the ordinary. He is fearful of the thorns, an image throughout the Bible with both positive and negative meanings. Paul's "thorn in the flesh" was what kept him from getting "puffed up" or inflated.[14] Thorns were a sign of austerity and deprivation as well as a sign of salvation, as in Jesus' crown of thorns. In much of Christian art, the portrayed crown of thorns also shows a radiating divine light.

The request for ribs by the two feminine figures also reminds some of biblical creation story of Eve being created from Adam's rib, but here the masculine is to provide nourishment by way of the ribs. With the deer being a spiritual animal it implies his payment or gift to them for the journey he is making.

Although most folks might first associate fire with a few biblical passages about destructiveness and the eternal flames, there are also many parallel ideas placing fire close to the Cherokee concept of purifying and the holy nature. The pillar of flames was to lead the Jews.[15] The light of Israel was to become a fire[16] and the Lord was to come in fire.[17] The Holy Spirit appears as tongues of fire[18] and the words of John the Baptist say that he baptizes with water but the one to come after him will do so with the Holy Spirit and with fire.[19] And there is the passage where Jesus is before the high priest and Peter follows at a safe distance, and sits and warms himself at the fire.[20] These and many more passages give functions of fire related to its central spiritual role including its use in being tested, being forgiven, and being welcomed. The power and captivating nature of fire is as old as humankind and calls out for spiritual reflection.

The Tsuwe'nahi story at first seems to run against the work ethic, the community and biblical value of each person carrying his or her own load. But one can see as it develops that there is something more, something higher at work here. Not unlike the parable of the loving father who accepts the prodigal who has squandered his inheritance, it reminds one that most are like the older brother who works hard and feels put upon by such folk. It challenges one to see that maybe there is spiritual food that is of as much value as physical food. It brings to mind the story of Jesus' visit to the house of Martha, also in a small village. Her sister Mary did not help with the serving and sat at the feet of Jesus, whereupon Martha chastised Jesus, asking if he did not care that she acted this way, leaving the work to her. Jesus' words to Martha are classic and speak to the core of both the Connestee and Tsuwe'nahi stories we have seen: "Martha, Martha, you are anxious and troubled about many things; one thing is needful. Mary has chosen the good portion, which shall not be taken away from her."[21]

Conclusion

This trip into the outer and inner world of the Cherokee has not only given some insight into their history and the ancient wisdom they contribute to all humans, but also has shown the need to keep those rich traditions alive for the great wealth they possess. The myths are psychological and spiritual journeys, metaphorical images about life carried in symbolic language. As noted earlier, dreams, like myths, use symbolic language to express messages from the world of the unconscious, often to give some direction or solution not easily reached in the outer, conscious world. The following dream serves as a metaphor that pulls the themes of the myths together. The context of the dream includes a group of people standing on the porch of history looking out on the following scene:

People watch as a hunt is about to begin, as if it were an English field hunt where the dogs chase an animal. It seems to be a wild boar that they hunt, and an older English gentleman in Wellington boots comes out to explain the hunt; he carries a long stick with a spike in the end to poke the boar, or to keep it in line in case it does not run where he wants it to. One can only watch as the hunt begins. The dogs are huge and vicious, bellowing as they run over the fields. Instead of a boar, two young deer spring forth quite near the observers with the dogs hot in pursuit. They come from the left. Someone says, "Watch them maneuver!" They suddenly split apart with wide arcs to the left and right then turn back toward the middle into a small herd of brown cows grazing in the field to the right. They drop their heads and graze and one observer whispers a prayer their way, "Keep your white tails down!" The dogs are confused and disoriented. They cannot figure where the deer have gone as they blend so well with the domesticated cattle. When they turn back to the left, toward the west, and resume the hunt, the deer look up cautiously and ease toward the woods, then lift their feet into that beautiful leaping dance that only deer can do. With white tails flagging their freedom they flee into their beloved woods.[1]

This metaphorical dream points to the fact that the Cherokee were themselves a hunted people. The literal, official history, including the Trail of Tears, shows the most primitive animal way of handling these natives of America. Those observers on the historical deck watching are shocked and helpless. They watch history unfold before their eyes and can do nothing. And the supposedly "sporting" way of it all makes it like a show, but it is life and death for the hunted, not just some sport. Why a hunting scene? Here is the "meat" of the stories, the focus on core issues raised by the journey. The Cherokee were, of course, hunters of game. Hunting was a common theme in most of the myths: Kana'ti and Selu were the original providers of game and corn; Judac-ulla was the keeper of all game and provided meat for others; the Connestee people were to get enough food in Pilot Knob, as was Tsuwe'-nahi, the "poor-rich" hunter. Spear-finger and Stone Man took advan-tage of hunters and were themselves evil hunters of people. Hunting and being hunted, or surviving, seems to be a major human theme.

Why an English context? Probably because historically, of all the different European settlers, the English had the most influence in the final analysis. The Cherokee sided with the British in the revolution, to their own detriment. The English language became the norm, with all the culture and psychology carried with it. The Englishman in Wellington boots seems to be a symbol for all those early settlers who used power to control both the direction and destiny of the Cherokee. They wear the high boots so as not to get their feet or personhood dirty as they make laws to give them legal justification for immoral deeds, to hunt them down. What an imbalance of power is captured in the symbol of these massive hunting dogs chasing the deer. The "director" makes it appear "proper," legal and acceptable.

Why a boar? He is a wild animal known to be dangerous. For sportsmen he is supposedly a good challenge because he is so danger-ous and will fight when cornered. He lives in the forest, foraging for food, mostly mast. This is the picture so often painted by those who wanted to destroy the Cherokee: "Let us declare them to be danger-ous, primitive and wild." Or: "We should take them out before they attack us." Or: "We are stronger but they might hurt us, so we must destroy them." But the story never lets one see any boar, as if to say it was only a game to justify the hunt. The powerful dogs bellow their cries of battle to seek out those who seem to threaten those in control.

So bellows the cry of racism to demonize and dehumanize those who are different, whose culture does not match one's own, to cover one's own aggression by declaring others to be worse, primitive and even dangerous.

Why two deer? Because the deer is a very spiritual animal and played such a role in all of Cherokee life. It is gentle, not destructive. It can see in the dark, symbolically into the depth of the soul. In a symbolic way these two deer capture much of the Cherokee personality. They are not the wild beasts (i.e. a boar) so portrayed in film, in history or in one's deeper anxiety. It seems that when the deer separate, moving from running parallel into two arcs, the movement captures the forced division into what became the Eastern and Western Bands in North Carolina and Oklahoma. The deer were forced into the maneuver in order to avoid clear destruction by the war dogs on their tail. The arcs are like symbolic shepherd's crooks, those staffs carried by shepherds everywhere to protect and rescue their sheep. This is an image for the Cherokee to protect those in their community. Those arcs or "crooks of salvation" stand in stark contrast to the destructive lance-type spear of the director of the hunt.

Why the cows as refuge? Cows are domesticated, not creatures of the forest. They are docile and productive. Mixing with the "domesticated" neighbors, as well as hiding in the remote mountains and trying to work with the new European system, is what saved the remnant Cherokee that eventually became the Eastern Band. The whispered prayer to be careful not to show that distinctive white tail is a call in essence to cover their rear. There they are, really looking like the cattle. They eat the grass, keeping their heads low as if they were just like everybody else. But the observer knows they are unique, and most of all smarter than their pursuers. They are special creatures of the Creator. They are survivors. They are not cows but truly are deer. But they can blend with the cows. Likewise, the Cherokee are not European settlers and have their own unique identity in spite of the context. They can adapt to the situation, blend with the settlers, a special Cherokee gift historically.

The escape is the call to freedom to escape from the beasts of the past as well as the present and future. That freedom is to keep their unique, ancient traditions and not just European traditions, to adapt to each situation with their unique Creator-given gifts. The dogs and hunter head west, perhaps symbolizing the Trail of Tears, thousands of Cherokee forced to move, with so many dying on the way. At a deeper level it may capture the past, the idea of riding into the sunset and the stereotype of history that the only good Indian is at least to be hunted. Whereas the other direction of the deer is to the East, the place of resurrection, of rising again for freedom. That sense of freedom is also captured by their white flags and leaping.

The deer-with-the-cows portion of the dream is reminiscent of the many gifts of friendship, of trust, of sharing between Appalachian neighbors and the Cherokee over the years. The metaphor is hopeful, optimistic in the escape to a natural element, into the beloved mountains. The mountains and woods are safe.

It was previously noted that one early English map in 1733 described the Appalachian mountains as the Cherokee Mountains. Most of the myths considered carry a deep attachment to this Cherokee homeland: the powerful creation story shows the Great Buzzard's flowing wings touching the earth to make these majestic mountains. The collective community pilgrimage of the Connestee community leads some into the safety of Pilot Knob. Those who finally believe go with the poor-rich hunter, following his individual spiritual pilgrimage into Pilot Knob. And of course the Keeper of the Game, Judaculla, and his wife and family not only reside on top of his Tsunegun'yi, Tanasee Old Fields mountain farm, but keep calling to enter that deeper spiritual mountain where one could hear joyous celebration. And the home of Kana'ti and Selu, the Cherokee equivalent of Adam and Eve, is also Pilot Knob. Almost every major religion has some connection to a holy mountain, some special place where one is closer to the divine. The mountain captures the senses both of height and center. By reaching up, climbing upward, one feels closer to the heavens. Earth and heaven meet. A connection to God is felt.[2]

The stories carry deep wisdom, including psychological, social, spiritual and other dimensions, and this is something the Cherokee can contribute to modern society. The stories are reminders that all of creation carries the beauty of the Creator and that one is to be thankful. In whatever way those first Cherokee heard the missionary story, there are many parallels, especially in the Psalms and other places, where pure thanksgiving is expressed in the context of the ancient Appalachian mountains. There is simply no separation into physical, mental and spiritual in either Judeo-Christian faith traditions or in most Cherokee thinking. This holistic perspective is often lost in the reduction to categorical theological statements, in "head" statements with loss of "heart." (Of course, the other extreme is also possible where only subjective feelings count, no matter what one thinks.)

In reminding others of this holistic approach, traditional Cherokee healer Amy Walker once spoke of their understanding of what we call God. She explained the difficulty in describing the Great Mystery that people call God, noting that many Native Americans do not even have a name for something so huge and so mysterious. Some tribes use "Father" or "Grandfather" and the Cherokee talk about the "Healer," or "Giver of Life," or "the Creator." She said that there are many names trying to describe it but that cannot really do so, as everyone understands.[3]

This Cherokee sense is amazingly close to some of the more personal statements of Dr. C.G. Jung, three of which are simply noted:

• God is a mystery, and everything we say about it is said and believed by human beings. We make images and concepts, and when I speak of God I always mean the image man has made of him. But no one knows what he is like, or he would be a God himself.[4]
• What men have always named God is the unfathomable itself.[5]
• For me "God" is a mystery that cannot be unveiled, and to which I must attribute only one quality: That it exists.[6]

At the core of this wisdom from those ancient Appalachian ancestors one finds not just some unique theological connection, even though there are some parallels to the Judeo-Christian traditions, but rather an issue of a simple, basic connection to the Creator and to Creation itself. In the past, they did not worship animals or trees, but they were deeply connected to all of creation. That connectedness is captured in the sense of thankfulness—for each day, for life, for each being whatever it might be.[7]

This connectedness is captured most clearly in the words of Freeman Owle, a Cherokee story teller, teacher and artist in stone. He says that the Cherokee "secret" is that we are all part of creation. Owle notes that the Cherokee went out to the river early in the morning and would wade into the water waist deep and throw the water over their head and say, "Creator, wash away anything that may hinder me from being closer to you."[8] He declares that the birds by the thousands sing a thank-you for the new day and in the evening the whippoorwill will signify that the new day goes on, and everything is fine, all is good. And with the ending of a new day would always come a new morning or a new beginning. [9]

Owle declares that his people have an ability to feel life in all things around them and that the Creator "is not able to be placed into a small box, or even one church, or into one place, because the Creator was with everybody in all places at all times. Someone said that the Creator is so massive, he's like a circle where the circumference can not be found. And the center is everywhere."[10] Many Cherokee know in their hearts that they are a very special part of the creation.

His final statement sums up the simple, yet profound application of this Cherokee wisdom:

> So when you're able to go out and sit quietly by the streams and listen to the waters, or when you're able to go out ... and listen to the mountains while the wind rushes and roars over the mountaintops, and if you're able to see the first butterfly in the spring, and if you're able to still take your shoes off, and — like you were three years old — stomp in the first puddles of water, then you are showing the gift the Great Spirit had given you as a child. You loved life, you loved the waters, you'd take those shoes off and run in the water and chase the butterflies.... But truly to be Cherokee is to know life itself, and to know all those things that are alive around you.[11]

An old Latin quote that Dr. Jung favored for life and death and for his psychology is amazingly similar to the Cherokee wisdom. It is on the door of his home and on his gravestone in Kuesnacht, Switzerland:

> Called or not called, God is present.[12]

Appendix A: Summary Notes on Dr. C.G. Jung and Analytical Psychology

Adopted from Aniela Jaffé, ed., C.G. Jung: Word and Image

Carl Gustav Jung (1875–1961) was born in a rural Swiss setting to Johann Paul Achilles Jung, a Swiss Reformed pastor, and Emilie Preiswerk Jung. Both grandfathers had been professors of theology at Basel University. C.G. Jung studied medicine and qualified to practice in Basel. Further psychiatric studies were in Zurich with Eugen Bleuler and at the Salpetriere in Paris with Pierre Janet. He married Emma Rauschenbusch, and they had four daughters and one son.

Jung served in various psychiatric staff roles: most clinical positions were in the Burgholzli, the insane asylum of the Canton Zurich, and the psychiatric clinic of the University of Zurich. His early work with Eugen Bleuler was with the association experiment and schizophrenia (then called dementia praecox). Various teaching responsibilities included positions on medical faculties at the universities of Zurich and Basel as well as the Swiss Federal University (ETH).

Correspondence with Sigmund Freud began in 1906 and they first met in Vienna in 1906, talking 13 hours nonstop on topics on depth psychology, dealing with the unconscious. Freud, Jung and Alfred Adler are considered the fathers of depth psychology. Jung was elected the first president of the International Psychoanalytical Association. The dialogue with Freud continued until 1913, at which time differences in approach led to a break. Jung named his approach "Analytical Psychology" (at times "Complex Psychology") to differentiate it from Freud's psychoanalysis.

His world travels for teaching and research included trips to Algeria, Tunisia, Kenya, Uganda, England, India, and various U.S. locations including Clark University, New England, New Mexico (to the Pueblo Indians), and New Orleans among others. Many honorary doctoral degrees were conferred upon him by universities: Oxford, Harvard, ETH (Swiss Federal University), Geneva, and Calcutta.

Jung saw the dynamics of the unconscious differently than did Freud: Life forces are seen as more positive and play a role in healing. Religion is a major positive life force. Myths and fairy tales carry unconscious materials and many common motifs are found in various cultures in all times. Those common universals are called archetypes. Healing and wholeness of the psyche comes through dealing with unconscious materials and in bridging the opposites in life; coming to grips with religious issues and with the transcendent element in life are parts of healing.

Jung's psychology sees two attitude orientations: extraversion and introversion. There are four functions of the conscious world, two for perceiving the world or taking in information (sensing and intuiting) and two for judging or deciding on the information (thinking and feeling). His own perception of his work was that he was a radical empiricist, that is, he observed phenomena and reported on that. The world of the unconscious was his field of concern. It contains a vast amount of material, including both our personal unconscious and the very deep collective unconscious. His work focused on complexes and the shadow. The language of the unconscious is symbolic; and dreams, art and other expressions of the unconscious give pathways to reach their meaning.

Other terms and concepts used by Jung include alchemy, anima and animus, Self, persona, numinosum, synchronicity, soul, evil, and individuation. The goal of therapy is the individuation of the person, a process of working toward the whole, integrated personality by establishing a functioning relationship between the Ego (the center of the conscious personality) and the Self (the center of the whole personality, including the unconscious). His approach is synthetic and teleological in emphasis in contrast to causal and reductive. Wholeness is the goal, not perfection.

QUOTATIONS FROM C.G. JUNG, AS CITED IN JAFFÉ

1. "Here we must follow nature as a guide, and what the doctor then does is less a question of treatment than of developing the creative possibilities latent within the patient himself" (Jaffé 115).

2. "No matter what the world thinks about religious experience, the one who has it possesses a great treasure, a thing that has become for him a source of life, meaning and beauty, and that has given a new splendor to the world and to mankind. He has *pistis* and peace" (Jaffé 209).

3. "I don't overlook God's fearful greatness, but I should consider myself a coward and immoral if I allowed myself to be deterred from asking questions" (Jaffé 209).

4. "What men have always named God is the unfathomable itself" (Jaffé 209).

5. "God is a mystery, and everything we say about it is said and believed by human beings. We make images and concepts, and when I speak of God I always mean the image man had made of him. But no one knows what he is like, or he would be a god himself" (Jaffé 209).

6. "I thank God every day that I have been permitted to experience the reality of the *imago Dei* in me. Had that not been so, I would be a bitter enemy of Christianity and of the Church in particular. Thanks to this *actus gratiae* my life has meaning, and my inner eye was opened to the beauty and grandeur of dogma" (Jaffé 209).

7. "Life, so called, is a short episode between two great mysteries, which yet are one" (Jaffé 213).

Aniela Jaffé, ed., *C.G. Jung: Word and Image* (Princeton: Princeton University Press, Bollingen Series XCVII:2, 1979), 209 ff. Used with permission of Princeton University Press.

Appendix B: Wahnenauhi Version of Kana'ti and Selu

After the world had been brought up from under the water, "they then made a man and a woman and let them around the edge of the island. On arriving at the starting place they planted some corn, and then told the man and woman to go around the way they had been led. This they did, and on returning they found the corn up and growing nicely. They were then told to continue the circuit. Each trip consumed more time. At last the corn was ripe and ready for use."

Another story is told of how sin came into the world. A man and woman reared a large family of children in comfort and plenty, with very little trouble about providing food for them. Every morning the father went forth and very soon returned bringing with him a deer, or a turkey, or some other animal or fowl. At the same time the mother went out and soon returned with a large basket filled with ears of corn which she shelled and pounded in a mortar, thus making meal for bread.

When the children grew up, seeing with what apparent ease food was provided for them, they talked to each other about it, wondering that they never saw such things as their parents brought in. At last one proposed to watch their parents went out and to follow them. Accordingly, next morning the plan was carried out. Those who followed the father saw him stop at a short distance from the cabin and turn over a large stone that appeared to be carelessly leaned against another. On looking closely they saw an entrance to a large cave, and in it were many different kinds of animals and birds, such as their father had sometimes brought in for food. The man standing at the entrance called a deer, which was lying at some distance and back of some other animals. It rose immediately as it heard the call and came close up to him.

He picked it up, closed the mouth of the cave, and returned, not once seeming to suspect what his sons had done.

When the old man was fairly out of sight, his sons, rejoicing how they had outwitted him, left their hiding place and went to the cave, saying they would show the old folks that they, too, could bring in something. They moved the stone away, though it was very heavy and they were obliged to use all their united strength. When the cave was opened, the animals, instead of waiting to be picked up, all made a rush for the entrance, and leaping past the frightened and bewildered boys, scattered in all directions and disappeared in the wilderness, while the guilty offenders could do nothing but gaze in stupefied amazement as they saw them escape. There were animals of all kinds, large and small — buffalo, deer, elk, antelope, raccoons, and squirrels; even catamounts and panthers, wolves and foxes, and many others, all fleeing together. At the same time birds of every kind were seen emerging from the opening, all in the same wild confusion as the quadrupeds— turkeys, geese, swans, ducks, quails, eagles, hawks, and owls. Those who followed the mother saw her enter a small cabin that they had never seen before, and close the door. The culprits found a small crack through which they could peer. They saw the woman place a basket on the ground and standing over it, shake herself vigorously, jumping up and down, and lo and behold! Large ears of corn began to fall into the basket. When it was well filled she took it up and, placing it on her head, came out, fastened the door, and prepared their breakfast as usual. When the meal had been finished in silence the man spoke to his children, telling them that he was aware of what they had done; that now he must die and they would be obliged to provide for themselves. He made bows and arrows for them, then sent them to hunt for the animals which they had turned loose.

Then the mother told them that as they had found out her secret she could do nothing more for them; that she would die, and they must drag her body around over the ground; that wherever her body was dragged corn would come up. Of this they were to make their bread. She told them that they must always save some for seed and plant every year.[1]

Appendix C:
The Hunter and Selu

A hunter had been tramping over the mountains without finding any game, and when the sun went down he built a fire in a hollow stump, swallowed a few mouthfuls of corn gruel and lay down to sleep, tired and completely discouraged. About the middle of the night he dreamed and seemed to hear the sound of beautiful singing, which continued until near daybreak and then appeared to die away into the upper air.

All next day he hunted with the same poor success, and at night made his lonely camp in the woods. He slept and the strange dream came to him again, but so vividly that it seemed like an actual happening. Rousing himself before daylight, he still heard the song, and feeling sure now that it was real, he went in the direction of the sound and found that it came from a single stalk of green corn (selu). The plant spoke to him, and told him to cut off some of its roots and take them to his home in the settlement, and the next morning to chew them and to "go to water" before anyone else was awake, and then to go out again into the woods, and he would kill many deer and from that time on would always be successful in the hunt. The corn plant continued to talk, teaching him hunting secrets and telling him always to be generous with the game he took, until it was noon and the sun was high, when it suddenly took the form of a woman and rose gracefully into the air and was gone from sight, leaving the hunter alone in the woods.

He returned home and told his story, and all the people knew that he had seen Selu, wife of Kana'ti. He did as the spirit had directed, and from that time was noted as the most successful of all the hunters in the settlement.[1]

Appendix D: Judaculla's Judgment Seat Citation Giving the Popular Name of "Devil's Courthouse"

The following text from a popular book in sensational tabloid style was often used in the late 1800s as the authority for naming the peak associated with Judaculla. The so-called Devil's Courthouse forms a triangle with nearby Pilot Knob and Judaculla Old Fields, also related to Cherokee myths.

The Balsams are rich in legendary superstitions. The gloom of their dark solitude fills even the hurried tourist with an unaccountable fear, and makes it impossible to suppress the recollection of tales of ghosts and goblins upon which his childish imagination was fed. The mountains assume mysterious shapes, projecting rocks seem to stand beckoning; and the echo of cascades falls upon the ear like ominous warnings. No wonder then, that it was a region peopled by pagan superstitions, with other spirits than human. It is the instinct of the human mind, no matter what may be its degree of cultivation, to seek an explanation of things. When natural causes cannot be discovered for the phenomena of nature, the supernatural is drawn upon. The Cherokees knew no natural reason why the tops of high mountains should be treeless, but having faith in a natural devil they jumped to the conclusion that the "bald" spots must be the prints of his horrid feet as he walked with giant strides from peak to peak.

Near the great divide, between the waters of the Pigeon River and French Broad, is situated the Devil's Court-house, which rises to an altitude of 6,049 feet. Near it is Court-house mountain. At both places his Satanic majesty was believed to sit in judgment, and doom to punishment all who had been wayward in courage, or had departed from a strict code of virtue, though bravery in war atoned for a multitude of sins.[1]

Appendix E: "A Small Postscript of the ways and maners of the Indians called Charikees" by Alexander Long

David H. Corkran, editor of an article in the journal entitled *Southern Indian Studies*,[1] wrote: "Alexander Long's "A Small Postscript of the ways and maners of the Indians called Charikees" is one of the more quaint and engaging accounts of an American Indian tribe and is the earliest extant description of the Cherokee social and religious pattern. Written in 1725, it is the work of a man who knew the Cherokees well; for Long had been trading in the Cherokee country since before 1710, had been used by the South Carolina officials as an interpreter in meeting with Cherokees, and then had lived ten years as an exile among the Cherokees."

The long manuscript was originally in the files of the British Society for the Propagation of the Gospel in Foreign Parts. Photostats of the original were provided by the U.S. Library of Congress both to Corkran and to this author; the latter are in the archives of the Museum of the Cherokee Indian, Cherokee, N.C. The original text is difficult to read. David H. Corkran has produced a more readable modernized rendition, a small part of which is used here with permission. The part chosen is another tale of a disappearing town; this one is called "Agustoghe." Its people find refuge as in the Kana'sta story, and its images very much like the Judaculla story as well as the poor-rich hunter tale.

THEIR NOTION OF ENCHANTMENTS

I being in conversation with the priest at another time he told me as followeth: There was a town of our nation formerly called Agustoghe

191

wherein there was above 400 souls men, women, and children. There was one of the beloved senators who was a very wise man. This man fasted 4 days without eating anything. The fourth day he went out of the town and stayed 4 days more and then comes home the fifth day at night and comes into the temple and tells all the people to assemble in the temple. When they were all assembled in the temple, he stood up and said, My beloved townspeople I have been absent this 4 days from you and has been in one of the finest places that is not known to any in this world. All things come naturally without any trouble. The people never die there nor never grow old like but are always in the same as they were when they entered that country. There are all sorts of merry making there. The light never fails. In the midst of winter there is green corn. There is but all sorts that can be imagined; therefore all of you that will be councilled and ruled by me come join with me in fasting 4 days both young and old and be sure that you eat nothing whatsoever in that space; for if you do you will not be able to follow me. The fourth day at night you shall see plainly see that I do not impose on you for you shall see what a vast quantity of victuals shall be brought into this temple by these people. You see this great turn pool [whirlpool] in the river where you have brought water and drank thereof these many days. You think that it is a river; but I know to the contrary. It is one of the finest towns that I ever saw and speaks Cherokee as we do. You cannot see them although I do now, and here be some of them sitting by me now at this present. The whole town consented to obey his orders and began the fast. The fourth day at night this beloved man went out at sun setting and after daylight closed in he came and set up the warwhoop, and immediately all the town young and old was assembled in the temple. He went in and told them to put out all the lights in the temple. When so done there comes a troop of women with all sorts of victuals as green corn, pumpkin, water and muskmelons and turkey, deer, bear, and buffalo meat. This was in the middle of winter that this green provisions was produced although the Cherokee nation is rather colder than England. All that was in the house could hear the women laughing and speaking in their own language but could not see them as yet. As soon as this wise man told them they struck up a light.

When so done, they found the temple floor and empty cabins all covered with earthen pans of victuals above men's hand and the headman eat thereof first and then all the other people young and old. When so done the pans were swept away by invisible hands. When so done the wise man told one of the people to play the drum which is the music that they dance to.

When so done he takes the drum and gets up and said as followed: All you that has fasted the 4 days, viz., you that are able to go with me but you that has eaten anything are not able to go with me. Now is the time. Come follow me all of you. He went on before them beating the drum till he come to the turn pool. When he come to the water side, all those that had not eat anything in the 4 days went in after him; but those that had eaten anything was stopped by a rule of wood that passed before their breast that hindered them to advance. They say that the number that was forbid was not above 16 or 20 at the most. All the rest followed the wise man into the enchantment. The news of this came to the other towns. All the headmen of the nation assembled and came to that town and examined the matter of them that could not follow the others, who gave them this relation. They sent away them that were left into other towns and left the town a standing as it was with the provisions and all. They would not eat anything in the town counting it dreadful. This happened about 10 years before the English were amongst them. Now to fortify you of this, said the priest, if you will go there you will see the pillars of the temple and posts of the houses standing at this very day; and always when we go up and down that river and come nigh that pool, we hear those people hallowing and whooping and dancing and the drum beating. I'll show you three white men that was with me and can prove what I say to be true. They heard it as well as I. As he was speaking these words in comes James Douglas asked me what it was. I told him, who made me this answer: I'll take my oath of it. I was with him. Not I alone, but Johnson's son and John Roe, all three of us heard what he hath told you and he told me the whole circumstance as he hath told you. The old priest spoke to me and said, are you persuaded now that what I have told you is true? I told him, yes, but that I believed that it was the devil that beguiled them. The priest replied that he thought the same. But let it be what it will they have got them so fast that they are lost forever. I believe they rue their change. You may hear us in all our speeches speak of that town and forewarn our people [not] to have any such thought as these people had. Yet I think they live a merry life; for go there when we will hear them singing and dancing. I passed a joke on the priest and said: You would to [do] well to fast 4 days and go to that place and stay there for some small time to see how things goes with them and come and bring us word and be sure that you look our all over their town and see if they have got a good quantity of deer skins. I'll go and buy them of these people. The priest said I'll take care that I'll not fast nor go there; for if I do, they'll not let me come back with news to you. I'll have nothing to do with them. I never had any thought to try any such project nor I never shall.[2]

Chapter Notes

INTRODUCTION

1. William G. McLoughlin, *Cherokees and Missionaries, 1789–1839* (Normal and London: University of Oklahoma Press, 1995), 12.

2. Winthrop D. Jordan, *White over Black* (Baltimore: Penguin, 1969), 453. Cited by McLoughlin, *Cherokees*, 40.

3. Andrew Jackson, "Message to Congress, December 3, 1833," Congressional Serial Set, House Executive documents, 23rd Congress, 1st session, vol. 254, 1833, doc. #1, p. 14. Cited by McLoughlin, *Cherokees*, 4.

4. John Ross, "Memorial of the Cherokee Representatives, submitting the protest of the Cherokee nation against the ratification, execution and enforcement of the treaty negotiated at New Echota, in December, 1835, 24th Congress, 1st Session, Document Number 286, House of Representatives, June 22, 1836, 2. This document may be found at the Museum of the Cherokee Indian Archives, Cherokee, N.C.

5. *Ibid.*, 15.

6. Stephen Trimble, *The People: Indians of the American Southwest* (Santa Fe: School of American Research, 1993), xi.

7. James Mooney, *Myths of the Cherokee and The Sacred Formulas of the Cherokees*, from the 19th and 7th Annual Reports, Bureau of American Ethnology (Washington, D.C.: U.S. Government Printing Office, 1900, 1891). Reprinted as *James Mooney's History, Myths, and Sacred Formulas of the Cherokees* (Asheville, N.C.: Historical Images, 1992). Hereafter cited as Mooney, *Cherokee.*

8. *Ibid.*

9. Brett H. Riggs, M. Scott Shumate, Patti Evans-Shumate and Brad Owen, "An Archeological Survey of the Ferguson Farm, Swain County, North Carolina" (Boone, N.C.: Blue Ridge Cultural Resources, July 31, 1998), 3.13.

10. "Kituwah Archeology Reveals Significant Finds," *The Cherokee One Feather*, vol. 36 (Wednesday, May 23, 2001) p. 1.

11. C.G. Jung, *The Collected Works of C.G. Jung*, 2nd ed., trans. R.F.C. Hull (London: Routledge and Kegan Paul, 1979), volume 8, paragraph 336. Hereafter cited as *CW* with volume and paragraph numbers following immediately.

12. Bill Moyers, introduction to Joseph Campbell and Bill Moyers, *The Power of Myth* (New York: Doubleday, 1998), xiv.

13. C.G. Jung, *CW* 6: 193.

14. C.G. Jung, *CW* 9i: 271.

15. See Gerald Keith Parker, "Folk Religion in Southern Appalachia" (unpublished Ph.D. dissertation, Louisville, Kentucky: The Southern Baptist Theological Seminary, January 1970), 247.

16. "Indian Country," *National Geographic* 206, no. 3 (September 2004), National Geographic Map Supplement.

17. C.G. Jung, *CW* 10: 967.

18. C.G. Jung, *CW* 10: 968.

19. C.G. Jung, *CW* 10: 970.

20. Mooney, *Cherokee*, 229 ff. Jack F. Kilpatrick and Anna G. Kilpatrick have collected similar stories in Oklahoma, translating them from older Cherokee-speaking story tellers. Many animal stories are told and the ones presented in this work take on forms modified from the older Mooney collection. Jack F. Kilpatrick and Anna G. Kilpatrick, *Friends of Thunder: Folktales of the Oklahoma Cherokee* (Norman and London: University of Oklahoma Press, 1995).

21. 1 Tim. 4:7.

22. Jn. 3:3 ff; C.G. Jung, *CW* 5:333 ff.

23. Richard Cavendish, ed., *Mythology: An Illustrated Encyclopedia* (New York: Barnes and Noble, 1992), 10–11.

24. Marie-Louise von Franz, *Problems of the Feminine in Fairy Tales* (Dallas: Spring Publications, Inc., 1992) 4.

25. C.G. Jung, *CW* 9i: 261.

26. C.G. Jung, *Jung Speaking* (Princeton: Princeton University Press, 1977), 370–71. Cited by Robert A. Segal, *Jung on Mythology* (London: Routledge, 1998), 107.

27. C.G. Jung, *CW* 9i: 261.

28. Raymond D. Fogelson, "Cherokee Little People Re-considered," *Journal of Cherokee Studies*, fall 1982, 96. Cf. Mooney, *Cherokee*, 345–347. The Norwegian stories of trolls were greatly influenced by the fearful paintings of Theodor Kittelsen (1857–1914), who also influenced the writings of Tolkien and subsequent movies of the *Lord of the Rings*. More recent Norwegian writers show some trolls as good, some bad and not all so dumb. Close to animals and sometime helpers, they are similar to the Cherokee little people.

29. Some of those stories are told by Cherokee artist and author Lynn King Lossiah in her illustrated children's book (also for interested adults) about the Little People. Lynn King Lossiah, *The Secrets and Mysteries of the Cherokee Little People, Yun'wi Tsunsdi'* (Cherokee, N.C.: Cherokee Publications, 1998). It should also be noted that in Indonesia, where stories of "Little People" have persisted, recent archeological discoveries have discovered early humans, named Homo floresiensis, who were just three and one half feet tall. These Hobbit-like people coexisted with Homo sapiens and died out about 13,000 years ago, according to the releases. *The Week* 4, no. 182 (November 12, 2004), 24.

30. James Adair, *Out of the Flame: Cherokee Beliefs and Practices of the Ancients*, reprint ed. by William H. Robinson (Tulsa, Oklahoma: Cherokee Language and Culture, 1998). Originally published in London, 1775, as *History of the American Indians*; reprint cited above was used.

31. Samuel Cole Williams, introduction to Adair, *Out of the Flame*, xxix.

32. *Ibid.*, xxx.

33. McLoughlin, *Cherokees and Missionaries*, 8.

34. *Ibid.*

35. *Ibid.*

36. See Theda Perdue, *Cherokee Women: Gender and Culture Change, 1700–1835* (Lincoln and London: University of Nebraska Press, 1998) 159 ff.

37. McLoughlin, *Cherokees and Missionaries*, 8.

38. *Ibid.* Rennard Stricklend, a lawyer of Cherokee and Osage descent and dean of the law school of the University of Oregon at Eugene, documents the development of Cherokee law from a clan system into an Indian version of Anglo-American law. Rennard Strickland, *Fire and the Spirits: Cherokee Law from Clan to Court* (Norman: University of Oklahoma Press, 1975).

39. McLoughlin, *Cherokees and Missionaries*, 8.

40. Mooney, *Cherokees*, 392. Popular author and illustrator Thomas E. Mails has attempted to portray earlier Cherokee culture and religion, showing the role of powerful priests who were gone before the arrival of Europeans. Mooney (*Cherokee*, 393) uses older documents to cite the existence of the Ani-Kuta'ni, a hereditary priestly class who apparently abused the power and privilege when they "became haughty, insolent, overbearing and licentious to an intolerable degree." Why and how the priests disappeared is a subject of much scholarly debate and beyond the scope of this work. At least one Cherokee writer, Robert J. Conley, has woven some theory into a novel. See Thomas E. Mails, *The Cherokee People: The Story of the Cherokees from Earliest Origins to Contemporary Times* (Tulsa, Oklahoma: Council Oak Books, 1992) and Robert J. Conley, *The Way of the Priests* (New York: Doubleday, 1992).

41. McLoughlin, *Cherokees and Missionaries*, 8.

42. *Ibid.*, 10.

43. Walker Calhoun, interview with author, March 17, 2001, Cherokee, N.C. In context, Walker indicated that he had never heard of the dances being "religious" until the preachers said so in very harsh ways. His gentle, soft way of expression underlined his lack of understanding of why they were so harsh in judgment. In fact, he wondered, did they really agree with their own religion, which taught "Ye shall not judge?" He expressed sorrow for those who could not accept some other cultural manifestations.

44. Elias Boudinot, *An Address to the Whites, delivered in the First Presbyterian Church, on the 26th of May, 1836* (Philadelphia: William G. Geddes, 1836), 73, in

Theda Perdue, ed., *Cherokee Editor: The Writings of Elias Boudinot* (Athens and London: University of Georgia Press, 1983; reprint, Brown Thrasher, 1996). This quote, among others, reflects the strong, formal Christian education of Boudinot who became increasingly separated from many Cherokee in his eventual support of removal as the only means to survive what he saw as eventual destruction by the army. Many traditional Cherokee would not have agreed with his idealization, which was clearly to speak a language of the Christian whites in hopes of saving the Cherokee.

45. Rev. Robert Bushyhead, interview with author, June 27, 1998, Cherokee, North Carolina.

46. Rev. Jesse Busheyhead was the great-grandfather of the Reverend Robert Bushyhead who assisted in this writing. (The original spelling was later changed to Bushyhead).

CHAPTER 1

1. Marie-Louise von Franz, *Patterns of Creativity: Creation Myths* (Dallas, Texas: Spring Publications, Inc., 1972), 5.

2. *Ibid.*

3. *Ibid.*

4. *Ibid.*, 6.

5. *Ibid.*, 8.

6. B. Lynne Harlan, "Where It All Began: Cherokee Creation Stories in Art," in *Where It All Began: Cherokee Stories in Art*, ed. Barbara R. Duncan (Cherokee: The Museum of the Cherokee Indian, 2001), 9–10.

7. Bushyhead, interview with author, June 27, 1998.

8. Mooney reports that the buzzard story is also part of the genesis myth of the Creeks and Yuchi, southern neighbors of the Cherokee. Mooney, *Cherokees*, 430.

9. *Ibid.*

10. *Ibid.*, 431.

11. *Ibid.*, 431.

12. William G. McLoughlin, *Champions of the Cherokees: Evan and John B. Jones* (Princeton, N.J.: Princeton University Press, 1990), 88. Most, if not all, Asian traditions have special water rites.

13. C.G. Jung, *CW* 7:103n.

14. Gen 1:3–4.

15. Gen 1:26 ff.

16. Matt. 4:19.

17. Luke 24:42.

18. Luke 9:13 ff.

19. Jon. 1:17 ff.

20. The word swastika comes from Sanskrit, and has to do with well-being, as in a benediction. Ancient in usage, the form made with extensions bent in a clockwise direction was adopted as the symbol for the party emblem in Nazi Germany, thus giving it a very negative racist image for most modern peoples. *Webster's New Twentieth Century Dictionary of the English Language, Unabridged,* 2nd ed. (New York: The World Publishing Company, 1970), 1841.

21. Gen. 1:31.

22. Walker Calhoun, interview with author, March 17, 2001.

CHAPTER 2

1. Mooney, *Cherokee*, 431.

2. Mails, *Cherokee People*, 157.

3. Ad de Vries, *Dictionary of Symbols and Imagery* (Amsterdam and London: North Holland Publishing Company, 1984), 187.

4. *CW* 9i; 627ff, *CW* 12:122ff. Jung actually defined the Self as both the center and totality of the personality or psyche. The central nature of Self in human personality is why it is capitalized in Jungian circles to distinguish it from other uses of the word self.

5. The second death is seen as a lake of fire in Rev. 20:14. Matt. 5:22 speaks of the lake of fire. And there are three men cast into a fire but not consumed in Dan. 3:24, ff.

6. Exod. 13:21; Isa. 10:17.

7. Exod. 3:2.

8. Exod. 40:38.

9. Jer. 23:29.

10. Mark 9:2.

11. Luke 22:55; Acts 28:2.

12. Rev. 3:15.

CHAPTER 3

1. A wild child born of blood drops is also found in other tribes, such as the Creek, Dakota and Omaha, according to Mooney, *Cherokees*, 431.

2. Mooney, *Cherokees*, 432–433.

3. C.T. Onions, ed., *The Oxford Dictionary of English Etymology* Oxford: At the Clarendon Press, 1966–1991, 740.

4. Lynn Lossiah, interview with author, Cherokee, N.C. January 4, 2005: Gregg Galloway, Ph.D., botanist, interview with author; and Jack Galloway, agriculturalist, in-

terview with author, Cullowhee, N.C. January 4, 2005.

5. Mooney, *Cherokees,* 420 ff. Selu is a strong presence in many forms of Cherokee art. Marilou Awiakta, a Cherokee-Appalachian writer, portrays Selu as a living spirit for Native Americans, a key to finding balance in persons and in the world, especially between the modern technological age and the ancient wisdom. Marilou Awaikta, *Selu: Seeking the Corn Mother's Wisdom* (Golden, Colo: Fulcrum Publishing, 1993).

6. Mooney, *Cherokees,* 434

7. Sometimes the Little People are called Thunderers for small rumbles of thunder, especially when they toss rocks down the mountain as in the Connestee story. At other times the Great Thunderer who brings the mighty storms such as hurricanes would be none other than Kana'ti. See Mooney, *Cherokees,* 435.

8. Mooney, *Cherokees,* 435.

9. Gen. 3:5.

10. Mooney, *Cherokees,* 248 ff. and 431.

11. Mark 3:17.

12. De Vries, *Dictionary of Symbols and Imagery,* 357.

CHAPTER 4

1. Perdue, *Cherokee Women,* 182. See also Strickland, *Fire and the Spirits,* 183ff.

2. Mails, *The Cherokee People,* 121. Chapter 1 notes the disappearance of the priestly order. In modern times some of those functions are assumed by healers or those practicing traditional medicine.

3. C.G. Jung, *CW* 10:846.

4. Mooney, *Cherokees,* 469.

5. Perdue, *Cherokee Women,* 4. Some Cherokee women, and others, have noted to this author how this is close to PMS.

6. *Ibid.*

7. Mooney, *Cherokees,* 469.

8. *Ibid.*

9. Deuto 15:7; Ps. 95:8; Mark 8:17; II Cor. 3:14, etc.

10. Matt. 10:16.

11. Gen. 2:9; 6:5; 8:21; Job 28:28; Amos 5:15; Matt. 6:13; Luke 11:13; Rom. 12:9; Heb. 5:14, among others.

12. Exod. 31:18; Luke 11:20.

13. John 8:6; 20:27.

14. 1 John 1:7; Rev. 7:14; Heb. 9:14; Rom. 5:9; 1 Cor. 11:25, among others.

15. Ex 12:13.

CHAPTER 5

1. Rev. Robert Bushyhead, interview with author.

2. Mooney, *Cherokees,* 335.

3. Rev. Robert Bushyhead, interview with author.

4. Jean Chavalier and Alain Gheerbrant, *The Penguin Dictionary of Symbols,* trans. John Buchannan-Brown, (1969; reprint, London: Penguin, 1996), 431.

5. "Intrigue of the Past: Lesson 5.2, Interpretation of Judaculla Rock," University of North Carolina, <http://rlas.unc.edu/Lesson/L502/H502b.htm>, January 24, 2005.

6. Mooney, *Cherokees,* 250, 435. For many years the U.S. Park Service used a wording from the writing of Ziegler and Grosscup for the official sign about the so-called Devil's Courthouse. Only after a plea in the 1990s from the Tribal Council in Cherokee was reference made to Judaculla. Wilbur G. Ziegler and Ben S. Grosscup, *The Heart of the Alleghanies or Western North Carolina* (Raleigh, 1883). Appendix D gives an excerpt from this work from which the "Devil's Courthouse" name was developed.

7. Chavalier and Gheerbrant, *Penguin,* 431.

8. von Franz, *Problems of the Feminine in Fairy Tales,* 153.

9. Mooney, *Cherokees,* 480.

10. Matt. 20:22.

11. Exod. 20:12, Ps. 146:9, I Tim. 5:5, Acts 6:1.

12. I Tim. 5:8.

13. Gen. 6:4.

14. Matt 6:22.

15. Job 31:1.

16. Ps. 121:1.

17. Ps. 149:3, Ecc. 3:4.

18. Luke 15:22–25.

19. Eph. 6:11.

20. Matt 6:25ff.

21. 1 John 4:18. Oskar Pfister, pioneer Swiss psychoanalyst, Reformed pastor and close friend of Sigmund Freud, built much of his psychology and treatment on this verse and the principle that anxiety and fear are at the core of mental illness. Oskar Pfister, *Das Christentum und die Angst: Eine religionspsychologische, historische und religionshygenische Untersuchung* (Zurich: Artemis, 1944).

CHAPTER 6

1. William L. McDowell, Jr., ed., *Documents Relating to Indian Affairs, May 21, 1750–August 7, 1754* (Columbia, S.C.: Archives Department, 1958), 86; George Chicken, Sr. "Travels to the Cherokee, 1725," in *Travels in the American Colonies, 1690–1783*, ed. Newton D. Mereness (New York: Macmillan Co., 1916); Mooney, *Cherokee*, 33.

2. Mary Jane McCrary, *Transylvania Beginnings: A History* (Easley, S.C.: Southern Historical Press, Inc., 1984), 7, citing Jones.

3. Selica is a Cherokee name for "sparkling waters" given by an Indian living nearby, according to McCrary, 8.

4. Joffre L. Coe, secretary of the Archeological Society of Brevard College, "Open Letter to the Citizens of the County" dated spring 1935, cited in *The Transylvania Times* (Brevard, N.C.), Monday, June 4, 1988, 7A.

5. Pat Holden, interview with author Rosman, N.C., April 1, 2000. A more recent archeological survey was done by Ruth Wetmore; "Transylvania County Survey" (unpublished, 1993).

6. H. Trawick Ward and R.P. Stephen Davis, Jr., eds., *Time Before History; The Archeology of North Carolina* (Chapel Hill and London: The University of North Carolina Press, 1999), 140, 141.

7. Holden interview.

8. Bushyhead interview.

9. In Judges 12:5 ff the story goes, in part: "And when any of the fugitives of Ephraim said, 'Let me go over' the men of Gilead said to him, 'Are you an Ephraimite?' When he said 'No,' they said to him, 'Then say Shibboleth,' and he said 'Sibboleth,' for he could not pronounce it right; then they seized him and slew him at the fords of the Jordan." Thus the term "Shibboleth" has come to represent a password or control word to check out another person.

10. Mooney, *Cherokee*, 480.

11. A copy of the original was graciously provided by the Library of Congress, Manuscript Division, and is now on file in the archives of Museum of the Cherokee Indian, Cherokee, N.C. Long's name is spelled Longe in some places.

12. David H. Corkran, Introduction to *Southern Indian Studies*, XXI, October 1969, p. 4. Appendix E gives the modern version of the text as prepared by David H. Corkran.

13. Luke 14:18.
14. Acts 13.
15. Luke 2:37.
16. Heb. 12:16.
17. Heb. 12:16.
18. Luke 15:11 ff.
19. II Sam. 22:02.
20. Ps. 19:14.
21. Ps. 31:2.
22. Isa. 26:4.
23. I Cor. 19:4.
24. Fanny J. Crosby, "Hide Thou Me," based on Ps. 32:7, and Rev. A.M. Toplady, "Rock of Ages," based on Ps. 94:22.
25. Matt. 27:60.

CHAPTER 7

1. Mooney, *Cherokees*, 540.

2. *Ibid.*, 481.

3. Jean Bushyhead, correspondence with author, February 18, 2005; and telephone conversation with author February 23, 2005.

4. Strickland, *Fire and the Spirits*, 13.

5. *Ibid.*, 12.

6. John Haywood, *The Natural and Aboriginal History of Tennessee* (Nashville: George Wilson, 1828), 246, cited by Strickland, 12, 21.

7. Quintin Ellison and Jeffrey Cantrell, "Potter awarded tribe's highest honor," *The Asheville Citizen-Times*, Friday, December 7, 2001, B1, 5.

8. Scott McKie, "Eternal Flame Rededicated at Mountainside Theatre," *The Cherokee One Feather* 36, no. 26 (Wednesday, July 4, 2001), 1.

9. Jung, CW 5:356, 480; 7:128.

10. James Mooney, *The Ghost Dance* (1896; reprint, North Dighton, Mass.: J.G. Press, 1996), 16.

11. Mooney, *Cherokees*, 481.

12. Geneva S. Jackson, interview with author, Cherokee, N.C., September 30, 2002. In context, "Mama Gene" said that when a midwife is "catching" the new baby as it is being born, there is that moment when "you feel the presence of the Great Spirit just behind you, looking over your shoulder, deciding to give the breath of life to that child."

13. 2 Thess. 3:10b.
14. 2 Cor. 12:7.

15. Exod. 13:21.
16. Isa. 10:17.
17. Isa. 66:15.
18. Acts 2:3.
19. Matt. 3:11.
20. Mark 14:54.
21. Luke 10:41–42.

CONCLUSION

1. Dream of author, Brasstown, Chero-kee County, N.C., January 22, 2002, after time with Glenn Rogers, member of Eastern Band of Cherokee Indians.
2. Hebrew and Christian scriptures use the mountain as a powerful symbol for a place of safety, of refuge (Ps. 30:7, Ps. 36:7, etc.) Even references to hopeful, almost paradise-like states for eternity give that sense of security, always associated with God (Ps. 48, Isa. 14:12 ff etc.). Prophets get their revelations on mountains. Of course, the Sermon on the Mount with crucial teachings of Jesus has been connected to the Mount Sinai experience of Moses. In addition, the Transfiguration of Christ was on a high mountain (Mark 9:2). To go into the mountain is to center oneself, to be tied both to earth and heaven, to find peace. The powerful Psalm 48 captures this spiritual symbolism of the mountain and perhaps could have been uttered by one of the Chero-kee elders long ago, with different terms: Great is the Lord, and greatly to be praised in the city of our God. His Holy mountain, beautiful in elevation is the joy of all the earth, Mount Zion, in the far north, the city of the great King, in the mountain of his holiness. Within her citadels God has shown himself a sure defense.... We have thought on thy steadfast love, O God, in the midst of thy temple. As they name, so thy praise reaches to the ends of the earth (Ps. 48 ff, RSV). These are only a few of the many biblical examples of the symbolism of mountains. Not all are good, for being so filled with holy and spiritual possibilities meant that they were also places where pride and destructiveness could arise. There humans would build idols and be filled with egotism and not worship God but rather themselves. Cf. Chevalier and Gheerbrant, *Symbols*, 682 ff.

3. Amy Walker, interview with author, Cherokee, N.C., June 27, 1998.
4. C.G. Jung, "Letter 17 August, 1957," in Aniela Jaffé, ed. *C.G. Jung: Word and Image* (Princeton: Princeton University Press, 1979), 209.
5. C.G. Jung, "Letter 12 June 1933," *C.G. Jung Word and Image*, 209.
6. C. G. Jung, "Letter 23 May 1955," *C. G. Jung Word and Image*, 209
7. Freeman Owle, interview with author, Waynesville, N.C., February 18, 2005.
8. *Ibid.*
9. *Ibid.*
10. *Ibid.*
11. *Ibid.*
12. "Vocatus atque non vocatus deus aderit" (author's translation). C.G. Jung, *Word and Image*, 217.

APPENDIX B

1. Mooney, *Cherokees*, 248–431.

APPENDIX C

1. Mooney, *Cherokees*, 323–324.

APPENDIX D

1. Wilbur G. Ziegler and Ben S. Grosscup, *The Heart of the Alleghanies or Western North Carolina* (Raleigh, N.C.: Alfred Williams and Company and Cleveland, Ohio: William W. Williams, 1883).

APPENDIX E

1. Corkran, introduction, 3.
2. Alexander Long, "A Small Postscript on the ways and manners of the Indians called Cherokees, the contents of the whole so that you may find everything by the pages," 1775; modern version edited by David H. Corkran, *Southern Indian Studies* XXI (October, 1969), 40–44. Courtesy of the North Carolina Archeological Society.

Selected Bibliography

Adair, James. *Out of the Flame. Cherokee Beliefs and Practices of the Ancients.* Ed. William H. Robinson. London: n.p., 1775. Reprint, Tulsa, Ok.: Cherokee Language and Culture, 1998.

The Archive for Research in Archetypal Symbolism. Moon, Beverly, ed. *An Encyclopedia of Archetypal Symbolism.* Boston and London: Shambhala , 1991.

Awiakta, Marilou. *Selu: Seeking the Corn-Mother's Wisdom.* Golden, Colorado: Fulcrum, 1993.

Bayley, Harold. *The Lost Language of Symbolism: An Inquiry into the Origin of Certain Letters, Words, Names, Fairy-tales, Folklore, and Mythologies.* New York: Carol, 1993.

Boudinot, Elias. *An Address to the Whites, delivered in the First Presbyterian Church, on the 26th of May, 1836.* Philadelphia: William G. Geddes, 1836.

Brown, Joseph Epes. *The Spiritual Legacy of the American Indian.* New York: Crossroad, 1996.

Bushyhead, Jean. Correspondence with author. February 18, 2005.

_____. Telephone conversation with author. February 23, 2005.

Bushyhead, Reverend Robert H. Interview with author. Cherokee, North Carolina, June 27, 1998.

Calhoun, Walker. Interview with author. Cherokee, North Carolina, March 17, 2001.

Campbell, Joseph. *Myths to Live By.* Toronto, New York, Sydney, Auckland: Bantam Books, 1972.

_____. *Transformations of Myth through Time.* New York: Harper and Row, 1990.

_____, ed. *Myths, Dreams and Religion.* Dallas: Spring, 1988.

Campbell, Joseph, and Bill Moyers. *The Power of Myth.* New York: Doubleday, 1988.

Cavendish, Richard, ed. *Mythology: An Illustrated Encyclopedia.* New York: Barnes and Noble, 1992.

Chavalier, Jean, and Alain Gheerbrant. *The Penguin Dictionary of Symbols.* Trans. John Buchannan-Brown. London: Penguin, 1996.

Chicken, George, Sr. "Travels to the Cherokee, 1725." In *Travels in the American Colonies, 1690–1783.* Newton D. Mereness, ed. New York: Macmillan, 1916.

Coe, Joffre L. "Open Letter to the Citizens of the County." Dated Spring 1935, Cited in *The Transylvania Times*, Brevard, N.C., Monday, June 4, 1988, 7A.

Conley, Robert J. *The Way of the Priests.* New York: Doubleday, 1992.

Corkran, David H. Introduction in *Southern Indian Studies* XXI (October 1969), 4.

de Vries, Ad. *Dictionary of Symbols and Imagery.* Amsterdam and London: North Holland, 1984.

Duane, O.B. *Native American Myths and Legends.* London: Brockhampton Press, 1998.

Dugan, Joyce C., and B. Lynne Harlan. *The Cherokee.* Cherokee: The Eastern Band of the Cherokee Nation, 2002.

Duncan, Barbara R., ed. *Living Stories of*

the Cherokee. Chapel Hill and London: The University of North Carolina Press, 1998.

_____. *Where It All Began: Creation Stories in Art.* Chapel Hill: The University of North Carolina Press, 1998.

Duncan, Barbara R., and Brett H. Riggs. *Cherokee Heritage Trails Guidebook.* Chapel Hill and London: N.p., 2003.

Ehle, John. *Trail of Tears: The Rise and Fall of the Cherokee Nation.* New York, Toronto, Sydney, London, Auckland: Doubleday, 1988.

Eliade, Mircea. *Myth and Reality.* Trans. Willard R. Trask. New York and London: Harper Colophon Books, 1975.

Ellison, Quintin, and Jeffrey Cantrell. "Potter awarded tribe's highest honor." *The Asheville Citizen–Times,* Friday, December 7, 2001, B1, 5.

Farb, Peter. *Man's Rise to Civilization as Shown by the Indians of North America from Primeval Times to the Coming of the Industrial State.* New York: E.P. Dutton, 1968.

Finger, John R. *Cherokee Americans: The Eastern Band of Cherokees in the Twentieth Century.* Lincoln and London: University of Nebraska Press, 1991.

_____. *The Eastern Band of Cherokees 1819–1900.* Knoxville: The University of Tennessee Press, 1984.

Fogelson, Raymond D. "Cherokee Little People Re-considered." *Journal of Cherokee Studies,* fall 1982.

French, Laurence, and Jim Hornbuckle, eds. *The Cherokee Perspective.* Boone: Appalachian Consortium Press, 1981.

Galloway, Greg. Telephone interview with author. January 4, 2005.

Galloway, Jack. Telephone interview with author. January 4, 2005.

Garrett, J.T., and Michael Garrett. *Medicine of the Cherokee: The Way of Relationship.* Santa Fe: Bear and Company, 1996.

Harlan, Lynne. "Where It All Began: Cherokee Creation Stories in Art." In *Where It All Began: Cherokee Stories in Art,* Barbara Duncan, ed. Cherokee: The Museum of the Cherokee Indian, 2001. 9–10.

_____. Interview with author. Cherokee, North Carolina, September 30, 2002.

Haywood, John. *The Natural and Aboriginal History of Tennessee.* Nashville: George Wilson, 1828.

Holden, Pat. Interview with author. Rosman, North Carolina, April 1, 2000.

Hultkrantz, Ake. *Soul and Native Americans.* Woodstock, Conn.: Spring, 1997.

"Indian Country." *National Geographic,* 206, no. 3 (September 2004), National Geographic Map Supplement.

"Intrigue of the Past: Lesson 5.2, Interpretation of Judaculla Rock." University of North Carolina Website. <http://rlas.unc.edu/Lesson/L502/H5 02b.htm>. 1/24/05.

Irwin, Lee, ed. *Native American Spirituality: A Critical Reader.* Lincoln and London: University of Nebraska Press, 2000.

Jackson, Andrew. "Message to Congress, December 3, 1833." Congressional Serial Set, House Executive Documents, 23rd Congress, 1st session, vol. 254, 1833, doc #1.

Jackson, Geneva S. Interview with author. Cherokee, North Carolina, September 30, 2002.

Jacobi, Jolande. *The Psychology of C.G. Jung.* London: Routledge and Kegan Paul, 1942.

Jacoby, Mario A. *Longing for Paradise; Psychological Perspectives on an Archetype.* Trans. Myron B. Gubitz. Boston: Sigo Press, 1985.

Jaffé, Aniela. *C.G. Jung: Word and Image.* Trans. Krishna Winston. Princeton: Princeton University Press, 1979.

_____. *The Myth of Meaning in the Work of C.G .Jung.* Zurich: Daimon, 1984.

Jordan, Winthrop D. *White over Black.* Baltimore: Penguin, 1969.

Joseph, Alvin M., Jr. *500 Nations; An Illustrated History of North American Indians.* New York: Alfred A. Knopf, 1994.

Journal of Cherokee Studies. Multiple volumes. Cherokee: Museum of the Cherokee Indians.

Jung, Carl Gustav. *The Collected Works of C.G. Jung.* 2nd ed. Trans. R.F.C. Hall. Eds. Herbert Read, Michael

Fordham, Gerhard Adler, and William McGuire. 23 vols. London: Routledge and Kegan Paul, 1979.

_____. *Jung Speaking*. Princeton: Princeton University Press, 1977.

_____. *Memories, Dreams, Reflections*. Trans. Richard and Clara Winston. Ed. Aniela Jaffé. London: Random House Inc., 1963.

Jung, Carl Gustav, M-L von Franz, Joseph L. Henderson, Jolande Jacobi, and Aniela Jaffé. *Man and His Symbols*. London: Aldus Books Limited, 1964.

Kelsey, Morton. *Dreamquest; Native American Myth and the Recovery of Soul*. Rockport, Maine: Element Books, 1992.

Kilpatrick, Jack F., and Anna G. Kilpatrick. *Friends of Thunder; Folktales of the Oklahoma Cherokees*. Norman and London: University of Oklahoma Press, 1995.

"Kituwah Archeology Reveals Significant Finds" *The Cherokee One Feather* 36 (Wednesday, May 23, 2001).

Klots, Steve. *Indians of North America, Native Americans and Christianity*. Philadelphia: Chelsea House, 1997.

Lefler, Lisa J., and Fredric W. Gleach, eds. *Southern Indians and Anthropologists*. Athens and London: The University of Georgia Press, 2002.

Levi-Strauss, Claude. *Totemism*. Trans. Rodney Needham. Boston: Beacon Press, 1963.

Lewis, Thomas M.N. and Madeline Kneberg. *Tribes That Slumber; Indians of the Tennessee Region*. Knoxville: The University of Tennessee Press, 1989.

Lossiah, Lynn King. *The Secrets and Mysteries of the Cherokee Little People, Yunwi Tsunsdi'* Cherokee, N.C.: Cherokee Publications, 1998.

_____. Interview with author. Cherokee, North Carolina, January 4, 2005.

Mails, Thomas E. *The Cherokee People; The Story of the Cherokees from Earliest Origins to Contemporary Times*. Tulsa, Okla.: Council Oak Books, 1992.

Mathis, Mark A., and Jeffry L. Crow, eds. *The Prehistory of North Carolina; An Archeological Symposium*. Raleigh: Division of Archives and History, 1983.

McCrary, Mary Jane. *Transylvania Beginnings: A History*. Easley, S.C.: Southern Historical Press, 1984.

McDowell, William L., Jr., ed. *Documents Relating to Indian Affairs, May 21, 1750–August 7, 1754*. Columbia, S.C.: Archives Department, 1958.

McKie, Scott. "Eternal Flame Rededicated at Mountainside Theatre." *The Cherokee One Feather* 36, no. 26 (Wednesday, July 4, 2001), 1.

McLoughlin, William G. *Champions of the Cherokees, Evan and John B. Jones*. Princeton: Princeton University Press, 1990.

_____. *Cherokee and Missionaries, 1789–1839*. Norman and London: University of Oklahoma Press, 1995.

Middleton, T. Walter *Qualla; Home of the Middle Cherokee Settlement*. Alexander, North Carolina: WorldComm, 1999.

Mooney, James. *James Mooney's History, Myths and Scared Formulas of the Cherokees*. Asheville: Historical Images, 1992. Originally published as *Myths of the Cherokee* (1900) and *The Sacred Formulas of the Cherokees* (1891) by the Bureau of American Ethnology.

_____. *The Ghost Dance*. 1896. Reprint. North Dighton, Mass.: J.G. Press, 1996.

Olson, James S., and Raymond Wilson. *Native Americans in the Twentieth Century*. Urbana and Chicago: University of Illinois Press, 1986.

Onions, C.T., ed. *The Oxford Dictionary of English Etymology*. Oxford: Clarendon Press, 1966.

Owens, Lily, ed. *The Complete Brothers Grimm Fairy Tales*. New York: Avenel Books, 1981.

Owle, Freeman. Interview with author. Waynesville, North Carolina, February 18, 2005.

Parker, Gerald Keith. "Folk Religion in Southern Appalachia." Unpublished Ph.D. dissertation. The Southern Baptist Theological Seminary, Louisville, Ky., 1969.

Perdue, Theda. *Cherokee Women: Gender and Culture Change, 1700–1835*. Lincoln and London: University of Nebraska Press, 1998.

Pfister, Oskar. *Das Christentum und die Angst: Eine religionspsychologische, historische und religionshygenische Untersuchung.* Zurich: Artemis, 1944.

Radin, Paul. *The Trickster: A Study in American Indian Mythology.* New York: Schocken Books, 1956.

Riggs, Brett H., M. Scott Shumate, Patti Evans-Shumate, and Brad Owen. "An Archeological Survey of the Ferguson Farm, Swain County, North Carolina." Boone, N.C.: Blue Ridge Cultural Resources, July 31, 1998.

Rosema, Vicki. *Footsteps of the Cherokees.* Winston-Salem, North Carolina: John F. Blair, 1994.

Ross, John. "Memorial of the Cherokee Representatives, submitting the protest of the Cherokee nation against the ratification, execution and enforcement of the treaty negotiated at New Echota, in December, 1835," 24th Congress, 1st session, Document Number 286, House of Representatives, June 22, 1836.

Samuels, Andrew, Bani Shorter, and Fred Plaut. *A Critical Dictionary of Jungian Analysis.* London and New York: Routledge and Kegan Paul, 1986.

Sander, Donald F. and Steven H. Wong, eds. *The Sacred Heritage.* New York, London: Routledge, 1997.

Segal, Robert A., ed. *Jung on Mythology.* London: Routledge, 1998.

Shaffer, Lynda Norene. *Native Americans before 1492.* New York, London: M.E. Sharp, 1992.

Siler, Margaret R. *Cherokee Indian Lore and Smoky Mountain Stories.* Asheville: n.p., 1993.

Spene, Lewis. *Myths of the North American Indians.* New York: Avenel, 1994.

Steele, William O. *The Cherokee Crown of Tannassy.* Winston-Salem, N.C: John F. Blair, 1977.

Stolzman, William. *The Pipe and Christ.* Chamberlain, S.D.: Tipi Press, 1986.

Strickland, Rennard. *Fire and the Spirits: Cherokee Law from Clan to Clan.* Nor-

man University of Oklahoma Press, 1975.

Trimble, Steven. *The People: Indians of the American Southwest.* Santa Fe: School of American Research, 1993.

von Franz, Marie-Louise. *An Introduction to the Psychology of Fairy Tales.* Dallas: Spring, 1978.

_____. *Archetypal Patterns in Fairy Tales.* Toronto: University of Toronto Press, 1997.

_____. *Problems of the Feminine in Fairytales.* Dallas: Spring, 1972.

_____. *Patterns of Creativity; Creation Myths.* Dallas: Spring, 1972.

_____. *Psychotherapy.* Boston, London: Shambhala, 1993.

_____. *The Psychological Meaning of Redemption Motifs in Fairytales.* Toronto: Inner City Books, 1980.

Walker, Amy. Interview with author. Cherokee, North Carolina, June 27, 1998.

Ward, H. Trawick, and R. P. Stephen Davis, Jr., eds. *Time Before History: The Archeology of North Carolina.* Chapel Hill and London: The University of North Carolina Press, 1999.

Weatherford, Jack. *Indian Givers: How the Indians of the Americas Transformed the World.* New York: Fawcett Columbine, 1988.

Webster's New Twentieth Century Dictionary of the English Language, Unabridged. Second edition. Cleveland and New York: The World, 1970.

Week, The. 4, no. 182 (November 12, 2004), 24.

Wetmore, Ruth. "Transylvania County Survey." Unpublished notes, 1993.

Williams, John Alexander. *Appalachia: A History.* Chapel Hill and London: The University of North Carolina Press, 2002.

Ziegler, Wilbur G., and Ben S. Grosscup. *The Heart of the Alleghanies or Western Carolina North Carolina.* Raleigh, N.C.: Alfred Williams & Company and Cleveland, Oh.: William W. Williams, 1883.

Index